The Music of Berlioz

THE
MUSIC OF BERLIOZ

A. E. F. DICKINSON

FABER & FABER
LONDON

First published in 1972 by
Faber and Faber Limited
3 Queen Square London WC1
Printed in Great Britain by
William Clowes & Sons Limited
London, Colchester and Beccles

Contents

Illustrations

Acknowledgments

I am glad to acknowledge the assistance and courtesy of certain institutions and individuals. Of the Council of Durham University for help with the expenses of travelling and visiting libraries, and of copying; of Reading University Library and Music Department Library for various facilities; of the staff of the Music Rooms of the British Museum and of the National Library of Scotland for general co-operation; of the editors of *The Music Review* and of *The Musical Quarterly* for consent to the reproduction of matter from articles in their journals; of Mr. Michael Wright for the loan of a copy of his recent bibliography of writings on Berlioz, with permission to make capital out of it; and of my wife for assuming a typist role with an erratic script. Musically, I am glad to mention the art of Raphael Kubelik, whose direction of *The Trojans* at the Royal Opera House in 1957 first revealed Berlioz's true dimension to me. Critically and documentarily, Dr. Jacques Barzun's fusion of life, art and books in his Berlioz book clarified many features in Berlioz's method and filled many gaps, besides being invaluable for classified references.

I am grateful to the following for granting permission to reproduce illustrations: Mr. Michael Ayrton, The Radio Times Hulton Picture Library and The Mansell Collection.

Preface

BERLIOZ's audiences in the concert-room and at home are now predictably wide and varied. If it is easy to underestimate the general grasp of the medium enjoyed by the kind of reader who will face an entire survey of Berlioz's music, it is also rash to assume generally an accomplished and sophisticated perception of the thematic distinction, textural adventurousness and structural mastery with which Berlioz confronts each situation of his choice. In striking a balance between these, I have had first in mind the isolated and comparatively rural reader, not necessarily in close touch with big orchestral or operatic events, nor able to command a vast supply of records at a touch, and not trained in the elements of structural dynamics and symmetry. Accordingly, I have not hesitated to go over details in slow motion. The impatient reader must accept this or quit. But I have kept steadily in mind what I think the composer is about, in the little and in the large. The selected examples of themes and textures are to keep discussion on the ground, but also to encourage the reader, as widely as possible, to follow or fancy a performance with the aid of a full (miniature) or vocal score. (Following a performance with a score is only a matter of practising rhythmic co-ordination of eye and ear with the rhythm imposed by the performer or conductor.)

In the matter of structure, I have not shrunk from emphasizing Berlioz's constant use of strophe, in the broadest sense, in the developed numbers as well as in the separate songs, his employment of more wayward shapes, and in the orchestral movements the subtle interplay of classical sonata form and cyclic or 'motto' theme. These and many other underlying connexions call for some preliminary anticipation, or at least for a check-up after performance. The second is ideally the best order, to ensure the freshness of impact, but it implies a further, corrective experience of the music. The first is so far usually the more practical order.

The literary and dramatic contacts of Berlioz's music are commonly treated lightly with a mere cross-reference, or else taken for granted. Yet as one finds him devising and selecting texts from Goethe, Shakespeare and Virgil, from Hugo and Gautier, from Humbert Ferrand and minor versifiers, one becomes curious to know what he condensed or subtracted from, and in the case of *Faust* and the *Aeneid*, in particular, an appreciation of the sense of the whole work is well-nigh incumbent, in order to realize the measure of Berlioz's transformation, for better or worse, of his great originals. Here, again, I venture to assume that consultation of sources, and of commentary and translation, is not necessarily ready to hand. Nor, again, are words sung easily audible in transmission.

An apprehension enriched with the products of leisurely observation or a thrilling slide over the surface? The confrontation of a 'coldly analytical' summary and of a positively disagreeable estimate on occasion, or an enthusiastic acceptance all along the line? A decision on such questions will incline the reader for or against the tour proposed. The independence is all.

A. E. F. D.

I

Berlioz the Progressive

BERLIOZ the composer is now accepted as a thorough-going romantic; as an individual artist of his time and ahead of his time. On the one side, he represents a substantive post-Beethoven period of constructive assertion, bringing into rich contact genres of expression previously departmentalized as operatic, devotional, poetically based or orchestral, and thus effecting a necessary extension of the frontiers of music. 'Dans la patrie de Beethoven, le français Beethoven'—Ernest Reyer's bon mot of 1869—remains a useful pointer to the composer's place in the concertroom. On the other side, Berlioz's development of clue-themes and scenes in free association with literary or dramatic ideas established a novel method of communication that was to dominate the next hundred years of music, without involving the exhaustive thematic development which accompanies Wagner's tireless declamation of phrase. So far Berlioz was the precursor both of Wagner, Tchaikovsky and Strauss, and of the anti-Wagner craftsmanship of the mood-music, more relaxed in terms of reference and so much the more concentrated in intention, of Mussorgsky, Debussy, Delius. It is useless to try to find a continuous programme at the back of Berlioz's music, as Wagner did with *Romeo and Juliet*.

Proliferating audiences still find plenty of valid statement, indeed, in Beethoven's orchestral and primarily symphonic works for the concert-hall, so signally and faithfully written to satisfy himself, not any performing body or patron, yet undoubtedly framed for a much broader audience than music had yet known. For these, Berlioz's concert works in bulk present an intelligible sequel without Beethoven's sense of compulsive and systematic development. The early period of maturity exhibits three extended symphonies: two orchestral but with a programme of a sort; the third substantially choral and 'dramatic' in tone and in its patent reference to Shakespeare scenes. (The *Symphonie funèbre et triomphale* was a *pièce d'occasion*, symphonic only in title.) There are eight supporting *Grandes ouvertures*, all with titles, three being overtures to operas. Their assured place in the concert repertory, except for *Rob Roy*, testifies to their musical stability rather than to their fitness to their title or implied content. The more than well-made funeral march for the end of *Hamlet* is also worth mentioning here, inconceivable as it is in any public performance of *Hamlet*.

The chief cantata, *La Damnation de Faust*, an obvious expansion of the early and remarkable *Eight Scenes*, is an extended work of over twenty numbers, symphonic only by the listener's consent. Yet cumulatively, in its four main stages, it adds up to an integral impression, propelled, as in *Roméo*, by the penetrating recollection of a recognized work for the threatre. *L'enfance du Christ*, a short Christmas oratorio with a difference, followed later. Its imaginative quality and firm plastic structure are now widely acknowledged. It remains a number-work (i.e. a work divided into separate 'numbers'). The two Latin works, the *Messe des Morts* (henceforward the *Requiem*) and *Te Deum*, similarly transcend their ecclesiastical setting and sectional construction. Their orchestral grandeur and overwhelming climaxes have encouraged the effort of keeping them alive, the *Requiem* more especially. An early experiment, *Lélio*, for a concealed orchestra and singers, is a miscellany of movements linked by a fanciful monologue on the stage. In this, rare beauties and robust, sometimes hammish excursions seem to quiz one another. The pronounced orchestral interest lends coherence to the series, quite apart from the animating monologue. It remains a respectable solecism, like the Sitwell-Walton *Facade*. Outstanding among single pieces, *Sara la Baigneuse* (Hugo) has nothing experimental about it except the multitude of verses and a lack of companion pieces for concert use. As an expansive document in *allegresse*, evocative and neatly assembled, it is unrivalled, and the long and total neglect of this haunting waltz-piece seems inexplicable. One might have expected an excess of performances.

At the outset of his musical career Berlioz wrote a cantata every year for four years, in competition for the French Institute's 'Rome-prize' gold medal, little as he aspired to residence in Italy. That he could confer distinction on a stylized mould of three numbers will become apparent later. Rarely performed (the fourth and medal-winning cantata surviving only in a torn-off fragment of the finale), these cantatas may be considered as a not unhappy augury of the composer's grasp of scene and mood, and firm sense of structure. The slightest perusal of the scores shows that the young ex-medical student, recently come to Paris from the country, was anything but an amateur with the orchestra.

Berlioz wrote about forty songs for solo voice or small ensemble and piano. He orchestrated and published sixteen of these, and even produced, late in his career, an orchestral version of *Erlkönig* for a particular singer. These miniature but often richly featured Scenes, of which *La Captive* (Hugo) and the six Gautier settings of *Nuits d'été* are the best known, form a recurring background and supplement to the extended cantatas; veritable tone-poems in their strophical way. The songs with piano must be regarded as the products of an ancillary craftsmanship, recurrent rather than characteristic, and sometimes negligible, yet exhibiting considerable melodic power. They remain the home musician's sole companion, apart from the piano duet arrangements of various overtures published in the composer's lifetime. Unfortunately, only *Nuits d'été* is easily obtainable.

From the earliest period of extended composition Berlioz was interested in opera, and there can be no doubt that his greatest ambitions lay that way. After what proved a prolonged but false start with a grim liberationist-*versus*-tyrant plot, *Les Francs Juges*, Berlioz found what he wanted in *Benvenuto Cellini*, a romantic and crucial episode in the career of a famous craftsman, spiced with sophisticated stresses, stratagems and the exercise of pompous judicial authority, but releasing waves of creative energy in the seesaw polarization of congenial elopement, carnival commotion, feverish sculpturing and sundry diversions. The failure of this work to take root at the Opéra left Berlioz none the less involved in a sense of total theatre. He kept up a dramatic connexion in *Romeo and Juliet* and in *La Damnation de Faust*, while framing an essentially imaginative, anti-theatre communication for these concert occasions. He continued the process later in *L'enfance du Christ*. Meanwhile, a third opera, *La Nonne Sanglante*, had folded up, like the first, in fragments, with the text left to Gounod to take over. But eventually Berlioz settled down to shaping a theatrical work based on the *Aeneid*, which had been long in his mind. He called it significantly *Les Troyens*; two acts are placed at Troy and three at Carthage. In his lifetime only the Carthage acts were performed. For complete performances the world had to wait around forty years (Karlsruhe, 1899; Paris, 1903), with Covent Garden following in 1957. But however untimely the public response, the work marked the crucial point in the establishment of Berlioz's claim on audiences of the future. The culmination of his artistic life was at last exposed, strongly French in character and not without patriotic undertones, yet absolutely capable of breaking through beyond the immediate frontier; the more so to audiences now richly acquainted with national advancement through native opera and quasi-mythical epic. A stage was essential for such an historic projection of the familiar Troy-to-Carthage events in true perspective, as the operation of the *daimon* in an unparalleled concourse of men and peoples in a struggle for survival. The triumph is that this longest possible evening of music has been given an extraordinary unity, both through the composer-dramatist's stamp of historical vision and in the calculated blend of speech-song, chorus and orchestral refrain. Nor was this achievement at all superseded by Wagner's more systematic cultivation of the Beethoven orchestra and heroic myth. Berlioz had long declared in advance his independence of Wagner's methods.

Béatrice et Bénédict, a nimble excursion round *Much Ado*, followed *Les Troyens* (what was left of it) on to the Paris stage. It showed fresh personal touches rather than an advance in style, and the appeal of its successive scenes reminds the mere listener of Berlioz's leanings towards tableau-music.

This expansion of the conventional ranges of orchestral, vocal and operatic music, now summarized, confronted audiences over four decades (1830–70) in the middle of the century, when an original appeal was far from being a conscious desire in public. Today the composer's adventurous spirit, steady pursuit of genuinely literary contacts and consequent avoidance of mutually exclusive genres are taken for granted as far as they go, but his musical intentions are apt to be under-rated, as strokes of resourceful opportunism, bolstered by a fresh command of the orchestra, rather than as constructive utterance. His raw spots of empty or pre-tentious rhetoric can become a focus of disapproval for a work of genuine char-acter, and a certain section of the public in the concert-hall and opera-house remain undecided about Berlioz's appeal for them. This is partly because they miss the more consistent course of Beethoven's craftsmanship in symphony and concerto, or the intellectually conceived progress with which Wagner's mature music-drama transcended number-opera in work after work, in an historic exhibition of clue-theme development and an 'endless' flow of declamation, interlude and postlude. Compared with these demonstrations of method—and they are the obvious basic exemplars of the expanding symphony and transformed opera of the century—Berlioz's work can sound wayward or lacking in ulterior relevance. The Hungarian March is merely the best known instance of a brilliant episode which yields nothing beyond itself; it tells nothing of any consequence about Faust, nor does it hint at the later course of the music. Even in *The Trojans* the general lack of connexion between the Troy and Carthage acts is a stumbling-block to some listeners. Was Berlioz out-witted, paradoxically, by his own scenario? To explain a distaste does not amount to a critical acceptance of it. But the insecurity of Berlioz in any stage repertory can hardly be doubted, and fifteen annual renderings of the *Carnaval Romain* are no rejoinder.

An extension of live performances, and of recordings and broadcasts, will do much to conquer disbeliefs and to demonstrate that Berlioz's best works not only improve with deeper acquaintance but need it to reveal their true shape and quality; and by shape I mean, not the bare sonata or number-on-number structure, but the sense of succession, development and return. Nothing can replace this act of com-munication, whether direct or transmitted at one remove or another to an imagina-tive listener. But it is possible to record on paper a fresh examination of Berlioz's main works, for the purpose of distinguishing their musical or more than musical impact in terms of their known inception and growth, frequently in relation to a literary text, and of framing a reappraisal of the relation between the cantatas, operas and symphonic works. From this might emerge a broader conception of listener-identification. *L'enfance du Christ*, for example, has from the start been readily received as a musical interpretation of a familiar situation (the flight into Egypt of Christ's parents and their child), or at least as an acceptable extension of it in oratorio style, part narrative, part didactic or devotional. It only needs intelligence to recognize the same method working in less established successions of dramatic or quasi-dramatic or lyrical involvements, from the unpredictable sweep of the *Faust* scenes and cantata to the rather more pre-determined courses of the *Requiem* and *Te Deum*; from the concentrated settings of Gautier, Hugo and the rest to the passionate celebrations of Cellini, Roman Aeneas and Benedict, of Romeo and Lélio. Except for the lastnamed (and he is self-explanatory throughout) the literary ground is well known to any informed listener, and the inclusion of the obscurer terrain is a matter of time and private investigation. But the specific *treatment* of each text, amounting to anything up to total absorption in the musical product, remains a perpetual issue which is frequently ignored. It claims fresh examination. Moreover, it must be realized that music for Goethe or Gautier or Virgil, or a devotional commemoration, is not better but only more intelligible for being so; 'intelligible' carrying the implication that the burdened mind of Faust or Gautier's restless lover, the carefree mood of Hugo's bathing girl, have each a certain universal appeal, not merely the situations of high political or social tension, with their contemporary overtones. What matters is the musical projection from the base given. This should be clear to any one seriously acquainted with the many important works of the nineteenth century that have a story to tell but are no easier to evaluate. Berlioz's music, as the first, surprising and outstanding vindication of an unclassical approach—Beethoven's dramatic concert-music being confined to one tremendous finale and overtures intended for a stage performance—calls particularly for the scrutinizing ear. It remains to size up the successive works in relation to the pattern of expression adopted, from a titled overture to a fully staged music-drama. For this purpose, a hearing or two even of Berlioz's ten to twelve major works in a convenient sequence is normally not only an arduous and improbable proposition but, even if achieved, a confusing experience. A token round of measured acquaintance at second hand, supported where necessary by the hardy repetitions of the gramophone and whatever word-and-tone associations a full or vocal score may lend the reader, is an expedient stage of auditory accession, if the significance of each genre is to acquire some order of perception. This is where discussion on paper can supply what no concert performance can furnish: chosen order.

2

Berlioz's composer craftsmanship has had surprisingly little critical attention. T. S. Wotton's valuable and pioneering survey of 1935 exposed many misconceptions but it was too selective in its range to become a standard book. Of the many life-and-art books, in which the art inevitably suffers from the limitations of space, if not also from divided attention, Mr J. H. Elliot's (1938, 1967) is candid enough, but his steady scepticism amounts to a declaration of distaste without any of the redeeming enthusiasm which might give meaning to his exposures. He seems determined to demonstrate that the composer is so abnormal as to be negligible. By contrast, a militant, almost forensic promotion of man and musician colours (no more) Dr Jacques Barzun's capable and coherent account (1950) in two volumes. A luminous compendium of legomena about Berlioz, supported by a monumental and orderly index, makes this the inevitable start of an inquiry into the composer's aims and methods and into the history of readings and misreadings of the various works. Criticism so eclectic is apt, however, to leave a trail of dotted lines in the gapped procession of critiques—gapped by narrative—in the absence of personal and particular judgements.

Among books in French, J.-G. Prod'homme's (1904 etc.), preceded by brochures on the two French choral works, heads a procession of volumes more introductory than critical, where they touch on the music (See Appendix 2). The prime Berlioz scholar, Julien Tiersot, never published a book bearing directly on the composer's development. His long series of extended articles on the composer's scripts in Paris, in *Le Ménestrel*, was an unrivalled piece of research, but these footnotes and careful observations lack the critical thrust to make them into a book. Somehow the publication of the collected edition at the turn of the century did not have the effect which might have been expected of the critical world in Paris and beyond.

I turn to the present attempt to fill a gap. It will not be my aim to direct the listener's taste into certain grooves, but rather to clarify the intentions of each work, as they spring from their context of poetic thought, traditional drama or sheer invention. In nearly every extended piece of coherent music will be found some pivotal balance between an initial thought or train of sensations and a fresh turn of mood or thematic development, and between this diversion, however contrived, and a reverberation of associated phrases, which may in turn invoke further innovations and renewals in persuasive sequence. Without this balance of effort, of travelling up and down hill, the listener's way can be irksome, and the structural art lies in preserving this balance over the widest possible field in one orbit. In the nineteenth century the recurrent but variable strophes of an air, the developments and reprises of a symphonic movement, the harnessing of totally different movements by means of an *idée fixe* or commanding theme, became almost routine facilities for ensuring this swing of the pendulum, without which music moves either in one deepening track or in a baffling restlessness. Berlioz was not slow to exploit these structural devices and to amplify them in his own way. He could also be almost as anti-symphonic and anti-symmetrical as a composer of today. However, the total artistic effect depends partly on such calculated juxtaposition of like and unlike, forward and returning gestures, and without an appreciation of the kind of balance struck the musical impact is vague and misses its mark. It is obvious that the final parody of the *idée fixe* in the Fantastic Symphony is meant to be something more than a *jeu d'esprit* in sound. Much more is it emotionally significant that the *Romeo and Juliet* symphony mingles musical movements of dramatic import with definite tableaux in music, reflecting Shakespeare. The artistic situation can be tabulated in terms of its successive movements, and ceases to be coherent without its *points d'appui*. But the resulting symphonic mould is capable of much discussion.

Finally, Berlioz's blend in *The Trojans* of independent and strophical movements, declamatory interludes and riveting complex structures, calls for a fresh assessment in the absence of regular performances.[1] The meagre summing up in all books but Barzun's denies the work the justice which a monumental five-act *Aeneid* opera, one epic for another, demands from contemporary criticism.

Preserving, then, a working modicum of informed listening, while not stinting my survey in the larger instances, I propose to build up my impression of the composer, neither treating him as a controversial rebel against the classical style and therefore as perpetually on probation as a newcomer to musical history, nor adopting the equally aggressive, anti-critical tone of the listener for whom Berlioz cannot put a step wrong. (Both attitudes are far from uncommon today.) I shall not hesitate to reject or question works that seem to belie the composer's own standards of continuity and imaginative grasp, but without assuming that every raw spot of rhetoric or malconstruction betrays more than an exaggerated emphasis. I shall take it for granted that a trained, widely experienced and inventive composer wrote down what he meant, and meant what he wrote, and that a generally impressive intention is not vitiated by a partial miscalculation or by some lapse into what seems dull to our ears. At the same time, faithful to Berlioz, the pronounced and outspoken critic of others and a genuinely self-critical artist himself, I shall take leave to record the non-acceptances of an open mind in another era. This recognition of a sometimes baffling duality of level may shock some readers, in individual cases, but a rational intolerance should strengthen the dynamic of admiration for the genuine triumphs. Berlioz frequently worked in a public arena by no means favourable to art for its own sake. His true appeal lies partly in his capacity to realize his own level and leave public taste where it belongs. For over half a century we have taken this perseverance for granted in Beethoven's art, after a much longer period of indecision. We are still reluctant to admit the same claim in Berlioz's more erratic and perilous course of production.

It has been observed that the Berlioz output reflects varying opportunity for a direct hearing or for the amplifications and verifications of an accessible score. The three main symphonies, all the overtures but *Rob Roy*, the two French and two Latin major choral works, are in general circulation at all desired levels, except for the full score of the *Te Deum*. The same goes for *Nuits d'été*, except for the full scores of the orchestral version, but the most other songs are out of print and out of mind. For nearly all these and other missing links the enthusiastic inquirer has to fall back on what he can experience from a reading of the original published orchestral and vocal scores, or of the scores in the collected edition of twenty volumes, published at the beginning of the twentieth century, wherever they can be consulted.[2] (The new collected edition has issued five volumes to date.) Even the old collected edition did not include the scores of *Benvenuto Cellini* or *Les Troyens*, and at present only the latter is obtainable, by those who can afford it. A miniature full score of *Les Troyens* is the most urgent call on modern publication within the orbit of the average music section of a library. The present gaps in popular publication are a severe restriction upon a listener's desire for a wider minimal acquaintance, and for the following up of obscure references. Nevertheless, this wide output was Berlioz's creative life, and the reader must be prepared to take in his stride baffling references to a very inaccessible score. The magnitude of the printing and reprinting effort in early attendance upon most of Berlioz's works in the last century has been brought home by Mr Cecil Hopkinson's authoritative bibliography of editions. Apart from these limitations on the fringe of a comprehensively empirical identification of Berlioz's published compositions, his output is not so tremendous in extent as composers go: three operas, four sizeable choral works, four symphonies, six independent overtures, a dozen songs with orchestra and twenty with piano, in the main. The journey is nothing but monotonous.

Berlioz's wider grasp of music as at once a deliverance of spirit in a context of lyrical drama, an exercise of craftsmanship and a collective impresario activity challenging, or not challenging, public taste, informed the journalistic existence which for many years he was forced to lead, in order to be free both to compose and to produce his own music. His *Voyage musical* (1844), nominally a compilation of memoirs, contains many revealing declarations of artistic aim, and his renowned *Traité d'Instrumentation*, much more than a textbook, exhibits his wide and exact knowledge of current scores and his most favoured exemplars; not to mention at least three collections of earlier articles. These form an historical addition to the record of composer-criticism at a crucial point of musical development. But a portrait of Berlioz the ubiquitous musician is not within my terms of reference. Nor am I concerned with details of his career, apart from works not performed. Everyone knows that it was Paris-based, and therefore conducted in an environment of opera of varying status (grand, comic, grotesque) and a limited dispensation of orchestral music, with a corresponding burden of proof on what was none of these things. It is also well known that whenever possible Berlioz rehearsed his works with much patience and forethought, and was not one to supply a reduced-score alternative by cueing the indispensable bars of absent instruments in other parts. A glance at the scores, with the string numbers prescribed, shows that Berlioz saw no call to economize, by present-day standards of professional performance, in the forces demanded. Spontini and Meyerbeer had seen to that issue earlier. The burning question was reception and reasonable maintenance in the opera-house, or a denial of these. A decided romantic, Berlioz chose his own line of production and wrestled with it, immediately or on a long term, until he had achieved something. If opera was barred to him, another kind of stage must, without any illusion that it was a real stage, be devised.

Apart from this central issue, it is usually idle to attribute the character or origin of works to events in the composer's life, except for the slowing down of output, owing to declining health, in what proved to be the last fifteen years of his life. To do justice to the courage and bitterness, to the impromptu affections and genial wit, to the unruffled perseverance, with which Berlioz faced the world of his family life in youth and maturity, his patrons, interpreters and rivals, is matter for a book in itself, and at least one is called for, to bring research up to date and to broaden the understanding of character. It should be a thrilling narrative, but it will endear (or alienate) the composer to the contemporary public without explaining the music, which rarely lacks its own credentials. The art and life of Beethoven and of Schubert give every encouragement to this view.

In constructing a survey of Berlioz's development, I shall begin with the discoverable influences: what he must have heard in Paris, what he could assimilate from score, and what composers and literary figures impressed him. Then, there were the preceptors at the Conservatoire, for what they were worth. In sorting out Berlioz's own music, it is advantageous to proceed by genres rather than by arbitrary chronological stages. The number-cantata of detached scenes, moods or invocations shows its obvious developments and variants according to the nature and length of the text. The separate songs with orchestra, on the fringe of this genre, form a natural link with the songs for voice and piano of which a certain number later acquired orchestral settings. The four nominal symphonies claim a chapter. With the more casual and perfunctory overtures may be placed various stray orchestral pieces. After this the operatic output may claim a sense of climax, stage by stage in every sense. Finally, the impact of all these different levels of musical thought may be summarized, aspect by aspect, in the common or recurrent habits of melodic, harmonic and textural appeal by which one identifies with Berlioz's message in and beyond his century, sometimes reminiscent of the past, more often a hint of the future, and most often itself.

NOTES

1. The astonishingly incomplete recording under Scherchen, confined to the Carthage acts, has long been deleted. The 1969 revivals under Colin Davis at Covent Garden, following stage performances at Glasgow and Manchester and elsewhere, removed many misgivings for the metropolitan audiences who were able to attend. The complete recording now at last available (as I write) should do much to establish the general acceptance of *The Trojans* in depth, such as *The Ring* has long enjoyed in a similar transference from the opera-house.

2. The cavalier 20-volume edition of Malherbe-Weingartner (1900–), besides excluding *Cellini*, *Troyens* and sundry unfinished works and sketches, saw fit to bring Berlioz's scoring into line with standard (German) resources, chiefly by replacing the ophicleide parts by tuba parts and so forth—an incredible attitude for Weingartner to adopt (or consent to), as Balakirev hastened to point out to Malherbe. For details, see the fifth Supplement in Barzun's *Berlioz* (1951).

2

Forward from Gluck and Beethoven

THE two chief musical influences in Berlioz's formative years appear to have been French opera and Beethoven symphonies. This is the strong convergent impression that comes, first, from the listing of works known to be in the current operatic repertory up to 1830, or available for consultation in score in the Conservatoire library; then, from a survey of Berlioz's highly distinctive journalistic work, published memoirs, and often revealing letters. Most of all, it arises from observing the character and development pattern of his own music, located materially in Paris.

Let us assume that music, at this point in its history, is basically national and depends on the further cultivation of national opera for the acquisition of style. In this context, Italian opera, so long an established event in the way of popular art-music (if any) as to have crossed many frontiers, has so far been held at bay by French opera of various kinds. For the average opera-goer, not bent on comedy, this might have meant Salieri's *Les Danaides*, Catel's *Les Bayadères* and Spontini's *La Vestale*; works all published at the time, for a listener to rehearse or ponder over, not just an evening's entertainment. The plot of *Bayadères*, presenting a Hindustani myth as an actual event, maintains a certain degree of suspense up to the moment of supernatural revelation, but the artificial atmosphere is thinly concealed by the blend of temple ceremonial and discipline and human declarations (by Lamea, the 'heroine') of affection and calm resignation to death-by-agreement. The music is bland and conventional, and must have owed its incredible run at the Opera (140 performances cited) to its singers, its spectacular and *bayadère* appeal, and its mystical touch. *Danaides*, also myth-based, maintains a much more intense atmosphere of overhanging horror. The intentions which King Danaus soon discloses, that his fifty daughters shall murder his brother's fifty sons on their bridal night, truly overshadows the dialogue and cantabile. All but one daughter carry out his orders, and are consigned to perpetual and savage torture in Hades. The exception, Hypermnestra, saves Lynceus, now her husband. At first romantic and confident about her love affair (duet in **A**), she is soon grief-stricken at her father's decision, and then tormented by her double involvement in it, to which her own extinction,

Ex. 1.1

HYPERMESTRA: Par les lar - mes dont vo - tre fil - le ar -
(to Danaus)

- rose en trem-blant__ vo - tre sei - ne

Ex. 1.2a

HYPERMESTRA: Mon pè - re! Mon é - poux! Dieux,___ quel af-freux mar -

- ty - re, Dieux___

Ex. 1.2b

HYPERMESTRA: ne voy-ez vous pas que j'ex - pi - re d'a - mour, d'a - mour?
(to Lynceus)

Ex. 1.3

HYPERMESTRA: Pè - re bar - ba - re, ar - ra - che moi la vi - e, ar -

Vln.(colla voce)

- ra - che moi la vi - e! Joins ta fille

Plate 3 A lithograph of Berlioz in Vienna, 1845, by von Kriehuber

Plate 4 Caricature of Berlioz   Plate 5 Caricature of Berlioz

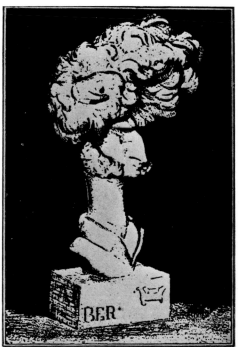

Facing page 24: A portrait of Berlioz in 1832 by Signol
Opposite: Paganini, a drawing by Ingres, 1819
Overleaf: A lithograph of Berlioz in Vienna, 1845, by von Kriehuber

as well as Lynceus', is preferable. Some key-phrases may be quoted. The recurrence of **G** minor is noticeable, and the insistent phrase (**Ex. 1**.2b) almost anticipates Cassandra's soft centre. The Hell scene, however, does not live up to its horrific text. Originally attributed to Gluck, the music reflects his pungent tone without his personality, but a capable singer could have made Hypermnestra a live passing echo, for the informed, of Aeschylus' portraiture in the *Supplices*.

Berlioz was very much more stirred by Spontini's *La Vestale*, which happily and beyond all reasonable expectation unites in story the Roman general, Licinius, with Julia, a vestal virgin. A rich succession of temple scenes, serene or fearful, encloses a more than hazardous struggle between the ill-assorted but mutually and passionately devoted pair and an inexorable priestly sentence of death. This fate is finally and visibly deflected by an overruling and beneficent goddess, as Julia is being led off to die for her impious defiance of all her sacred obligations to Vesta, as Diana is named (as at Nemi). Two ballets and an overture complete the table of events. The absorbed mood and developing tensity of the various situations are matched by the music. Not only by an eloquent top line, but by an orchestral accompaniment to suit it and set it off. One may recall certain features here, for the opera is still given from time to time: in Act 1, the sensitive blending of voices and woodwind in the morning 'hymn' to Vesta, and the striking and Weberish juxtaposition of trombone chords and tremolo strings, new in French opera, in the subsequent love-denouncing air of the high priest. The middle act is without doubt one of the most memorable events in early nineteenth century French opera. There is a fervour of which Meyerbeer was incapable, and yet something of his fastidious instrumentation. After the vestals' delicately scored, serene evening hymn and a pathetic prayer from Julia, reflecting Ilia from *Idomeneo* (Mozart), Julia meets solemn priestly intervention with an air of desperation, mingled with intoxicating spasms of all-risking devotion to Licinius; an eloquent and suggestive number, which prepares psychologically for conventional, blasphemous transport (duet). In the finale, a penetrating appeal to Latona underlines the pitiless **E** major climax, compounded of relentless choral rhythm and strident chords in torrential flow. After this rehearsal, as we may think it, of some of the conflicting currents of desperation and imperious self-dedication in *Les Troyens*, the sinister trombone-haunted march to ritual execution, and Julia's farewell to her lover, with its truly poignant close, are good points in a final act whose facile and contrived release of spirit is closely matched, and not transcended, by the choral and ballet material, though the scoring is piquant enough (**Ex. 2**.1 and 2.2).

In one of his later reminiscences, *Evenings with the orchestra*, Berlioz shows why he regarded *Vestale* as not only an advance on trivial earlier operas to Italian words, but an outpouring of ideas which found the composer impoverished for the succeeding *Cortez* and *Olympie*. If Berlioz's fondness for *Vestale* as a whole is less easy to understand, it certainly fixed itself in his affections as a stage event which, with the right Julia, demanded singers, orchestra and a responsive direction at any time. Even as late as 1852, when he performed generous selections in his London concerts, Berlioz was embarrassed at the critics' lack of response.

The main inspiration for opera, however, came from Gluck, with all of whose mature classical operas, and *Armide*, Berlioz was well and early acquainted. The connexion needs some clarification. Berlioz admired Gluck for his nominally

Ex. 2.1

uncompromising stand (preface to *Alceste* etc.) for a truly dramatic, or at least drama-respecting, conception of opera, and for his creative efforts to break down the stereotyped schedule based on Metastasio's texts, namely secco recitative and da capo aria, and too imperious soloists, and to substitute a more subtle process of number-succession than stop-go, in which simplicity of means was displaying a fresh magnetic quality. But Berlioz did not accept Gluck's contention that in opera music must be the servant of the drama; a thesis which, indeed, Gluck himself often

Ex. 2.2

ignored. On the contrary, Berlioz steadily asserted that music, whatever its point of application, should be characteristic in itself, and that to subordinate music to a dramatic situation was to mistake its nature. What he discovered in Gluck was not so much his projections of grave and enthralling situations, in *Orphée*, *Alceste* and, most of all, *Iphigénie en Tauride*, but chiefly his revelation of the power of the orchestra to make itself indispensable in scene after scene.

In a well-known letter to his sister Nanci, dated 1821, Berlioz sketches vividly his impressions of *Iphigénie*: the orchestral presage of a storm, the later piquant portrait of the matricide Orestes, vocally calm but guilt-conscious in the 'persevering mutter' of the violas. There were to be many more examples in the explicit *Traité d'Instrumentation*. Recently Beethoven had opened doors, for an imaginative score-reader, to a new sort of dramatic music in the orchestra, which Berlioz called '*genre instrumental expressif*'. In his late operas Gluck had particularized this way of expression in his typifying style of character-portraiture; the desperate resolution of Iphigeneia, Alcestis and even vestal Julia differing in quality rather than in its ambivalent kind. As a precisian, however, Gluck appeared no model. His carelessness over scoring detail, like his bursts of indifference as to the relevance of an overture or interlude, did not go unheeded by his successor.

The upshot was that with Gluck on their side in tragic opera, and harmless and industrious producers like Boieldieu in comic opera—his early rescue opera, *Beniowsky*, having flopped—the promoters of this national, 'literary' drama could for a time hold their position strongly enough to render Italian opera an intrusion in style as well as in organization. Apart from singers of telling personality like Madame Branchu, improved conditions of stage management furthered any artistic expression that might be available. Besides, a more resourceful system of scenic lighting and the installation of the more speedy gas lighting in place of Argand lamps, the darkening of the house for the production and the lowering of the curtain between the acts, removing scene-shifting from the public view, appear now as essential aids to the enhancement of a proper atmosphere.

His Gluckian faith made Berlioz antagonistic to the dramatic insouciance of Bellini and his pathetic dressing up of Shakespearean characters in the luscious cantabile of *I Capuletti e i Montecchi*. He was equally allergic to the thrusting parvenu of the Paris scene, Rossini, with his 'melodious cynicism' and automatic spinning-top crescendo, while not being indifferent to his dazzling stage qualities, delicate instrumentation and, as in *Le comte d'Ory*, marked elegance. Gluck's statuesque operas assured Berlioz that a strongly conceived stage situation could be matched by a growth of musical style involving the whole orchestra, whether in recitative burgeoning into a pulsating arioso, in a cantabile shared between singer and orchestral soloists, or in a scene in whose shaping Gluck had gone some way but not compulsively enough.

Berlioz might have drawn similar constructive conclusions from Mozart's Italian masterworks, in which sophisticated, sparkling and sometimes sociologically ruthless comedy had released an outpouring of vocalized line, cantabile or voluble speech-song, and orchestral movement, without parallel before or since; not to mention the experiments in a different, German, operatic genre, or the late symphonies. But if he did so conclude, Berlioz knew that he was moving away from prevailing taste, which, if it considered Mozart at all, dismissed his work as a thing of brittle elegance. The fact remains that no more convincing precedent could be named for the development of the plastic kind of richly characteristic, precisely toned and firmly structured music for which Berlioz, as we know, was searching all through his career. In his more systematic exploitation of the numerous combinations made practicable by the enlargement of the orchestra and the historical improvement and extension of the wind instruments, and in his steady concern for exact detail, Berlioz blazed his own trail, but a broad acquaintance with Mozart's later scores must have brought home to him how much he was pirouetting on Mozart's acrobatic shoulders.

There was precedent, too, in the spasms of orchestral eloquence that rise to the surface in Schubert's operas, cluttered with all the idle mockeries of plot with which the composer let himself be handicapped, yet evocative and forcible by turns in their fantastically complicated scenario, *Fierrabras* especially. Then, there were the nine Schubert symphonies, the last two of incredible originality of expression, for all their steady adherence to sonata form, but *terra incognita* to Berlioz. Nor apparently was he acutely aware of the piano concerto genre brought into being by Mozart and Beethoven. He had no personal interest in the piano. Schubert's songs began to appear in Paris, mostly in the egregiously flowery and often fictitious translations of the mysterious Bélanger from 1833 onwards. A miscellany of six was followed by 'Le roi des aulnes'. In 1839 Émile Deschamps took a hand, while Bélanger, undismayed, continued in full spate.[1] Berlioz must have known some of these. His recorded comment seems at first curious: 'Il est certain que Schubert ne contient rien de ce que certaines gens appellent de la mélodie—fort heureusement!' (*Journal des Débats*, 25 January, 1835). It appears, however, that he is replying to a notice by Fétis on 'La jeune religieuse' (as sung with orchestra), in which the critic found in the vocal part nothing but ineffective recitative. Berlioz, sensing what Fétis meant by melody, jumped on the other side of the scale. Could he genuinely have regarded Schubert as no melodist? It is hardly conceivable. But the intimate communication of singer and piano, with which Schubert had made history and

29

given home music a new life, somehow passed Berlioz by. 'Le roi des aulnes' roused him, not to emulation but, years later, to orchestration. Schubert's piano duets appeared in Paris by 1835. It is surprising that they did not tempt Berlioz to run off a march or two on similar lines, choosing a suitable dramatic occasion for a title.

The Beethoven symphonies were another story. It is not likely that Berlioz gained any keen sense of recognition of Beethoven's calibre from François Habeneck, who in the late twenties, armed with violin-conductor scores, set himself to introduce the Paris musical public to Beethoven the symphonist with more resolution than practical judgement. But the scheme, which to this day repeats itself annually somewhere in the westernized world in a less exploratory setting, provided a platform for an essay on each symphony, in which the writer's admiring but discerning study of the scores is left beyond doubt. As a set, Symphonies 1–8 revealed not only a range of mood, a definite sense of purpose and a compulsive logic without precedent but, in a given movement, a juxtaposition of the kind of contrasts that one associates with Berlioz's own music. After the very first performance of the Fifth symphony, the Vienna correspondent of the *Allgemeine musikalische Zeitung* had found the Andante original and attractive with its blend of 'heterogeneous ideas—gentle reverie and warlike fierceness' (Barzun's translation). 'Reverie' nicely summarizes the absorption that Beethoven could put into a theme designed for formal variation, and equally the kind of music which Berlioz was to produce in many an interlude, symphonic or dramatic, from a severely pressurized and vocal Cellini to a silent Romeo or Lélio.

Beethoven's Third symphony, which with the Fifth and Seventh Habeneck put first in his series, was no less a document in emotional exploration and instrumental adventure, yet in its stalwart accumulation of four out-size movements a whole experience; the Fifth, with its overwhelming third-and-last movement, using the gloomiest of scherzo-movement as a kind of catalyst for the release of the most assertive C major sequel possible, was demonstrably integral. But it was the Ninth which showed Berlioz the way to the symphonie dramatique, fusing characteristic movements of sheer music with others displaying a text sung, as a clue to the intention of the whole work but no less generously releasing rhythm, melody and whatever in their own right and in calculated relation to the other, non-vocal movements. Beethoven's resort to a chosen text as a necessary treatment, with symphonic variations, to complete three tremendous movements could be credibly extended to a working relation with a text and singers from the start, whether preserving a symphonic pattern or developing a more multifarious scheme of number-work, proceeding fitfully from one 'number' to another. No slackening of detail was implied by a reliance on a text. Rather, it was a challenge to find new life in the *genre instrumental expressif*.

Berlioz could have had no doubts but that in the release of his musical powers the blaze of Beethoven's undiminishing creativity left Gluck's service to drama in a diminished light, when he came to consider the degree of musical impact in a work as a whole. 'Forward from Gluck' meant continuing where he had made progress, in the confidence of new standards of breadth and precision. 'Forward from Beethoven' involved competing with Beethoven's sweep and powers of definition by means of an imaginative approach, with fresh organization of existing structures and more research into textural combinations and antitheses. As Berlioz's most constant and sophisticated stimulus, this message will recur throughout our narrative.

In this research the orchestrally skilful but aesthetically compromising craftsman-ship of Meyerbeer could not dent Berlioz's quest for a characteristic style, except in so far as Meyerbeer's insistence on a grand and balanced orchestral establishment, and his fastidious care for precise and fresh scoring, set a firm public standard, even if the new and affluent public cared more for the processions, the horrors and the orgies involved. It was the ultimate fate of Meyerbeer to be remembered intrinsically for what he did not write, namely, as one of the obvious 'credits' in the colossal production represented by the name of Wagner, and, indeed, as an orchestral talent taken over by Wagner and expanded in more vital contexts—rather than as a force in musical history. Meyerbeer's eclectic style of Weberian romanticism, chivalrous, sinister and ebullient in turn, converged in a tremendous boost for French grand opera from *Robert le Diable* to *L'Africaine*, the latter with its still bravo-worthy 'O Paradiso' from da Gama but also its *Liebestod* from the resolute Selica, not to mention many other contrasted solos and ensembles. Even the tam-tams in *Il Crociato in Egitto*, the first Parisian première, are dramatically relevant. Yet 'an irreparable loss' seems now a strange parting assessment of so uncertain a musical craftsman.

So much for the given and identifiable impulses towards the re-making of char-acteristic music, in a guiding but not restricting stage context, actual or imagined, or in a fresh deployment of the orchestra in the delineation of musical ideas and in their orderly pursuit to a richer conclusion. If the guiding hand was to be that of late Gluck, soloists might have to give up their sovereignty, but they were assured of a true melodic line along with novel excursions *dramatis causa*, and a developing orchestra could not be kept out. It need not be the comedy for which the new rich public were inclined, but it would be the kind of storied music that a cultivated Frenchman could take in. If, on the other hand, Beethoven was to be the prompter,

31

general expectations of enjoyment would be low, since even the self-styled cogno-scenti at the Conservatoire regarded his music as disturbing, subversive and at best not properly intelligible. Nevertheless, 'more Beethoven' made attractive programming to a young and clear-headed composer, and it drew Berlioz along, as it was to draw Wagner and Borodin in their equally individual ways.

Another genius struck early upon Berlioz's mind from outside music. The appearance of an English company in Paris with *Romeo* and *Hamlet*, besides being severely impressive in itself—the fascinatingly artless Juliet-Ophelia especially—awoke Berlioz to the higher potential of harnessing different scenes and different levels of existence in a new and sweeping vision of life. Music, specializing in char-acterization in depth, and already promising an expanding range of rhythmic movement, from a short arioso to a pounding Allegro vivace or brooding Adagio, had received, for a newly responsive Shakespearean viewer, important encourage-ment to project its control of quickly defined or gradually unfolding moods on to, or rather from, a vividly human scene. Actually, not to name various preludes and interludes, a symphony and an opera, both Shakespearean in origin, appeared at wide intervals, and it is not fanciful to attribute the breadth of *Cellini* and *Faust*, and of the dramatization of Virgilian Aeneas' adventures at Troy and Carthage, to Shakespeare's methods of treatment. Goethe himself had betrayed the same in-fluence in his scene-upon-scene handling of the Faust saga. Certainly Berlioz gained increasing confidence in his capacity to edit and augment, and finally to compose, his scenarios.

Further and steady reminders that Shakespearean creations of character and thought became part of Berlioz's imaginative life appear in the many apt quotations scattered about his scores, from the reflections of *Hamlet* and *The Tempest* in *Lélio* to the scene where Dido and Aeneas actually take their cue from Lorenzo and Jessica at the richest moment of their exchange of passionate declaration. It is an attractive hypothesis that at a period when in our own country Shakespeare was never more forcibly played to audiences, as to people ready to be involved in whatever tensions or releases the staging may offer, the dramatic appeal of Berlioz has a good chance of falling on alert ears.

Nor must Goethe's *Faust*, Part 1, be under-estimated in this context. With its typical succession of scenes, the work made an instant impact on Berlioz's mind, aided by de Nerval's recent translation. The *Eight Scenes* (opus 1) and the cantata developed from them in late maturity illustrate his dependence on Goethe at crucial points. One might have expected to observe a different urge from the creator of *Ernani* than the setting of *Sara la baigneuse*, delicious as it is; but so it was with Hugo on the surface. Thomas Moore and Gautier evoked a song-set each.

Berlioz ended by becoming his own librettist and scene-compounder. He worked out his own text and scenario for his free settings from *Matthew* and the *Aeneid*. Having learnt not to be afraid of Shakespeare or Goethe on his chosen ground, Berlioz formed a habit of consulting a similarly 'universal' text for the plan of subsequent major work. He thus forced his way hither and thither with a textual backing, just as Wagner did in a consistently stage setting, in a closer relation to his own text and consequently in a systematic progress of style not so easily detected in Berlioz.

Let us turn aside to consider the immediate incentives to the formation of a musical style provided by the tutors and textbooks known to be available to the learning composer. It does not need much knowledge after the event to visualize a somewhat grotesque situation at Berlioz's entry into the Academy. By the special intervention of J. P. Lesueur, one of the chief tutors, Berlioz was enabled to take both the 'composition' and the 'counterpoint' courses in his first year; one with Lesueur himself, the other with Anton Reicha. Before we try to size up the true nature of this confrontation, let us glance at the harmony book previously used by Berlioz, the *Treatise on Harmony* (1803) by Citizen C. S. Catel, composer of *Les Bayadères* and other operas. He had been commissioned by State authority to lay down a system. This consists chiefly of a parade of the accepted chords of the mid-eighteenth century and various established semitonal variants, with their uses in modulating to fresh keys; in short, a harmonic grammar and syntax, prescribing procedure without any reference to its exemplification in approved music. None of this can have been news to an already practising composer. (Barzun's picture of him trying out the chords on his guitar seems naïve.) Still less can these elements of harmonic progression have stimulated Berlioz in the slightest.

When we come to the supposed academic tutoring, it must be said that in Lesueur and Reicha Berlioz enjoyed the society of two musicians of character and parts. An eminent teacher-composer who had survived many régimes by sheer authority and independence in controversy, Jean-François Lesueur (62) had begun his career as a church musician with his own ideas about the way that devotional music should go, but he had also, under the favour of Napoleon, produced *Ossian* and other full-scale operas. These two lines of production, of a historically and culturally informed approach to creative work and a more spontaneous reach for passion and dream in music, combined in a new conception of dramatic Mass-music or oratorio, supported by an early *Exposé d'une musique, une, imitative et particulière à chaque solennité* (1786–7). The liturgical text was to be polarized, in effect, by being presented as the symbolic contribution to a scenario based on Gospel narrative, devised according to the calendar-occasion. The clue to making this recital expressive was rhythm; but timbre also had its place. Further, the ordinary structural genres of aria, imitation and recitative were to be reinforced by the interpolation of suitable traditional tunes. (Inquiring scholar as he was, Lesueur was not to know that he had been signally anticipated in musical principle by J. S. Bach's many cantatas in the vernacular, written round a text reflecting the Gospel of the day, dramatized in an aside (recitative) as a contemporary spiritual event, with recurrently cited chorales.)

Lesueur's Christmas Oratorio, with its seven movements incorporating *Kyrie* and *Gloria* in a series at once picturesque and devotional, is a typical example of his 'freedom through unity' method. It may have given Berlioz a stimulus to the fresh treatment of traditional dramatic material and scriptural narrative in scenes made characteristic by musical means. The resemblances have been much pressed by O. Fouque in *Les révolutionnaires de la musique* (1882). But it seems much more probable that Lesueur's work was taken by his infinitely more critical pupil as a warning that elaborate didactic intentions are no substitute for hard workmanship. As exemplary music, Lesueur's oratorio leaves much to question. The movement-structures are arbitrary and whimsical, and the themes, where not formal inflexions, are rarely made for growth or wear. I quote two fragments, the *Laudamus te* figure, common to Movements 3, 4 and 5, and the start of the main strophe of the final movement.

Ex. 3.1

lau - da - mus, lau - da - mus_ te_____

Ex. 3.2

Premier strophe moderne

SOPRANO
SOLO: Qui na - tus est de vir - gi - ne

The most impressive sound-element is the elaborate texture, such as accompanies the climax of the opening *Kyrie*. The same line of criticism may be offered for the imperialist dream of heroes and prophets, *Ossian*. The bards of whatever tribe are on the dull or solemn side, and so is Rosmala, Ossian's intended bride. The fresh

Ex. 4

(*Entrée des jeunes Calédoniens dansants.*)

Vivace

Vln., Fl., Hp.

air comes from the supernumeraries, the junior bards and their girls. This at least is nineteenth-century perkiness (**Ex. 4**).

The closing of the medical school in Paris, as a purge of 'liberalism', had determined the career-change of at least one student there. When Berlioz had therefore decided to approach Lesueur, of whom he had heard through a pupil named Hyacinthe Gerono (composing under his first name), he submitted a vocal piece, *The Arab mourning his steed*, and a canon. Lesueur found 'warmth and dramatic movement' in the 'cantata'(?) but faulted the 'harmony' and recommended Gerono as a coach. What were 'our principles of harmony' (derived from Rameau) one can only guess, for in a few weeks Berlioz was accepted. (The evidence for all this is contained in the plausible write-up of his entry into the Academy, in the *Memoirs* composed two decades later.) Lesueur's sense of harmonic progression and modulation can now only be regarded as stilted, awkward and elementary. The benevolent tone of this and many other recollections of Lesueur, as leading figure in the world of Paris music, makes it clear that, if his counselling was less than shrewd and his experience of classical music such as Beethoven quite imperceptive, fundamentally Lesueur encouraged this self-helping student to develop his talent. And the support of J. F. Lesueur was never to be taken lightly, least of all in 1826. Yet one infers that his main influence on Berlioz was to help him to think out what music could do for a literary situation by way of augmenting the listener's sense of involvement in a wider and more intense order of experience. Subsidiarily, what orchestral timbre could do; thus reinforcing Gluck as an aid from history.

Antonin Reicha had also been an opera composer, and he proved a methodical teacher. Bohemian born, he had come to Paris in 1808 via Bonn and Vienna. At Bonn he learnt to speak German and French as well as his native Czech, read mathematics and Kant at the university, and played in the electoral orchestra, where he formed a warm acquaintance, cemented by a Gluck air, with another player, his exact contemporary, Ludwig van Beethoven. At Vienna there were Albrechtsberger and Salieri and Haydn to expound, each in his own way, what every composer needed to know. What this meant to Beethoven is on detailed record in *Beethoven's*

Studien as transcribed by Gustav Nottebohm. Reicha, now recognized as the pioneer in French wind ensemble music, emerged as something of an individualist on the surface. His impulsive *Thirty-six fugues* for piano, with their kinky subjects and kinkier answers, have even been compared with Hindemith's *Ludus Tonalis*, but he remained an entire conformist in the bulk of his industrious output. At Paris he was eventually put in charge of the counterpoint class in 1818, where the distinctness of his ideas and the precision of his methods attracted pupils in general. His main opera, if that is not too strong a term, was *Sapho* (1821). From 1814 to 1833 he published an impressive-looking series of textbooks, in French in the first place: one on melody and accompaniment (later, in Italian), another on composition and harmony (going into German, Italian and finally English); a third on advanced composition and harmony, and a fourth on 'dramatic' composition. He also left a handwritten book of practical illustrations, used later by César Franck. From these several transcriptions of his teaching one may judge to some extent what Reicha stood for as an analyst and historian, if any, of method.

'La melodie est le language du sentiment', yet, declares Reicha, it needs the logic of balanced phrase-groups, punctuated by cadences, and of thematic development. By melody he means the melodic line of an operatic aria. His treatise consists chiefly of analyses of cited arias by Mozart, Piccinni, Zingarelli and their respective like. Possibly Reicha made his pupils write airs after these models. Anyhow this sort of rationalization of familiar practice might have been stimulating to a student feeling his way about construction. The *Cours de composition musicale* is an elementary manual of harmonic processes, of no interest here. The exhaustive *Traité de haute composition musicale* is educationally no better. It covers a wide field of contrapuntal and other devices, with mocked-up illustrations and a general lack of penetrating comment. In his *Art du composition dramatique* Reicha, returning to the medium in which, one suspects, he felt most at ease, formulates from A to Z the craft of the operatic composer, since no style was established for concert vocal music. Recitative, air, ensembles, orchestral interludes, the stimuli of singers, decor, situation, the slow wearying business of putting a score into production—all is considered. But the illustrations are from Reicha's own opera, pedestrian except where, as in the moving Phaon scene from *Sapho* (Ex.64), the pulsating harmony moves to its hesitant cadence in an almost Schubertian style. The general effect is musically nugatory. Near the end Reicha refers sceptically to the 'genre romantique', in which the composer enjoys all freedom of taste and treatment, and he recalls his friend Beethoven's extemporizations in this context. But he goes on to decry Beethoven's early resolution (*c.* 1802) to write at the bidding of his imagination, because in fact Beethoven's compositions of that period affirm the beauties of science, logic and planning! A curiously incomplete portrait, as we now know from the sketch-books of the time, of Beethoven wrestling with his material till he had shaped it to his thought. This a textbook could not teach, but at least it could imply that workmanship is not enough. Reicha thus supplied a shape to composing, for the stage or apart from it, which he *inferred* from his studies but rarely or never felt. Barzun's dismissal of musical dogma in the Academy as 'deceptively "rational"' seems a fair report on the Reicha curriculum. What Reicha thought about, say, the *Faust* scenes, is not known. He remains an enigma as far as Berlioz's progress is concerned.

Breathing, then, Gluck, Beethoven and endless French opera, Berlioz sallied into the virgin territory of his own ideas, in music for orchestra and voices. There let us observe him.

NOTE

1. The main stages in the striking growth of Schubert in French were as follows:

Table 1

Date	Publication	Translator	Publisher	City
c. 1830	Die schöne Müllerin	Bélanger	Diabelli	Vienna
1833	Six mélodies célèbres	Bélanger	Richault	Paris
1834–35	Quatre nouvelles mélodies	Sivol	Prilip	Paris
c. 1836	Collection des Lieder de Schubert	Deschamps	Schlesinger	Paris
	La jeune religieuse	Nourrit	Richault	Paris
1839–40	12 mélodies	Deschamps	Schlesinger	Paris
1840–50	367 mélodies	Bélanger	Richault	Paris
1850	40 mélodies	Deschamps	Brandus	Paris

It may be noted that Nourrit and Deschamps had one method in common. Ignorant of German, each would obtain a translation of a song from a more linguistic friend, and then put this into verse. Bélanger, one thinks, never bothered his head about translation. He used his 'imagination'. On the whole background of Lieder in French, see F. Noske, *La mélodie française*, pp. 23–30, to which certain references above are indebted.

3

Cantatas and Scenes

MOST of Berlioz's early works are lost. Known titles include 'Le cheval arabe', presumably a setting of a long 'chant élégiaque' by C.-H. Millevoye, taken seriously enough to be submitted to Lesueur through his pupil Gerono, as already related; *Estelle et Némorin*, idly dramatized by Gerono in order to release for Berlioz a personal confession of longing for a real Estelle; and *Beverley ou le joueur* (bass and orchestra), a series of scenes based on a current melodrama in what seemed a modern realistic style. But also lost is an oratorio, *Le passage de la Mer Rouge*, with the composer's own version of *Exodus* 14. This composition may be attributed partly to the influence of Lesueur, who approved of the work for performance, and partly to the growing reality of Egyptian culture after Bonaparte's expedition. A full-scale performance in a Paris church (St. Roch's) had to be abandoned after an unsatisfactory rehearsal, due to poor attendance and fatally inaccurate parts. Having learnt his lesson, Berlioz destroyed this record of his grand oratorio manner, as a potential analogue of the Empire style or of a modernized biblical event. But surely more than the ghost of the song of triumph, at least, must have survived in some extant work.

The *Mass* music of 1825, revised under Lesueur's scrutiny and copied out, part by part, by the composer, *was* performed at St. Roch's with H. I. Valentino of the Opera and the Opera orchestra, the engagement of whose services had been graciously permitted, at the composer's expense. (For the outlay of 12,000 francs he was indebted to a loan from a loyal friend, Augustin de Pons.) Lesueur attended, hidden behind a pillar, and afterwards gave his opinion, 'Too many notes, but every intention carries', and adjured his pupil to take up music, not medicine as his father had planned. Without entertaining any illusions about the more-favourable-than-not notices of the press, Berlioz felt encouraged enough to have no further doubts about what his future career should be. He was aware, however, that the *Mass* needed re-casting. In the end he discarded it, including even the brilliant but light-weight 'Gloria' which the public had liked. Only 'Resurrexit' remained; that is, from 'Resurrexit' to the end of the Creed. This appeared in 1829 by itself, with eight extra kettledrums, as *Le Jugement Dernier*; a Lesueur touch? Then it was to form part of an oratorio, later opera, *Le dernier jour du Monde*, on the scenario of which Berlioz worked spasmodically from 1831–33, with the entire non-cooperation of his friend, Humbert Ferrand, and others over the book. Further musical intentions were fortunately scotched by refusal at the Opera. In 1835 the basic chorus figured in a commemoration of France's famous men (see page 155). Even that did not secure publication.

This compound of energy and solemn admonition, singled out from the rest of the *Mass*, thus became the first of many early pieces, fragments of which can be found in later works. The details of the eventual inglorious dispersal may be summarized as concerning the chorus, published in the first collected edition and then in vocal score, so that it can be found in many English libraries. (1) The **G** major section of 50 bars, 'Et ascendit . . . Patris' came in handy for the more direct 'Christe, rex gloriae' (in **A**) of the *Te Deum* (1849). Meanwhile (2) the 30 bars of brass prelude and bass declamation for 'Et iterum . . . Tuba mirum . . .' had duly appeared for 'Tuba mirum' in the 'Dies irae' of the *Requiem* (1837). (3) A year later the Allegro settings of 'Et iterum' and 'Cuius regni' became, incredibly, the stuff of a milling, minatory crowd-episode in the finale of *Cellini*, Act 2, opening with an indignant 'Assassiner un capucin!' and ending with 'Ah! quel chaos! . . . scélérat!' So far, in reverse charge, so to speak, those works of ten or twenty years later betray these derivative patches and audacious extractions. They have their parallels in other Berlioz works as well as numberless precedents in eighteenth-century opera and oratorio, Gluck included. Yet all such borrowing must be justified in its context, and pending such examination must be written down as an economic mannerism.

'Et resurrexit' thus retains unsullied its coherent conception as a completion of the Creed with 'Tuba mirum' boldly inserted after *vivos et mortuos* and unexpected resumptions of the end of the second main paragraph in the middle of the third. Its occasional revival today would mark Berlioz's first significant work, as well as a notable setting of a text which the greatest composers have exalted with their most strenuous efforts. Here the arresting start (from a prolonged expectant chord of **D** major for *sepultus est*?) in a pulsating **G** minor maintains suspense, which a melodious **G** major for 'Et ascendit' rather extends than dispels, since its cadential phrases can only be a pause before the next train of musical thought. This proves to be unswervingly in **E** flat. A declamatory 'Et iterum venturus', dazzlingly punctuated by full brass, prepares for an expansive Allegro in which fresh and rhythmic iterations for 'Et iterum venturus' assist the systematic, rather unyielding, cultivation of a plainly shaped, scarcely evocative, phrase, with a highly coloured finish. Yet the gradual release of spirit as this theme (**Ex. 5**) takes command makes a

40

Ex. 5

stirring projection of a vision of transcendent judgement and authority without end. It still speaks piercingly to men of belief and men of unbelief. A remarkable surviving number of a larger work assumed not to have been commensurate, this chorus showed at once the imaginative range of Berlioz's art, apparently indebted to Beethoven but in fact unaware of it.

A little later Berlioz worked at a text supplied him by Ferrand, *Scène héroïque* (*La Révolution Grecque*), a tribute to the recent revolt. It was not performed at the time, but it was included in Berlioz's (and any Frenchman's) first one-man concert in 1828, along with the *Francs Juges* and *Waverley* overtures and *Et resurrexit*. It was received with enthusiasm and, incidentally, preferred to the *Mass* chorus. In 1833 Berlioz revived the work, in rehearsal under Habeneck, indoors—a valuable aural test. This was for inclusion, with the *William Tell* overture and other warhorses, in the ceremony of putting Napoleon's statue back on the Place Vendôme; an eleventh hour manoeuvre on Berlioz's part. But in the next hour the *Heroic Scene* was cut out of the programme, and anyhow the musical part of the celebrations was drowned by political demonstrations. The Opera announced a performance. This, too, was cancelled. An ironic finish to a work that had gone off with a bang.

Projected from ancient history, with a somewhat confused invocation of Leonidas, the renowned Spartan commander, but later of Tyrtaeus, the fervent poetic supporter of a war of conquest two centuries earlier, this picture of a revisionist movement is romantic from start to finish. 'Greeks,' cry a hero and supporting priest, 'Let us march together to immortality and world-renown in the sacred cause of our country.' Prayer to a star makes an interlude. Berlioz takes all this in his stride, as the framework for two developed choruses divided by a contrasted movement. The first contrives to be the most eventful. Instant, terse recitative and a short, jejune air lead to a firmly shaped Allegro. Here two successive phases ('Hellènes', 'À ses clartés') for solo and answering chorus and more urgent antiphony initiated by the priest arrive at a period of thematic insistence ('la voix du Dieu des armées').

41

Increasing speed, a vibrant continuing bass and a sharp turn to flattened sixth tonality reach a point of no return in the succinct intensification of 'À ses clartés'. So to a brusque, almost comic, exit by the sixfold repeat of 'Marchons!' up the scale.

The use of the female chorus for the prime devotees of the Larghetto is effective. The informed ear may even flash forward to recall the more trenchant texture, similar in kind, of Cassandra's stoic band in the temple of Vesta (*The Trojans*, act 2). The later accession of male voices, heavily accompanied, serves to release subsequently a graceful coda ('sans crainte') of receding tone, tempting to quote (**Ex. 6**).

Ex. 6

This, however, is only an interlude before a tumultuous finale sweeps all before it, including the bombastic text. A rousing tune (**Ex. 7**) and its grand recurrence encloses an extended, importunate, aggressive period of typically saccadic rhythm and stubborn, unprogressive tonic or fifth-degree bass. This period bursts forth from a portentous discernment of Tyrtaeus' spirit in the distance, plucking two harps (**Ex. 8**). A vivid turn to flattened-third tonality lends point to the renewed call to arms, a vague echo of the reiterations of Beethoven's **C** major closes.

Ex. 7

Allegro non troppo

TENORS: Le monde en - tier_____ pré-pa - re la tro-phé - e.   Que nous pro -

-met,   que nous pro-met un   si beau sort.   Le monde en - tier

BASSES: Le   monde   en - tier   pré - pa -

Ex. 8

Doppio movimento

crescendo sempre ma poco a poco

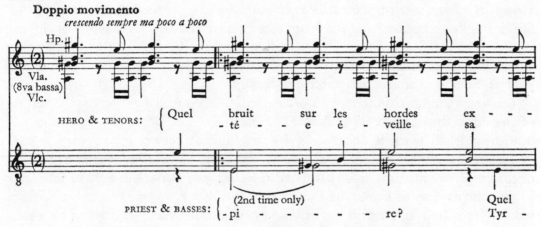

Hp.

Vla.
(8va bassa)
Vlc.

HERO & TENORS: { Quel   bruit   sur   les   hordes   ex - - -
-té - - e é - veille   sa

(2nd time only)

PRIEST & BASSES: { -pi - - - - - re?   Tyr -

Quel

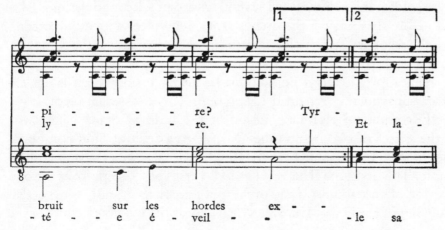

1   2

-pi - - - - re?   Tyr -
ly - - - - re.   Et la -

bruit   sur   les   hordes   ex - - -
-té - - e é - veil - - -le sa

43

This detailed account of Berlioz's first sizeable production seeks to do justice to a work entirely unperformed in modern times. While the massing of State troops or a volunteer faction, for an attack on or by those of another, could happen almost anywhere today, the steady summons to *gloire* may fall on deaf ears among modern performers and audiences. Yet the music is not dependent on the text and its genres of exclamatory and visionary expression except for connecting detail. There is enough of musical interest, constructive or faltering, to leave a characteristic mark on the ear. Forward, then, from the inaugural concert of 1828, supported by *Waverley*.

With this demonstrable capacity apparent in 1826, it was something of an affront to Berlioz's creative talent to have his bluff called, and to be subjected to the academic test of setting a prescribed text of a certain pattern, in competition year by year, until the award of the first prize should provide the necessary kudos, and a period of study in Rome for which, spurning Italian music, he had no inclination. However, there was no alternative way of building up recognition, such as his father might appreciate, and for four years Berlioz provided annually a qualifying fugue and a cantata, the fourth cantata securing him the gold medal. These four works will be considered later, as closed-circuit compositions, to be abandoned or kept as 'Sketches' after a few public renderings.

Ten years after writing *Scène Heroïque*, Berlioz produced *Le Cinq Mai*, a setting of an ode on the death of the emperor Napoleon by P. de Béranger. This short and undistinguished work is doomed by its structure. A serviceman, a very solitary grenadier making for France from a distant country, has fleeting, falsified glimpses of the emperor emerging from captivity, the enemy of none; but only to sink back in pathetic dreams of France and a peaceful end. Every escape of the music from tedious brooding in animato incident and orchestral vivacity is dogged by a fatal *da capo* of 'Pauvre soldat' and a diminished seventh chord of false modulation. 'Ah!' sigh the chorus before they answer the orchestra, as one voice, with a pulverizing last repetition of the recurrent self-pitying phrase. Tyrtaeus had served the composer far better.

In the same vein, approximately, Berlioz wrote, nearly twenty years later, *The Tenth of December*, subsequently renamed *L'Impériale*. This occasional piece, however, is a directly communal utterance, in aid of the head of State. The music spreads round the verses of two hymn tunes ('hymn' in a dedicated but non-devotional sense), set to texts by Captain Lafont. Samples of each will show the difference in vocal style. The first tune (**Ex. 9.1**) has two verses and one more at the end for a brilliant fusion of choral unison and orchestral punctuation; not, as expected, in its original key but in the key of **Ex. 9.2**, which avoids the inconveniences of the

Ex. 9.1

Du peuple en - tier les â-mes tri-on-phan - tes on tres-sail-li

Ex. 9.2

Dieu qui pro - tè - ges la Fran-ce, Veil - le sur son Em-pe-reur

first key for choral unison. The second tune (**Ex. 9.2**) is ushered in by recitative and runs to four verses. These clear strophical assertions are skilfully separated by short episodes, substantial or sonorously digressive. Once again, this précis is called for. It is commonly assumed that because this *Emperor* hymn is optimistic and breezy, it must be negligible. The elementary appeal of its tunes and pattern, and its evocation of the motherland, are obvious, but do not disqualify. Berlioz had a definite command of infectious melody, and here he had virtually been asked for it. There is no call either to cry the piece down or to magnify it above its genre.

These two mini-works approximate in type to the orchestral songs to be surveyed in Chapter 7, and Berlioz actually added the first to his later collection of *32 Mélodies* for voices and piano. The *Hymne à la France*, *La menace des Francs* and the *Chant des chemins de fer* are similar patriotic odes of a more songful character. They will be treated in chapter 7.

It remains to sort out briefly the four *cantates de concours* of 1826–29. They do not present a progressive series to our ears, but they share a common problem and a common status as produced for Conservatoire consumption. Materially, they were intended to be for solo voice and orchestra. Actually a chorus appears in the first and last. Presented to the judges in the usual full score, each cantata had to be performed before them in a voice-and-piano rendering, in order that the broadly-based citizen committee should all hear something of what was involved by way of sound-relationship; what Stanford later called the black and white test. It was no hardship to most candidates, having written an accompaniment on piano staves and then scored it, to have it reduced back. For a composer who thought in orchestral terms from the start, a pianistic version spelt travesty and confusion. It is not surprising to learn that Berlioz's first cantata, *La Mort d'Orphée*, was pronounced unplayable at the piano session. (Obviously the pianist was no Liszt.) With this

45

penalty mark, the judges had no hesitation in passing over Berlioz and awarding the first prize to J. B. Guiraud, the script of whose cantata can still be seen in the Conservatoire library, and makes a useful comparison, as do others in the next three years of the composer's life. The script of Berlioz's cantata-score is not there—borrowed for performance and not returned?—but a copy of it survived. After being lost for forty years, this turned up again, and a photographic reproduction was published in Paris in 1930. The work has had occasional broadcasts in recent years. It is demonstrably a very remarkable early score.

The text, by 'Berton', presumably the established composer of light opera, presents Orpheus confronted and cruelly massacred by the Thracian women whom he had scorned. After formal expostulation with the hostile 'priestesses', Orpheus apostrophizes his lyre, voice of sanity, in such terms as (1) 'O seul bien', (2) 'Art séduisant', (3) 'O prodige étonnant', and at the last moment (4) plunges into a desperate and vain appeal to Apollo to save him from the Bacchantes' fury. Guiraud sets all this in measured terms, with arias at points 2, 3 and 4 above. Only in the last does Orpheus appear agitated, and then in plenary sonata form, with reprise. Berlioz read up the story, no doubt, probably in Ovid's 11th *Metamorphosis* ('En hic est nostri contemptor'). His Orpheus sees murder in the women's eyes almost from the start. He comes on as the dedicated, innocent artist, whose sublime calm is to pervade the world. But as soon as the women are in sight, all careless talk of the all-soothing lyre is off. In a troubled context of nagging strings and explosive tuttis, Berlioz concedes one developed aria for 'O seul bien' (given a passing intensity by Guiraud), and then, skipping entirely the text around 2 and 3 above, makes for the passionate prayer to Apollo. Nor is he content to leave the menacing women to the imagination. Ominous brass chords (**Ex. 10**.1) (well, fairly ominous), an agitated string motive (**Ex. 10**.2) and aggressive percussive features prepare for the entry of a double chorus of women, whose crude antiphony is easily moulded into dire gestures; trombones, creeping up semitonally, as in the furies scene in Gluck's *Iphigénie*, reinforce this (**Ex. 10**.3). The soloist's renewed appeal (*da capo*) escalates the demonstrations of hatred. With 'Eurydice!' wrung from his expiring breath, the liquidation of Orpheus is celebrated in a snarling, triumphant **C** major, mingled with echoes of 'Eurydice!' in declining rhythm. The story is told, and the nominally third aria completed. But a tremulous shift of harmony shows that this is not the end. The opening image of Orpheus' magic power is now reproduced, upon the fancy of the wind catching Orpheus' lyre and a piping shepherd taking up his song (**Ex. 11**). So a work that started in **D** and moved to **A** for one aria and **C** minor for the other, finishes up in **A** flat, a key in no relation to **D**.

On these lines a memorable polarization of a mood eloquently in tune with

Ex. 10.1

Ex. 10.2

Ex. 10.3

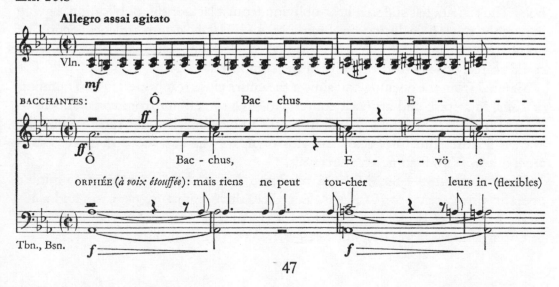

Ex. 11

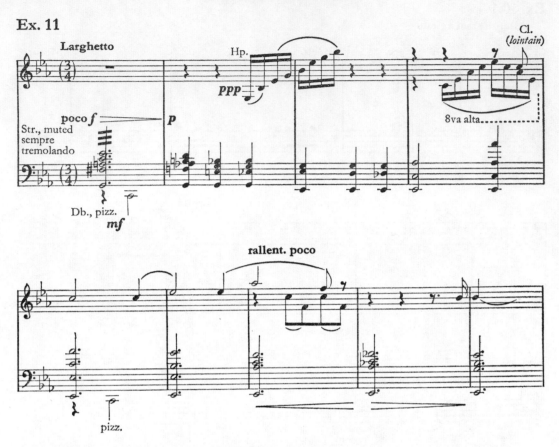

nature and of overwhelming fears of Bacchante intentions (furies grounded on earth) is effected by a masterly instrumentation of poetic ideas and a few plain symbols. The cantata has suffered near-oblivion from a lack of full publication, having inevitably missed inclusion in Breitkopf and Härtel's admirable collection of vocal scores around 1905. It is still neglected. Any one who has heard the work could scarcely doubt of the quality of the composer.

Material from the opening and almost the entire close reappeared in two numbers of *Lélio*, in a fresh and artificial context, to save something from consignment to the awful shelf. Thus the essential magical-Orpheus music is the most commonly known feature. But Orpheus claims his own, for his hazardous mastery over a cruel death. With it come art's survivals.

Nearly a century later, Milhaud produced *Les malheurs d'Orphée*, a 45-minute opera in three scenes for Orpheus, Eurydice, three miniature choruses and a 13-piece orchestra. (Revived in 1962 for the 'festival' at Aix-en-Provence, where it had been written, it was described in *The Times* as 'a gem'.)

Here the myth is modernized in a simple Provençal setting. Orpheus, a village healer of men and wild animals (second chorus), marries Eurydice, the prettiest of four gypsy sisters, the other three of whom take vengeance on him. Eurydice also dies from a sickness. Which Orpheus will be remembered in a hundred year's time, and for what?

Berlioz's second cantata, *Herminie*, is on more regular lines. The subject, derived from an episode in Tasso's *Jerusalem delivered*, had already been treated, to different texts, by Halevy (1819) and recently C. S. Paris (1826), with whom Berlioz would have competed if his qualifying fugue had not been turned down. Viellard's fresh text was now shared entirely by Berlioz with, amongst others, G. Ross-Despréaux, whose cantata survives and shows arias in **A, C** minor and **E** with the same intention as Berlioz's coincident arias in **C, D** minor and **E**; each promoted by explanatory recitative, enriched with orchestral motives. Herminia, a heroic 'unbeliever' in a city besieged by the Christian officer, Tancred, whom she loves and who is wounded in an attack, is torn between simple happy love, a desperate longing for Tancred to keep out of danger, and her own resolve to go into battle herself, coupled with a prayer for Tancred's safety to the god in whom she disbelieves.

The airs represent points 'taken' from these three trends. Despréaux portrays Herminia in a whirl of agitation, ending in a lengthy exhibition of the ever-womanly, exulting in perilous rescue. Berlioz is at once much more subtle and more musical. His first air is not the predictable three-beat cantabile in **A** of all his predecessors, but cast in a vaudeville, near-patter style (two beats, in **C**), skilfully shaped. The second air balances a tone of stern desperation by a melodious *meno mosso* in the relative major key, recalling the initial theme of the cantata, for 'J'exhale en vain ma plainte.' From the latter Despréaux derives a piquant finish; Berlioz allows his opening to return, intensified, because so strong a rhythm cannot be held back, and this is true to character. But it is in the last aria, 'Venez, terribles armes', containing the unbeliever's prayer, uttered as she sallies forth armed, that Berlioz showed his shrewd response to a complex situation. Despréaux treats this ejaculatory prayer as a midway melodic phrase in an expansive onset of declamation and orchestral repartee, pressed home by a quivering tonality and ending on a note of heroic bravura, faithful to the last as a woman in love. Unswerving, vigorous, it gained the composer the first prize; and in confirmation of this success, Despréaux went on to write *Le souper de Mari* and other operas, with the full score published, not hastily improvized for a production.

Berlioz, avoiding Despréaux's rather obvious preparatory recitative, dashes into his *impetuoso vivace* after a stage of oscillation, making it easier to have an absolute break for the prayer; a *largo* three-beat affair with a self-contained tune in **G**.

49

4

(The composer mistakenly revived this for a setting of the *Chant sacré* in *Mélodies irlandaises*.) After this a speeded up *Tempo primo* soon runs its course, leaving a vacuum. It is filled by a renewal of the *largo* tune, its 7-7 bars spread over 21-21 four-beat bars, while the resolute rhythm confidently continues in diminishing tone, sealing the music with the genuine calm of a decision taken. It conveys, one may think, an assurance of the integrity of the new vows. So, an award of a second prize: 'let us see what comes of this sort of gimmicky finishing-off'.

Ex. 12

To a modern judge the cantata seems a capably written work but not distinctive enough to rise above its conventionally emotional text as *Orphée* (1826) does. Meanwhile, for future purposes one must note the handy method of combining opposites, as in **Ex. 12** above, with full significance in the mind's drama. And here, firmly on the ground for any faltering examiner to notice, is the opening theme, a forecast of Herminia's jaunty approach, to be softened for her insouciant gesture in the second aria (j'exhale en vain ma plainte'). There it might have rested. But this was not to be. It was only the beginning.

Ex. 13

Next year Viellard produced another text, *La mort de Cléopâtre*, showing the queen communicating with herself at the last stages: facing humiliation by the Roman emperor, seeing a line of Pharaohs to welcome her after death, and increasingly aware of her approaching destruction by snake-poisoning. Berlioz penned an extended introduction, and struggled resourcefully with this train of introspection, not least in the vigour of the recitatives. In the first and third arias the pattern of formal reprise and fresh start is dogged by weakly repetitive elements, especially 'Du destin qui m'accable' in the latter aria. Only in the summons to the Pharaohs, in a kind of ritual dance, does the music take firm command. The final speech-song, 'd'une voix altérée . . . plus altérée', is a vivid and original suggestion of a mind overwhelmed but determined not to yield. The whole instrumentation is distinguished. The 'final aria' is left behind.

As the amiable Boieldieu explained the day after, the judges, or a majority of them, found the cantata so unconventional in treatment that it appeared to be a test of *them*, and palpably not to be entertained as a conscious improvement on *Herminie*. No prize, then, was awarded at all. The fatal rendering of the cantata by the in-adequate soloist, who was deputizing for the proper performer, her sister, called to the Opera for higher duties, aroused protests against a total no-award from Ingres and Pradier (Lesueur was ill), but the scandalously irresponsible conditions enabled the jury to postpone decision on Berlioz with a slight colour of correctness.

Berlioz retained some of the material in his mind's ear. An over-worked figure in the first aria was brought into *Cellini*, and hence into the *Carnaval Romain* over-ture; a similar feature of the third aria was worked hard in the *The Tempest* fantasia, later to go into *Lélio*; and on a full scale the second aria became the *Choeur d'ombres* which impinges on Lélio's inner ear as he recalls Hamlet's confrontation by his father, self-invited and as good as ten Pharaohs. (The music had originally been planned for a Juliet scene, in the vaults of the Capulets: 'But if when I am laid into the tomb'.)

In *La mort de Sardanapale* (1830) Berlioz was at last, owing to there being a *grand prix* in hand, declared first for the first prize, Alexandre Montfort second; and W. Millault received second prize, with an extra award from posterity for having his cantata and hence the official text preserved, as Montfort's was not. The first concert performance of Berlioz's cantata, at which the climax of explosive sound became a whimper owing to missed cues, was described in a letter to the composer's father. But the non-survival of any score, except for a fragment of the final move-ment (discovered by Tiersot in the same book as the script of the unfinished opera, 'La nonne sanglante'), makes a practical revival an impossibility. The richly remini-scent content, however, of this fragment, taken with Jean-François Gail's text as found in Millault's score, makes it possible to reconstruct with certainty some interesting musical facts.

The scene matches *Cléopâtre* with the more spectacular death-by-conflagration of Sardanapalus and his court. The king has three arias: (1) his address to his favourite concubine, 'Étoile du matin, Néhala, prends ta lyre'; (2) a declaration of being forced into an intolerable submission by a superior power; (3) a prayer to Mithras for salvation after death and to be remembered gloriously. The score fragment begins in the middle of the third aria, and shows a male chorus on the fringe, more vivid and less intrusive than trombones. After a wayward exchange the tonic springs back into focus and the aria moves to a firm climax. On that note of fantastic *gloire* the cantata might have ended, and must have done so for the competition. But for Berlioz such a routine finish was beneath him. For the concert platform, then, he cut out the final chord, in order to initiate, after an utter reversal of key, a kind of epilogue that makes every appearance of summarizing the cantata in a rapid and restless citation of motives, which can only make sense if they are allusions to earlier events, fervently collected before a manifest conveyance of the fearful cataclysmic moment, sinking down to a meditative close with the clarinet as the soloist, as in *Orphée*. We may without further argument accept in principle the bold 'addition' as an imaginative arrest of so contrived an aria, giving the whole cantata an individual twist; disorderly but unforgettable.

What is more, the themes quoted in the round-up can be identified with some certainty with (1) the address to Néhala; (2) the dancing girls, ordered to dance at the outset and now possessed with terror; and (3) the second aria. Now, these themes are all familiar today from other works. The first is the Larghetto theme introduced by the oboe in the 'Roméo seul' movement of *Romeo and Juliet*. The second is near the main subject of the ensuing Allegro, and becomes the counter-subject figure of the oboe theme later. The third resembles the start of the first tune of *L'Impériale* (**Ex. 9.**1, page 45). Thus the plaintive melody now associated by modern listeners with Romeo, hungry for Juliet, was first intended for this distracted, sensual oriental potentate's tender image of his favourite. The jarring revelry of the Capulets came from the same scene. The salute to the Emperor was suggested by the bitter reference to the all-highest from a ruler in desperate defeat. The cantata thus joins its fellows, in spite of its fragmentary condition, as a commonly unrecognized source for features of later works. It is of course impossible to judge it as the last of the composer's efforts in the quasi-academic field.

This being so, it may be said that the freer course of *La Mort d'Orphée* leaves far the most refreshing impression of the early composer at work; something which will continue to invite involvement in its stress of mind where *Herminie* and *Cléopâtre* remain impersuasive as wholes; with some reservations in favour of the latter.[1]

Three minor works for chorus and orchestra remain to be considered: the *Eight Scenes from 'Faust'*, *Lélio* and *Sara la Baigneuse*. The first of these, written after *Herminie* and published as Opus 1, was Berlioz's outstanding commitment to public notice. He regretted the decision and tried to withdraw all unsold copies of the score; he wanted to be able to revise. The work remains extant in select copies. The nine 'scenes' (two joined in one setting) are an assembly of isolated numbers of varying substance in extremely random sequence, some based on the incidence of a song in the drama, others on a chosen opportunity for developed music. While Scenes 1, 3 and 7 are expansive, the remaining five are simply strophical and based on one verse-setting. However, to further immediate contact with an audience used to stage events rather than to dramatic lyric, the scenes were provided with quotations from the dramatic context or auxiliary quotations, of varying relevance, from *Hamlet* and *Romeo and Juliet*, the two plays recently brought to Paris by Kemble's company. This approach was the republican tradition as borne out by Lesueur, and Berlioz favoured this method of outside communication of intentions from time to time, most transparently in *Lélio*, but more subtly in *Romeo and Juliet*. The upshot was a *Faust* rhapsody, stimulated by the appearance of De Nerval's translation. A contact begun in a ballet for the Opera, commissioned but overruled, and continued as an idea for a symphony, now materialized. The suite is 'Faustian' but a great deal else. The Goethe-filled listener feels au fait with each disjunct scene and at the same time carried into fresh worlds, namely musical ones.

There the contact remained static for seventeen years until *Cellini* and *Romeo and Juliet* had appeared. Yet when the composer embarked on an integral series, embracing the whole of Faust's rise and fall (part 1) in a blend of scene, episode and interlude, twenty-four in all, these nine scenes slipped readily into their place as basic material. Besides enlarging the orchestra, Berlioz made changes of detail, and wider alterations of two scenes. Otherwise the music reappears substantially in *The Damnation of Faust*, without any patent reversion of style. This is, indeed, the most comprehensive transference among Berlioz's many adaptations from one work to another, and the widest span from period to period. Accordingly, any estimate of the *Eight Scenes* can be postponed to the next chapter, where the suite will be noticed chiefly as background material. In itself it has ceased to matter, as it is unlikely to be heard. Of Berlioz's general and ultimate approval, in spite of the withdrawal, there cannot now be any doubt.[2]

The separate consideration here of the 'lyric monodrama', *Lélio ou le Retour à la vie*, to composer's words, may surprise some readers, in view of the instructions before the score that the work should be performed after the *Symphonie Fantastique* which it supplements and concludes. This programming, however, of a bipartite 'episode in the life of an artist' is rarely realized, apart from some studio presentation, and it is purely fanciful. The symphony was written to be, and is, conclusive in itself, so far as it goes; and in *Lélio* the opening reference to the lurid death-agonies contained in the original programme-note on the symphony is only a piquant start to the opening patter. The musically six-piece suite fulfils its own histrionic purpose, to connect the most unhomogeneous movements (the interlinked fourth and fifth excepted) by means of a witty, sometimes poetic, stream of consciousness. The clue-theme of the symphony that twice intrudes at the beginning and at the end is part of the game. Musically it is not at all necessary or relevant. Consequently, it is quite in keeping here to approach *Lélio* after sampling the *Eight Scenes*, whose random sallies into the pages of *Faust* are so strewn with citations on the title-pages from Goethe and Shakespeare and others that the introduction of a live commentator as link-man becomes a logical development. Here his special task is to promote six movements, of which five already existed in some form, while the remaining one, the 'Chanson de Brigandes', must surely have been based on the lost Pirate Song from Hugo's *Orientales* or other sketch, since it is so obviously dragged into the encircling gloom, a Western among Gothic tales.

Lélio was actually the product of pressing circumstances. In 1831, after doing statutory time in Rome, Berlioz came home, and resolved to make a fresh attack on the Paris public. He had a medley of potential movements in his portfolio: a Goethe ballad of youth and mermaid; a long choral fantasia on *The Tempest*, performed all too fittingly at the Opera to a house emptied in advance by torrential rain and political disturbances, but worth keeping up as a manifesto for 'classical and romantic music', the subject of an article in 1830;[3] a prelude and epilogue culled from *Orphée* (1827), focused on the Orpheus spirit; to which might be added Cleopatra's equally visionary second air and, for polarization's sake, a brigand song of jaunty-grim type, bringing in a chorus. Could not these be tied together by a scenario in the form of an introspective monologue, spoken by an actor on the front of a stage, with an invisible body of performers behind a curtain to illustrate invocations? Berlioz decided that this was practicable, and his audience found it entertaining and 'in keeping with the needs of the day, and attractively Shakespearean'. The idea of melologue (Thomas Moore's term) was not new, and, besides being tried in Mendelssohn's *Athalie* and Bennett's *Paradise and the Peri*, was taken up seriously by Schoenberg and others, but the original treatment here was Berlioz's, and he had no further use for it. All future linking episodes he cast in some musical shape, apart from the spoken lines of *Cellini* and *Béatrice et Bénédicte*. There is no point in dwelling on the extravagances and affectations of the text of *Lélio* as connecting thread. The only way of making sense is to take each movement as it comes, as in the *Eight Scenes*, and to leave addition to a computer.

Le Pecheur, then, is a neat strophical setting for voice and piano of a Goethe ballad, selecting Verses 1, 2 and 4, but interposing the *idée fixe* of the symphony after Verse 2 to illustrate the exclamation 'Sirene!', conflating the mermaid and the already abjured 'Bacchante' from the symphony but meaningless to the ear. The earlier version (1827, published 1835) has four verses and a less subtle rhythm, but no intrusion. (Schubert's simple setting of 1815 would have been available in Bélanger's translation at Richault's, Paris, but not till around 1838.) In the next number the spirit of Hamlet's father becomes a shade-chorus (but in unison and octaves). A single melodic line, richly and rarely accompanied, unfolds the sombre message, couched at first in the mystery-syllables of the damned, but in the published edition (1855) in plain French, in order to keep the infernal lingo for the Pandemonium of *Faust*. Cleopatra's 'angry shades' are thus transferred to the Elsinore underworld with a concordance worthy of *The Golden Bough*. A strange gloss, but a useful preliminary for the construction of the Hector scene in *The Trojans*, Act 2.

The repeated swashbuckling strophe of the bandit song, celebrating the romantic outlaw but not the tycoon of today, lowers the pressure with its facile male choral rejoinders, but it is effectively swept aside by a free vocal descant for the return of the extended, bustling orchestral prelude. A far from negligible interlude, after which the shapely and subtle melodic development of the 'Chant du bonheur' is satisfying, and proves its quality both in the opening and closing orchestral statements and in the distant response (clarinet) in the 'Souvenirs' to follow. While using the Orpheus theme, 'Bonheur' is a separate construction. 'Souvenirs' repeats the pattern of the coda of *Orphée* up to the final disruptive chord (a shade more disruptive than the end of Schumann's fourth *Scene from Childhood*), and it supplies a delicate postscript here.

The *Tempest* fantasia in **F**, longer than the rest put together, is no finale but an impulsive, irrepressible welcome to the now disclosed orchestra in the role of Prospero at work on 'a timid maiden, a passionate youth, a blundering savage' through his obedient spirits, who call Miranda to join her destined bridegroom in a new life of love, caution Caliban against Ariel's anger, and bid a gushing farewell to a receding Miranda. Berlioz wrote an Italian text to keep the audience from looking for clues. He seizes the occasion to devise many characteristic features, including piano duet as well as eight solo-violins. (The movement figures on that account in one of the examples in the *Traité d'Instrumentation*.) The last such opportunity had been the blackish magic of the 'Witches' Sabbath' in *Symphonie Fantastique*, or the Sylphs in the third *Faust* scene. The successive fascinations of the island of strange, delightful noises (an eloquent chorus of airy spirits, S.S.A.T.T.) are now combined with a built-in sense of growing power, in two stages. The first is a short, evocative chorus to establish the ethereal world in which Miranda is addressed. In the second and longer stage, an industrious rising-ninth motive at the outset leads to a sweeping,

Ex. 14.1

Ex. 14.2

and soon rather cloying, reminder of Cleopatra at her most sanguine (her third air), announced by the woodwind (**Ex. 14.2**) with a bell-like send-off from the chorus in unison ('Miranda!'). Relief comes in the blunt invocation of Caliban in a reiterated five-beat phrase and an explosive tutti (Ariel-*lo*). The Cleopatra motive slips back in **C** (primary key), now with a violin canon. There is also a sweeping impromptu tune, couched in the main key, which is most misleading, since it is quite transitional. However, a full and gracious reprise succeeds in acquiring a spontaneous, up-roarious coda. This gorgeous palace may seem to rock and lean at times, but it is cumulatively convincing and, after the unitary appeal of the other movements, dazzlingly rich in material. Here, if anywhere, Berlioz let himself go. Lélio is for-gotten. It is distressing to have then to return to Lélio and his little theme, suggestive as it may be of past reverie. The fantasia should be heard by itself, as a regular thing, creatively romantic, not part of a happening.

About the same time Berlioz wrote a very slight setting, for six-part chorus and small orchestra, of one of Moore's so-called sacred songs, 'Ce monde entier n'est qu'une ombre fugitive', and called it *Méditation religieuse*. The music certainly fades out, at the beck of a falling tone or semitone. Subsequently, Berlioz brought out this record of a ghostly world, together with *La mort d'Ophélie* and a funeral march for *Hamlet*, as *Tristia*, to express his Ovidian melancholy in 1848.

No one can listen to the foregoing works without being aware, on the one hand, of Berlioz's strong sense of music appropriate to a given text, whether soaring above it or exploding around it, and, on the other hand, of his command of the telling phrase, of the precise and absolutely refreshing texture, of the compellingly harmonized melody, for its own sake. If, nevertheless, one detects a trend towards a heroic or aspiring tone, and a certain struggle for cumulative expression, it may be pleasant to pass to a work which contrives to illuminate the many facets of a fragile and extended lyric without a sense of artifice or a lack of musical coherence: the full and final setting of Hugo's *Sara la baigneuse*. The nineteenth of the *Orientales*, this poem of 1828 had 19 verses, of which Berlioz has set all but five (omitting vv. 7–9, 14, 17). Originally appearing as a male voice quartet at a concert of 1834 (music lost), re-set for two voices with a piano part compiled by the composer's critic friend, Auguste Morel (revised by the editor in the old collected edition), the work found fulfilment in a setting published around 1850 for three choirs (1. S.T.B.B. 2. S.A. 3. T.T.B.B.) and an orchestra without heavy brass but with strings 12, 12, 10, 10, 8 (and drums).

Hugo's subject (after Watteau's *L'escapolette?*) is 'Sara, belle d'indolence', swinging in a hammock over a fountain, totally ornamental, meditative and detached. So, there are recurrent and piquant turns of phrase or texture for Sara (**Ex. 15.1**) in herself, an epitome of smiling insouciance (**Ex. 15.2a**) swinging (**Ex. 15.2b**) flying through the air (**Ex. 15.2c**) enjoying the freshness of the fountain water (or the perfume of an imaginary oriental couch). (**Ex. 15.3**) reflected as she swings (**Ex. 15.4**) showing her exquisite foot and neck (**Ex. 15.5**) treading in the water (**Ex. 15.6**) dreaming of undisturbed luxury; and more special episodes for fancies of solitary, naked delight (**Ex. 15.7, 15.8, 15.9**). That these thirty-odd successive fragments do not make up a restless diffusion may be experienced by hearing the music in its broad pattern of four strophical periods, each contributing its own developing features while supporting the general sense of the text with a firm core of associate

Ex. 15.1

Sa - ra   bel - le   d'in - do - len - ce

Ex. 15.2a

se____   ba - - lan - ce

Ex. 15.2b

se   ba - lan - ce dans un   ha - mac.____

Ex. 15.2c

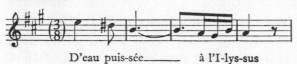

D'eau puis-sée_____ à l'I-lys-sus

Ex. 15.3

Et la frê-le es-ca-po-let-te   se re-flê-te

Et la frê-le es-ca-po-let-te

Ex. 15.4

on voit sur l'eau qui s'a - gi - te

Ex. 15.5

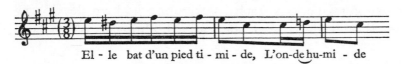

El - le bat d'un pied ti - mi - de, L'on-de hu-mi - de

Ex. 15.6

Oh!   si   j'é -tais Ca-pi - ta - ne   ou Sul -ta - ne

dans   un   bain de   mar-bre jau - ne   près d'un trô - ne

Ex. 15.7

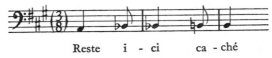

Reste   i - ci   ca - ché

Ex. 15.8

Je pou-vais   fô -la - trer   nu - e   sous la nu - e

Ex. 15.9

Ain - si   se parle au prin-ces - se,   et sans ces - se

phrases (**Ex. 15.**1, 15.2) as indicated above. The swinging movement never stops, but it avoids monotony. The bar-lengths indicate the degree of continuity in idea.

Such a squaring up of a rounded whole may seem to some readers to be a travesty of intelligent listening. All the same, if the opportunity is taken to hear the setting

Ex. 16

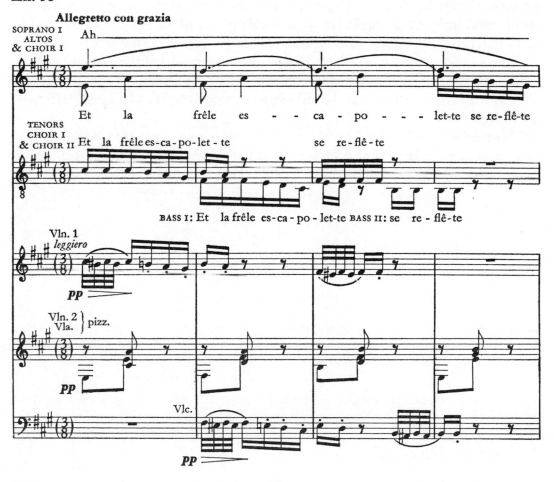

once thus symmetrically to verify the dovetailing of recurring phrases and impromptu sallies, or at least to absorb the pivotal phrases quoted (**Ex. 15.1, 15.2, 15.3, 15.6**), and once again to respond to the impact of a particular performance, the skill with which these fourteen verses are swept into a stream of orderly and diverting musical statement should be more apparent.

It might be added that the three 'choirs' are not used much antiphonally. One cannot be pompously admiring of this feat of relaxation. There is just enough imitation and cross-rhythm, or of substantive phrase and confirming touches (finally, some plain Ah-ing) to keep the pulse from sagging. Nor is there much real 10-part writing: five is the norm. The orchestra, never pursuing an independent line, gently and resourcefully reinforces and decorates, with an occasional dash of colour. For example, for 'reste ici' (v. 5), pirouetting flutes and dallying bassoons and drums; for 'le hamac de soie' (v. 12), woodwind triplets; for 'oublieuse des promptes aîles du jour' (v. 16), contrary triplet vibrations in upper and lower strings and insistent arpeggios in woodwind; bursts of energy for strings in 'Rit de la fraîcheur' (v. 4), for wind in 'folâtrer *nue*' (v. 13). A typical unobtrusive but engaging incident might be selected from this observation of the swinger and her reflection. In the repeat of this for verse 18, the intensification of the calm falling tone by means of a rising seventh, and vibratory woodwind for 'leur troupe frivole', are neat glosses.

This neglected miniature has suffered from having no ready place in any output that specializes in large dramatic works, and from having only obscure Schubert for company. It is time for a redress. There is nothing quite like this in Berlioz.

NOTES

1. A more detailed account of these cantatas, and of the competing entries, can be found in an article in *The Music Review*, Vol. 25. No. 3 (August, 1964) with full quotations from the Berlioz works, including a reproduction of two pages of the surviving score of *Sardanapale*, showing the 'horrific climax of gathered forces and tumultuous figures of catastrophe', including a glissando on the harp, which might claim precedence of the example in Liszt's *Mephisto Waltz*. Evidence why this cannot, as Tiersot supposed, have been a final Berlioz score is summarized.

2. An article summarizing the revisions of each scene, with some quotations from the original Easter Hymn, can be found in *The Monthly Musical Record* 89. 995 (September–October, 1959).

3. *Le Correspondant,* 22 October.

Table 2

Musical strophes	Verses	Content	Musical phrases and bar-lengths		Length
I	1, 2	Sara swinging	**1 2a 2b 1 2a 2c 3**		
			8 4 6 4 4 5 12		43 bars
II	3, 4, 5, 6, orch.	over the shimmering water (stay where you are, undisturbed!)	**1 2a 2b 4 5 2c 7 7 1**		
			8 4 5 6 9 5 19 18 4		78 bars
III	10, 11, 12, 13, 15,	The nonchalant! Dreaming of marble baths and unashamed nudity	**1 6 6 6 8 6**		
			12 14 11 4 15 14		70 bars
IV	16, 18, 19a, 19b, La, La,	Musing, chuckling; joined by her carefree playmates.	**1 2a 2b 1 9 3 5 coda**		
			6 4 5 4 9 22 8 20 10		88 bars

Figures in bold type refer to Music Example 15.

Mio Caro Amico

Beethoven spento, non c'era che Berlioz che potesse farle rivivere. ed io che ho gustato le vostre divine composizioni degne di un genio qual siete: credo mio dovere di pregarvi a voler accettare, in segno del mio omaggio, Ventimila franchi i quali vi saranno rimessi dal Sig.r Baron De Rothschild, dopo che gli avrete presentato l'acclusa.

Crederemi sempre

Il Vostro aff.= amico

Nicolò Paganini

Parigi Li 18 Decembre 1838

18 Décembre 1838

Ô digne et grand artiste

comment vous exprimer ma reconnaissance !! Je ne suis pas riche, mais croyez moi, le suffrage d'un homme de Génie tel que vous me touche mille fois plus que la générosité royale de votre présent.

Les paroles me manquent, je courrai vous embrasser dès que je pourrai quitter mon lit où je suis encore retenu aujourd'hui.

— H. Berlioz

Paganini's letter to Berlioz and the composer's reply

62

4

The Damnation of Faust

IT was not until 1846 that Berlioz, back in Paris after attending the Beethoven celebrations in Bonn, and once more conscious of the prevailing apathy and complacency about any sort of musical development, decided upon a full-scale work based on Goethe's *Faust* (part 1). Between the *Eight Scenes* of 1828 and this project, he had covered a wide stretch of experiment, achievement and frustration. In the field of opera, apart from attempts at two separate libretti, each abandoned for various reasons after the scoring of four or five numbers, Berlioz had produced *Benvenuto Cellini*, a sizeable work which, as recent audience reception has shown, deserved much more than the grudging four performances allotted by a timid and too much pressurized management with an impoverished artistic policy. Berlioz knew that he was on to a main road of emancipation for French opera. However, this setback and the uncertain prospects of any work for the stage prompted him to look elsewhere. Some years earlier he had written two orchestral symphonies, the *Fantastic* and *Harold in Italy*, the concurrent performance of which had gained him a handsome sum of money from the violinist Paganini, to afford him leisure and freedom from the journalistic distractions which had dogged his career. He settled down in 1839 to compose what he eventually called a 'symphonie dramatique' from *Romeo and Juliet*.

Here each of the seven separate movements involved retains a connexion with some feature of Shakespeare's scenario, explicit in the odd and vocal movements, implicit (as suggested in the titles) in the even and non-vocal movements. But the development of motives and progressions and the rest is primarily musical, including the use of voices from the start, with their established patterns of recitative, aria, arioso and fugue to reinforce the symphonic order. Indeed, the last movement, obviously balancing the opening narration by a positive colloquy, partakes of the nature of a compound oratorio number, inviting audience involvement and so far differing from the Ninth Symphony finale in the concreteness of its situation rather than in the tone of address. The result was a symphony with a decided slant towards something else; an issue to which we shall return in a later chapter.

Yet this fusion of genres, in Berlioz's fiery imagination at least, must have settled for him the lines on which, abandoning his original grand notion of a *Faust* symphony, he might construct a concert work that would at once reflect Goethe's elaborate morality, with its flow of scene, and make its own impact as a series of music periods, each with its component numbers. Such a cantata (which Berlioz's *Dramatic Legend* may more plainly be styled for purposes of comparison) need not be dramatic—and Goethe's stage work is book-drama in many senses—but it can conjure up an atmosphere of dramatic tension, and it can amplify moods recalled from an informed recollection of one of Goethe's scenes as a whole, or of the suggestion of a single line, or by fresh creation. The composer is thus free to draw up his own scheme of reference, with a view to shaping movements in a new compulsive order, as mental pictures recorded in sound. Here Berlioz often seems to be guided more by Gerard de Nerval, the translator, than by Goethe.

In *The Damnation of Faust* (the first and more commonly known part of Goethe's highly composite rendering of the sixteenth century tale) there is no need for an explanatory prologue, as in *Romeo and Juliet*, or for preliminary dialectic at the highest level, as in *Faust*. Instead, Berlioz starts three of the four unequal parts into which he divides his cantata by exhibiting Faust in various moods, beginning, not with world-weariness, but with an almost Wordsworthian naturist reverie, on which the ordinary world of merry-making peasants and advancing troops lightly impinges. Mephistopheles, Faust's evil self, assumes full command (without wager) in Part 2. Margaret becomes a vocal and responsive lover in Part 3 and, abandoned, dominates the start of Part 4, after which Faust's career is securely in the hands of evil. The *Eight Scenes* can fill in this scheme with the provisional settings of six songs and three episodes, some needing only sharper definition.

Thus, while *The Damnation of Faust* is not without its operatic touches—in the Auerbach scene especially—the cantata presents a series of situations, primarily involving Faust, which require no stage to prompt their musical projection. On the contrary, the whole compression of Goethe's surging scenes to three leading characters excludes opera, and it becomes apparent that even the recitatives are much more narrative or emotional leads to more sustained music than demonstrations of character or action. This understood, it will be convenient to indicate at once the mood-pattern and linking dramatic encounter underlying the musical development, with a comparative glance at the relevant scenes of lines of *Faust*, as cited after each part, with mentions of minimal connexions placed in brackets. (The useful numbering of Goethe's twenty-five scenes, as in some editions, will be followed here. It will show where Berlioz jumps about in his scenario.)

Part 1

scene 1 Faust, culture-hero, in tune with nature's spring.
scene 2 Enjoying life with the folk.
scene 3 Admiring an army of liberation, marching to the frontier.
  [*Faust.* Scene 2. Lines 903–6; 949–56, 965–72; (861–2).]

Part 2

scene 4 Faust, fled to town, sick of nature and tired of life, is about to take poison when he hears an Easter hymn being sung near by. He regains confidence.

scene 5 But a mocking, overpowering spirit (never named in colloquy) appears to his consciousness and promises him his fondest desire.

scene 6 Challenged to show his demonic powers, he first conducts Faust to 'Auerbach's cellar' for a brash evening of drinking, with erotic and satiric song.

scene 7 Thence in easy flight (*O tempora, O mores*) to a voluptuous dream-world, in which the sleeping Faust identifies Margaret. On waking, his only wish is to find her.

scene 8 His attention is sidetracked to crowds of troops and students, singing of conquest and possession in patent metaphor.
  [*Faust.* Scene 1. Lines (656), 720, 737, 742; (scene 3, 1436); scene 5, 2073, 2126–49, 2211–18, 2223–38; (scene 3, 1445, 1506); scene 7, 2671; scene 2, 884–902.]

Part 3

scene 9 The sounds of the Retreat mark the end of the day. Faust, utterly captivated, visits Margaret's room in her absence, luxuriating in the silent messages of the 'sanctuaire inconnue'.

scene 10 Mephistopheles hides Faust behind curtains.

scene 11 Margaret enters, troubled with dreams of her handsome lover, idealized as the king of Thule in the old ballad, faithful as his queen; faithful as she innocently believes Faust to be.

scene 12 Mephistopheles casts a spell over her, adding glib warnings against too friendly men in a mock ballad-to-guitar.

scene 13 Faust and Margaret exchange protests of devotion.

scene 14 They continue to do so in the teeth of avidly gossiping neighbours. In the background, the evil spirit gloats over his conquest.
  [Scene 8. Lines 2687–90; (2729); 2753–82; (scene 21, 3860); scene 19, 3682–97; (scene 12, 3163–4); scene 13, 3027; scene 17, 3544; scene 16, 3795–3500.]

Part 4

scene 15 Margaret, abandoned, crazily recalls all that Faust meant to her, and reveals her loss of all mental calm. The singing of soldiers and students, reminders of a heedless world, leaves her more desperate than ever.

scene 16 Faust, in a spasm of guilt-consciousness, falls back upon the worship of nature in storm.

scene 17 Mephistopheles breaks in with news of Margaret's judicial condemnation for giving her mother a drug that proved fatal in excess. To save her, Faust must sign an agreement to serve Mephistopheles 'tomorrow'. Faust signs, and hastens (as he thinks) to Margaret's assistance.

scene 18 Mounted on horseback, he is conducted to his real destination, the abyss, leading to scene 19.

scene 19 The kingdom of the now unmasked Devil, so alien in its pompous cow-towing that its speech is unintelligible to mortal ear! An accessory 'chorus' closes this historic case of 'Il dissoluto punito', distancing the human element.

scene 20 An angelic welcome to a soul pardoned for 'loving much' frames Margaret's ascent to heaven.

   [Scene 15. Lines 3374–3413, scene 2, 891–902; (scene 14, 3217–34); scene 14, 3251, scene 25, 4507, scene 4, 1715, 1741, scene 24, 4400; scene 24, 4398; —; (scene 25, 4607–12).]

This précis of Berlioz's text, as freely adapted from de Nerval's translation, is intended to serve various purposes: to show the selection of interest and resultant compressions and distortions of *Faust*; to tabulate what Berlioz planned to render instead in characteristic numbers, evocative episodes and cumulative parts of varying dimensions; and to suggest what sort of communication is involved. We may now try to gauge Goethe's intentions in brief.

It is common knowledge that Goethe achieved his masterpiece by very gradual stages, stretching from the first draft of 1773–5 and the published and essential *Fragment* of 1790 to the published Part 1 of 1808, and then to the Part 2 of 1831. Berlioz was concerned only with Part 1, leaving Part 2 to Schumann (and Mahler) to render in musical scene and conflation in the concert hall. In making poetically credible the restless scholar of legend, so bitterly aware of the vanity of human knowledge that he is ready to call up spirits, Goethe leads Faust, in a quest for experience under diabolical direction, from the Auerbach carousals to the witch's kitchen, where he receives as an elixir a tremendous rejuvenation. Attracted now by Margaret to the point of seduction, he suffers pangs of revulsion to himself, and a wounding sense of continued dissatisfaction. Later, he makes a symbolic excursion into the forest, to the amusement of an uncomprehending Mephisto. (As a young man Charles Darwin found conviction by gazing upon nature.) For this inner conflict Goethe eventually found creative shape in the clarification of a confused but suffering, striving man. When, at the outset of his involvement with Mephistopheles, Faust stakes his soul on the declaration that he will never be satisfied, he is sure that he will keep true to himself. The end of Part 1 finds him in the utmost straits, in a confusion worse confounded. In Part 2 Faust continues his search in a vastly wider world. Plunged in yet more guilt, he receives deeper insight into life, and he dies still 'striving', thus making his salvation through grace possible.

Margaret's pathetic story, quite additional to the original folkbook tale, is, paradoxically, incidental to this exposure of Faustian man. Margaret is an artless, naïve girl, accepting a superior worldling as her lover; encouraged by her dubious friend, Martha, and an object of shame and unconcealed contempt for her brother Valentine, another figure in the 'small world' into which Faust has been drawn by his evil genius, and for which concert music has no place. Mephistopheles, who as Faust's mysterious associate arouses in Margaret a certain ineffective resistance, is partly the rake's friend and tormentor, partly the cultivated arch-cynic, but always, openly or by insinuation, the spirit of denial, of self-destruction. His lyrics are all sinister, including his final guitar-song of prudish warning to 'Katie', which Valentine fatally challenges.

In Berlioz's Faust the subtlety of this inner tension is missing. He walks the world as a Byronic hedonist of wide interests, enjoying life as a young man may. On his cool abandonment of the poisoned cup, when he hears the Easter hymn, the music is oddly silent.

Part 1 of *The Damnation of Faust*, quite out of order, is a bland sequence of spring song, rural song and intrusive nationalist march. Musically, the style veers between the expansively arioso, easy-going strophical measures for solo with chorus, and a

Ex. 17

resolute interlude-finale with a compulsively established reprise, incorporating the Rakoczky March as delivered previously to a Hungarian audience (with its provocative quiet start) in a context highly charged with nationalist emotion. The presentation is of an outdoor culture-hero (**Ex. 17**).

Part 2, the longest continuum of expression, reveals Faust's oscillations of mood

Ex. 18

and morale, with the usual adhesive recitative in scraps of monologue or dialogue: melancholy study; an accession of hopefulness, induced by the hearing of an Easter hymn in rich harmony, the second verse of which marks the addition of Faust's personal concern amongst other intensifications of the first of the *Eight Scenes*, as in this naturist climax to a simple Resurrectionist sequence (**Ex. 18**). Nominal participation in the convivial pleasures of the academic underworld, with a brash 'rat' song capped by a much more eloquent 'flea' song, leads on to a total involuntary submission to the gorgeous night-club life conjured up by Mephistopheles (chorus and ballet). In a foretaste of Orff, soldiers and students of the waking world cool the air, in a refreshing lyrical mood, with amorous songs (**Ex. 19.1 and 2**). (Early German audiences were scandalized at this realistic picture of university youth (**Ex. 19.3**).) The songs are, of course, riotously combined, possibly under the stimulus of the egregiously square co-scoring of two folkish songs in the second act of Monsigny's *Le Deserteur*. The jubilant cultivation of the present moment fades into marching steps.

Ex. 19.1

Ex. 19.2

(*The spirits hover round Faust, asleep, then gradually disappear.*)

Ex. 19.3

In Part 3 a simple but extended aria of expectation attends, lamely enough, Faust's twilight entry into Margaret's room. He conceals himself. Margaret, entering, is aware only of a strange pressure in the ether. In an entirely abstracted fashion (*without expression* is the score-direction) she rehearses child-memories of the old story of the king of Thule and faithful love. (The sub-title, 'chanson gothique', meant 'popular song'.) The haunting stanzas are deepened by the refrains of an eloquent viola solo over decorative arpeggios. Outside, Mephisto prepares to soften her resistance (little in evidence here) with a mesmeric dance borrowed from the Walpurgis Night crew. A prolonged but capricious 'Minuet' adroitly suggests a performance under strict remote control. The Devil adds his amoral 'Katie' ballad, his insinuations supported by an obedient elf chorus in the second verse. His guitar, literal in the original setting in *Eight Scenes*, Number 8, has become a lively pizzicato band. No Valentine leaps to smash the permissive instrument and pronounce a devastating curse (Gounod's finest accession). All this conditioning is a prelude to Margaret's uninhibited response to Faust's instant and urgent declaration (v. 1) in dialogue, descant (v. 2) (**Ex. 20**) and laboriously prolonged coda. An intrusive neighbourly chorus, obviously compounded of the Marthas and

Ex. 20

Lieschens of *Faust* but of both sexes, sharply intervenes before a further and spirited duet resumes relations, Faust again calling the tune in each verse. To this Mephisto adds his superfluous Italianate rejoinder ('Je puis, donc, à mon gré te traîner'), somewhat as Fieramosca, unseen, contributes his double-talk to the elopement plotting of Cellini and Teresa, but 'trio' is a wrong description of this continuing exchange of pledges. The menacing tongue motion of the returning neighbours avoids a trite finish to this encounter by spreading confusion. So psychological a scene is anything but concert-opera (the misleading term put about by the composer at one stage or another), but the opportunity for a brisk ensemble to sweep aside the illusions of a masterful, rejuvenated lover and responsive, innocent-sophisticated girl with a vivacious, almost conventional mix-up of personalities seemed, no doubt, a convenient exit and a persuasive choral finale to a well-knit part.

Lastly Part 4. Margaret has had one song to herself, the 'Thule' ballad, a slight extension of Number 6 of the *Eight Scenes* and the earliest to be composed. For her final solo she is assigned a vital reconstruction of another of the *Scenes*, given the old-fashioned title of 'Romance', a generic term for the predecessor of the 'Mélodie', not for any sentimental ballad. 'D'amour l'ardente flamme' (**Ex. 21.1**) is, in fact, **a** re-translation, presumably Berlioz's, of De Nerval's version of 'Meine Ruhe ist hin', already celebrated by Schubert in three riveting strophes, illustrative, trenchant and musically cogent. 'D'amour' is an elaborate cantabile lament in an absorbed, part dreamy style, in which the cor anglais is co-conspicuous with the voice in refrain and

Ex. 21.1

Ex. 21.2

Ex. 21.3

71

repartee. Schubert, relishing the spinning-wheel symbolism so convenient to his piano, contrives varying outcomes of a masterful recurring strophe (to vv. 1–3, 4–7, 8–10 of the text), only once relaxing the main unswerving rhythm for sheer introspection ('sein Kuss'). Berlioz, allowing his maturer Margaret all the time in the world, extends the main mood of mental disturbance (1, cor anglais, 8, 10, cor anglais) in four succeeding episodes, contrasted in tempo or metre, to amplify her feverish recollections of her departed lover; each with its identifying string figure except the last one (**Ex. 21**.2 and 3). (These echo vv. 2–3, 6–7, 5–9 in Goethe.)

Ex. 21.4

This last, introducing the distant sounds of troops, marching to bugle and drum, and of straying students, with their now familiar wenching songs, has at first the appearance, after so conclusive a cor anglais refrain, of being a fresh number. In Number 7 of *Eight Scenes*, virtually a double number, such an episode proved, indeed, a self-contained sequel to Margaret's 'Romance'. But here, for any one able to recall the full scene at the end of Part 2—**Ex. 19**.3 (see page 69) does not figure here, but a later fanfare—the interruption soon shows itself to be a cinematic, compressed flash-back in Margaret's mind of the indifferent outside world, plus the blunt reminder that now 'il ne vient pas'. Thus firmly internalized, the persuasively fragmentary episode yields to a brief, tranquillized entry of the cor anglais against a dry pizzicato, for Margaret's barely articulate 'Hélas!' The semitonally strained assertion of **F** major in each previous refrain now relaxes to a plain cadence, followed by a long silence, all underlining Margaret's pathetic state (**Ex. 21.4**). On these carefully fashioned lines Part 4 opens with a most striking solo and a musical reading that seems to set aside Schubert's formal agitato, as a period setting of the past.

A further outburst from Faust, in his resort to nature's powers of consolation for his sense of guilt, makes the most abrupt transition and tests severely Berlioz's method of selective treatment, but the composer's own rendering of 'Forest and caverns' evokes strong and ultimately spontaneous music. In the ensuing tussle with Mephistopheles over helping Margaret out of prison, the sudden invocation of an unholy agreement ('sign today and be mine tomorrow'), obviously borrowed from the crucial soul-wager on which *Faust* so vitally hinges, is most disarming.[1] The hunting-call phrases which propel the angry dispute suggest a vindictive world. So to the horrific ride to the abyss and beyond, in which a strange but methodically equipped musical journey, with a spare, basic counterpoint (or rather textural combination) and a spreading hymn-tune in reserve, arrives at the realm of the fantastic. The minatory pomp of the 'furies' of the infernal regions (Orestes' demons in Gluck's *Iphigénie* could give them several points) celebrates desolation with nonsense language and brief barbaric songs. No chorus can normally feel happy about this dubiously mocking declamation, borrowed from Swedenborg's *Memorabilia*, 1224, 262–67, as Barzun explains. Nor is all this readily forgotten in the suddenly emerging apotheosis scene, which depends on its textural elaboration of dovetailed phrases, led by solo-violin arpeggios, rather than on any forward movement in melodic line or harmonic progression, or on the probation-officer trend of admonitory welcome to the erring girl. Moreover, to dwell on Margaret's salvation, ignoring Faust's condition, is an easy way out, although well founded on the almost final 'ist gerettet' ('is saved') of Goethe's text. The conductor, in short, has a pronounced task to bring this tortuous part of Berlioz's mosaic pattern to a close in a convincing manner. (Not that the other extreme, the loud, securely motivated, coda of Mahler's Eighth, ending a multiple setting of *Faust*, Part 2, is beyond question.)

Some textural features may be underlined. First, the soloists. Faust's tenor (with optional descents to avoid going above **A**) must range from a recurrent cantilena and a lyrical *chant récitatif* to the sombre, concentrated tone of one striving desperately for consolation in 'O nature immense'. Mephistopheles, bass with options for a baritone, can be lightly satirical at times, and the Serenade admits a cutting ironic relish if it is not taken too fast. He must expose his sinister vein in the dark and vibrant tone of his recitatives of suppressed exaltation. Snarling will not do, still less a comic manner. The magic of 'Voici de roses' must be insinuating. Margaret's comparatively small part entails a blend of different facets. A full tone is not enough. First, a simple tone but articulate phrasing for the dreamlike pathos of the 'Thule' ballad, maintained by a not too static tempo. Then, the straight cantabile for the conventional duet with Faust. Finally, the inward heart-break of 'ah! la paix de mon âme a donc fui'. This Margaret is far removed from the pathetic Gretchen and from the sentimental, luckless Marguerite who is nevertheless the chief *persona* (or at least the principal emotional byway) of Gounod's *Faust* (1859), hence called *Margarethe* by the Germans to avoid confusion with holy Goethe. Berlioz's sparing use of soloists, outside opera, is nowhere more evident than in this romance. Brander's blunt but resounding rat song, unchanged from *Eight Scenes*, Number 4, offers its grim underground humour as a foil to the sharper wit of the visitor gentleman. How far Berlioz would have accepted or not accepted the foregoing interpretations, it is most likely that he wrote, as always, with definite singers, or singer types, in mind. (Cf. p. 79.)

The chorus, whose resourceful part made *The Damnation of Faust* a long-standing favourite with English choral societies, ranges from straight devotional oratorio to parody oratorio, and from the developed quasi-psychedelic session summoned by the Devil to the open-air anticipations of lovemaking by the troops and students and the more involved intrusions of milling neighbours on the absorbed lovers in the next part. There is the appeal of precise chording and vigorous part-singing, but also of sustained cantabile and eloquent pianissimo. The chorus is a recurrent and varying presence in Faust's consciousness, in waking life or in dreams; in Margaret's hardly at all. It is always a singing body, not a bunch of extra reeds.

All the same, in many performances one is tempted to go along with those who name the orchestra as the composite and masterful hero of *The Damnation of Faust*. Historically so, arguably. (The early French critics set down Gounod's *Faust* as 'German . . . all the effects in the orchestra.' Also by the same token 'lacking in melody except in the soldiers' chorus', intended for *Ivan the Terrible*.) For score-readers it may be explained that the transference of ophicleide parts to trombone is one of many misleading features of the old collected edition, reproduced in the current miniature score; especially in the Auerbach scene. Otherwise Berlioz's orchestra has a normal Paris complement, with 3, 2, 3, 4 woodwind, cornets in the brass and two harps. Some detailed observations on the scoring may be assembled here to indicate the inventive colouring and resourceful nuances which make this work sound so fresh and 'early'. Meanwhile it may be suggested that in the purely orchestral set pieces an assumed invitation to increase speed is a false clue. Even the long march profits by a slow building up of the climax, and the automatous minuet makes elegant puppetry at a moderate speed, with a rousing wild *presto* to follow.

74

Part 1

scene 1 The open scoring of the *tutti* at the climax (*ff*) of the postlude exhibits the main motive in violins and wood, spread-out chords in strings and brass—not a dense continuum.

scene 2 The vibrating wood-horn background, yielding to strings only for Faust's entry, almost forecasts Troy on armistice night.

scene 3 In the march, a similar reed-band basis for the redoubtable minor-key opening is lightened enough to let through the glistening **A** major tune on the violins *et al*. Reprise can afford to be heavy; yet the tune is never embarrassed by a too clinging brass, harmonically or rhythmically.

Part 2

scene 4 In the first verse of the hymn, wood and horns having at first identified with the male choir, the woodwind can then elaborate arpeggios, steadied by plain horn chords. In the mainly subdued second verse, the full choir with wind as before becomes ballast for a throbbing string 'fingered tremolo' (i.e. repeated figures), which passes to the woodwind. Finally, a united choral-orchestral impact (*ppp*) is *held* briefly over brisk, ecstatic bells, per pizzicato bass.

scene 5 The sensational climax of Faust's repentance is blown to bits by a sliding trombone outburst for the descent of Mephisto upon the scene, with the last chord caught up by vibrating strings (cf. scene 10) for a working background to the intruder's black satire.

scene 6 For the dive into Auerbach's the full orchestra, of course; yet here, too, the open scoring conveys the tone of men still relaxed when it thunders. In the 'Flea Song', (v. 3), the 'scratching' in answering strings is proportionate and witty.

scene 7 Equally apt is the brief but delicate Andantino air (violins and violoncelli) that ushers in Mephisto's short air. The brass accompaniment in the latter, sometimes criticized, *can* sound a miscalculation, but obviously Berlioz wanted a dark preparation for his main seduction scene, the sylph chorus and dance. In the former, the agile, quasi-orchestral use of the voices in the rapid accompaniment of the main theme (**Ex. 19.1**, page 69) with a flow of text is followed by transparently vocal harmony as the general basis of 'Le lac' and after; leaving to the end the finesse of gliding scales and tongueing woodwind for 'Partout l'oiseau timide' and of low-pitched string harmony for 'Dors!' In the dance, the reduction of

75

the main theme of the chorus to essentials finds delicate elaboration below or above it.

scene 8 The lightly percussive string background and brass fanfares for the soldiers, the sophisticated wind/string bravura for the students, and the heavy string harmony for the otherwise vocal-lined conflation of tunes, make up the cumulative effect of this ominously congenial finale, easily identifiable in Margaret's recall (part 4, scene 15) but artfully careless here.

Part 3

scene 9 Muted strings for twilight and sanctified bliss, as later for Faust's declaration to Margaret, changing to unmuted strings in the duet verse.

scene 11 An ensemble of solo viola and viola-violoncelli soli enhances the sensation of dropping into the depths of Margaret's mind.

scene 12 In the minuet of elves the wind-band setting of the principal phrase of eight bars assists the gathering feeling of the controlled automation of 'bent' natures. In the second reprise a distortion of key facilitates a take-over by strings in a heightening rhythmic and percussive context. In the final Presto the wind take control, prompted by pizzicato up to the humorous ending. In the 'Serenade' that follows in the same spirit of unyielding conquest, a jaunty pizzicato pattern wittily represents the unseen guitar (the sole vehicle in *Eight Scenes*), with a growing sostenuto of wind and chorus in Verse 2.

scene 13 A restrained accompaniment for the serene duet, with graceful woodwind figures for Verse 2 (**Ex. 20**, page 70) and only finally an intrusion of agitated strings, rests the ear before the turmoil of scene 14.

scene 14 Here hurtling strings (bass tune), punctuated by wind chords, yield to the sostenuto of Faust's pained farewell to his finest hour before energetic string passage-work drives behind the entering chorus, which carries the rest of the orchestra along with it.

Part 4

scene 15 The alto oboe, at once identified with Margaret's absorbed melancholy, can take charge of the first ritornello (or returning section) without the singer. Her ecstatic recollection of Faust is shaped by voice and strings, first in various species of sustained agitation (up to his *kiss*), then in entirely broken rhythm (**Ex. 21.3**, page 71) as a longing for what *was* overcomes her. The ceaseless distant drums of the fourth episode pass adroitly to the equally symbolic pizzicato background of the concluding, simplified ritornello.

scene 16   The tense string harmony is set off by the repartee of the basses (including all bassoons) in an embroidered style, conveying the deviant depths of 'nature immense'. The entry at the end of a regular, substantive all-string figure simulates a ritornello, but actually it is a florid impromptu bass to the wind harmony. An odd touch, but not the massing of strings for a bass, shared with many a Mozart imbroglio. But '*nine* beats a bar!' (B.)

scene 18   The almost early eighteenth-century scoring of oboe, violins and basses in close harness enhances the relentless conduct of the anxious but so far unaware Faust to the abyss. As he drops headlong, the whole texture loosens up to more variable genres.

scene 19   *Pandemonium* is painted pompous, and the composer makes the most of it, with well stuffed chording in all ranks, a rogue bass and otherwise massed entries, and plenty of tremolo, bowed or tongued. Although still *tutti*, the triumphal song of greeting for the prince of darkness is distinctly easier on the ear: the words could be heard, if they were intelligible. 'Diff! Diff!' (3/4) makes a positively light dance round Mephisto, with off-beat guitar strokes where first it was tam-tam etc. In the rapid collapse of the final *tutti*, the tortuous descent of the towering string tremolo harmony makes an effective prompter for the reduction of the wind.

scene 20   A firm harmonic progression is delineated by lofty strings over active harps, and then by equally elate solo-violin arpeggios, deftly punctuated by woodwind flutters, over the choral phrases (S.A.T. reinforced by a second chorus, S.A., of 200–300 children, or if necessary 30 boys). Tremolo strings finally add their punctuation-marks. Given the resolve to make perpetual harping typical, the composer's solution of delicate string movement, lightly reinforced, is convincing.

It should now be clear that any assumption that *The Damnation of Faust* was meant to be an opera but was unfortunately diverted to the concert platform, is to mistake its nature. It is also to ignore Berlioz's method of treating an integral dramatic text, as demonstrated in *Romeo and Juliet*, as we shall notice later. Berlioz knew his *Faust* well enough to know what kind of stimulus the work offered him, and it was not to mount a musical version on the stage of any Paris opera-house. All that he gave Gounod was an idea for a libretto. The survival in the repertory of Gounod's rendering, with its provocative mixture of incidental qualities—the delicacy of the garden scene and waltz-chorus, the strength of Valentine's death scene, the jewel song and other ornamental features, and yet the dramatically negative or secondary impact of the whole, and its purely nominal contact with the Goethe version—does not disprove Berlioz's handling. Taking *Faust* as a classic, even in the terms of De Nerval's mainly prose translation of 1827, Berlioz had no scruples about projecting a dramatic episode on to *his* screen, which might at once recall a vivid scene in Goethe. But he chose *Faust* primarily for its masterly exhibition of changing mental states, especially those of the title-role, man more than life-size. This left him free to find or supply music in no strict obligation to the text, except that equal stanzas or pairs of stanzas might claim a common basic strophe, if musically convenient, as we have observed in most of the detached songs. The chorus can be what they like when and where they like, as indicated by their words. To put them on a stage would promote, not suspend, disbelief. So with the orchestra in detachment—in the march, ballet and minuet—given a modicum of recitative. The dances could be staged, as has been done successfully in the past, but the reduction of the Rakoczky march, so explosive at its rendering at Pesth at the start of 1846, to an escort of foot-soldiers in a chateau garden (as related of one performance) borders on the absurd. As for the main characters, the noticeably small and static part of a visible Margaret, the less than comic impression of a snarling or sinister or debonnair Mephisto in the flesh, the final grotesqueness of red devils and white angels, such as mark a misguided stage representation, are no criticism of a composer who knew what he was about. His advance in his chosen field lay in his sustained power to transcend situations, as vocalized or barely hinted, in music. It was part of his mission to extend genres. In this aim he was curiously like Bach. Unlike Bach, whose vocation and appointments called for a procession of works lasting under half an hour, he made only one further attempt, the subject of the next chapter, and a surprising move from a classic drama to a visionary gloss on *Matthew* 2. But no one after him could say that 'dramatic cantata' was an outworn method.[2]

NOTES

1. In a letter to his friend Griepenkerl, the Brunswick critic, confirmed in a footnote in the *Memoirs,* 1847 entry, Berlioz makes play with the patriotic Dresden critic's resentment both at this Frenchman's highly suggestive picture of students singing to the tune of *Per urbem quaerentes puellas eamus* (already, in fact, censored likewise at Moscow, for printing purposes, but so *sung,* unintelligibly enough not to cause scandal), and at his vilification of the good Mephistopheles by making him mislead Faust as to his destination, where in Goethe he had kept to his word. Dresden, Berlioz declares, was delighted. But the Dresden critic's second point holds water beneath the surface. Goethe, after long and earnest thought, was most precise about Mephistopheles' basic wager with *Faust*, since the validity of the whole issue of *Faust* depends upon it. (Mephistopheles is still acting under divine scrutiny. He can lead Faust on, but not mislead.) Berlioz's reduction of Faust's evil spirit, so well maintained so far, to the status of a mere con-man *is* a cheap device,

worthy of Scribe or some other operatic scribbler, and a parody of Goethe's creation of the situation. Some other exit to the abyss should have been prepared.

2. I for one regard the concert-hall integrity of *The Damnation of Faust* as the firm and self-evident testimony of the music in relation to Goethe's drama. It is disconcerting at first to learn that in 1847 Berlioz had a considerable correspondence with the leading Paris librettist, Scribe, on the project of a *Faust* opera to be mounted at Drury Lane, London, in December, 1848, by Antoine Jullien, an impresario who in his flamboyant way had established Promenade Concerts with an excellent orchestra; Spohr having been commissioned to write a *Faust* for Paris, thus ruling out a second one there. This new Faust was to be a moderate expansion of the existing score ('already lasting two-and-a-half hours'). It was to be called, Berlioz thought, 'Mephistopheles' in order to give the singer Pischek a more leading role, and would include, he hoped, an assembly of the princes of darkness to settle who shall go on earth to bring down Faust, ending in a flash of lightning on the naming of Mephistopheles. Margaret's role only needed slight expansion, by including the church scene with *Dies irae*. Faust's plate was full. To make the most of Pischek, he would need an air in two parts: (1) melancholy jealousy of Faust's success; (2) avowal of general hate and vengeance, furioso. After an immense *Pandemonium*, heaven would, in Jullien's intention, reproduce the impressions of the apocalyptic pictures of Martin. And other detail of the Lane's scenic resources.

Tiersot, who quotes the four letters to Scribe from which these details are taken (*Lettres de musicians écrites en français*, vol. 2. pages 188–93), pictures Berlioz as imagining that he had realized the end of his ambitions, to be music director (actually, only conductor) of a grand opera-house, and meanwhile trying to coax the desired scenario-supplement out of Scribe. Very soon disenchantment fell upon him: after putting on four operas (*Figaro* was one), Jullien went bankrupt, having actually taken on Drury Lane while heavily in the red. In a desperate attempt to recoup his fortunes, he toured the kingdom with the best part of his orchestra, whom Berlioz had trained. Berlioz himself arranged a concert of his works (the *Harold* symphony and parts of the *Requiem*) with the remainder, adequately rehearsed. It went down well, and a second concert was planned, although Jullien had made off with the proceeds of the first. *The Illustrated London News* had regretted that Berlioz had not been made music director at Drury Lane, in the interests of lyric drama. But no patron came forward to put him in charge. In Paris, February, 1848, the country was moving towards a republic. The end of monarchical interference with the arts, as Berlioz hoped? Rather, an end to cultural activity. Left without reserves, Berlioz could not continue to conduct in London. So goodbye for ever to *Mephistopheles* and its moody, almost Machiavellian prince.

As *Faust* history, this cumulative manifesto to Scribe is more than a little incredible. It reads as if Berlioz were leading Scribe right up the garden path, and trying to see how many ludicrous distortion of values he could swallow. As a serious proposal for an operatic book supplement to a text so demonstrably intended for the concert-hall, not the theatre, it makes rebels of every true Berliozian, and must be regarded as pathological. The intention to bend over backwards in offering Pischek a grateful part may record interestingly a current habit of writing, ideally, for a particular singer. One can only be thankful, however, that this surrender of all artistic principles to an easily understood longing to return to the opera-house as a composer, and to a smouldering of the total neglect of *The Damnation of Faust*, did not result in any musical products for a critic to choke over. Meanwhile, London held no future, although Mendelssohn's early death might have suggested an unashamed care-free opening for a Berlioz oratorio. It was left to Bénazet (see p. 195) to present *The Damnation* (Parts 1, 2) in 1853 to nine hundred people, as part of the new 'chic'.

5

The Childhood of Christ

BOUND up at almost every stage, both with its devotional text and with a certain grandeur of conception, Berlioz's next main work, a setting of *Te Deum*, falls for review with the *Requiem* in the next chapter. The ensuing major composition was in the cantata class with *The Damnation of Faust* in spite of obvious differences. *L'enfance du Christ* is the misleading title of a short oratorio, for the most part dramatic in character and dealing with an imaginary incident in the long flight of Christ's parents to Egypt, preceded by an account of Herod's fearful massacre decision. The inception of the work was apparently accidental. One evening at the house of a friend, Pierre Leduc, the composer sketched for his host a pastoral tune for organ. That somehow suggested to him an intimate farewell song for the shepherds to sing before the departure for Egypt, and he supplied a text accordingly. This set his mind seriously at work, and he added a short fugal overture and an extended number to cover the journey to Egypt. *La Fuite en Egypte (The Flight into Egypt)* was thus produced by the St. Cecile Society in 1850 in the name of 'Pierre Ducré (1679)', and when it was published in 1852 under the composer's name, it was still provocatively subtitled 'Fragments d'un Mystère en style ancien . . . attribué a Pierre Ducré, Maître de Chapelle imaginaire'. That the fantastic attribution had been successful, even amongst the 'critics', is a passing reflection of the low-grade perception of style, especially in the final number. However, the cantata met with a warm enough reception to encourage Berlioz to go further. He added a much longer and more strictly dramatic part to cover the arduous journey to Sais and sanctuary. Finally, to balance all this in advance he composed an extended part introducing Herod and, in contrast, the Holy Family at Bethlehem. The whole work was given in 1854.

These mainly dramatic scenes are framed by a didactic narrative at the start and finish, with devotional touches at the end of each part. Thus, the stretch of music drama from Herod's palace to the Ishmaelites' cottage is unmistakably presented with more than a gesture of identification with the historical hazards and revered personalities of the long trek to safety. A fragmentary but evocative epilogue at once avoids ending on a vernacular Good-night scene and sets its seal on the 'trilogie sacrée' as meaningful in a new way; bearing a sense of involvement in the Lesueur spirit but without any question of formal worship, and also without the flabby sentimentality of such an unconscious precedent as J. C. F. Bach's *The Childhood of Jesus* (1773), to Hender's text, which also contains a simple shepherds song.

L'enfance du Christ made a remarkable and immediate break-through. The directness of manner, combined with positive melodic outbursts, was popularly registered as a change for the more communicable. It was truer to say that the familiarity of all the characters but one (the Ishmaelite host) made the search for characteristic music more persuasive than any music for the legendary Faust and his Margaret. But the composer had not altered his methods. He had in mind a certain appeal to a remote and cherished past (as late as 1851 he was thinking of setting—so he told D'Ortigue—some poems on Joan of Arc by Canon Arnaud of Poitiers), and also certain strains of compassionate and minatory and formal music. From the virtual welcome to the coming of Christ on earth which had first sprung to his mind as a pastoral melody—almost a chorale—Berlioz moved on to the widening construction of successive mood-music, connected where necessary by plain or arioso recitative, and prompted but not confined by the scenes selected, with linking or preparatory instrumental movements as opportunity or improvisation suggested and, as in some Handel oratorio, a chorus standing not only in the drama but also apart with a contemporary glance.

What was new was a somewhat daring use of his scenic-musical art to illuminate this usually neglected part of the Christmas story with his own version of the text, reading between the lines. But this association, far from defying comprehension, enhanced it. In this way Berlioz at last clarified his position as a pioneer in concert music with a programme and text. In the process he showed that the association was melodically fruitful as well as structurally suggestive in its chosen stages. All this may be accepted today as an eventful leap in communication. What is surprising is the endorsement of a somewhat straggling structure and banal text. In Part 1, after the shattering portrait of a fearful, vindictive Herod in action, the dialogue on the lambs in a static manger scene is not impressive reading, and the closing hieratic angelic-warning scene, however delicately rendered, remains a desultory conclusion. In Part 2, again, the fine tenor solo wrestles with a prosaic narrative of the family resting comfortably in a green shade, with a perfunctory *Alleluia* finish. In Part 3, the change of view from initially didactic narrative to dramatic incident is animated by an ascending passion of distress and rejection, but the sudden release of tension for the Ishmaelites' welcome, and the total committal of the rest of the scene into the hands of the kindly and gracefully patronizing host strains credibility for a modern listener. Finally, however, the humanitarian message of this legend of the good Ishmaelite is sidetracked by a call to humbleness of mind 'devant un tel mystère'. Identification gives way to a distancing pious gesture. This may be a minority impression, but the occasional naïvety of Berlioz's own text must be recognized as a restriction which it falls to Berlioz the composer to absorb in a wider musical appeal. In a scenario which, in the watchful Roman guard, in a nerve-ridden Herod, and in the desperate, importunate Joseph invites Berlioz to find various ready tokens of mounting emotional strain, the meditative and devotional elements challenge the composer to maintain the quality of spontaneous utterance by other means without a positive change of style. We may now survey the musico-dramatic development in its three stages with these problems of continuity in mind.

After the recital of the causes and circumstances of the flight to Egypt (tenor, wind and strings), the Herod drama unfolds. First, a long nagging night-patrol, conveyed by a crescendo from a relentless, capricious bass, quickening from one to two notes a beat, and a furtive melodic descent (**Ex. 22.1a**) which moves irresistibly from strings to wind in the alternating keys of a fugal exposition. An oscillating, non-committal figure (**Ex. 22.1b**) in the woodwind serves as a token second subject,

Ex. 22.1a

Ex. 22.1b

enough to lend substance to an immediate restatement of the two phrases with fresh features, and to further elaboration after a piece of Roman-officer dialogue that explains the inner focus of attention, King Herod's traumatic state. The reverberation of x as a bass maintains the nervous tension to the end. (For the performance of *The Damnation of Faust* at Covent Garden in 1933 Beecham inserted this march between Scenes 3 and 4; as a bridge between military grandeur and a soul under siege?)

This dark and penetrating sketch of an uneasy provincial city in the Empire prepares for Herod's melancholy mood, as declared in a recitative and formal aria, in which the initial and characteristic violoncello theme, ominously accompanied by vibrant pizzicati, enlists the listeners' sympathy for a worried governor. It also serves to bring his consultation of the soothsayers into the same emotional environment. The ensuing cabbalistic exercise-music may seem at first a forced seven-beat prancing about, but the texture is inventive, and brings out the exotic gestures of truth-scanning, before the more conventional vindictiveness of Herod and assenting soothsayers breaks out, somewhat in the daggers-blessing style of a well known *Les Huguenots* scene (**Ex. 23.1a**). Here wild scales, imperious saccadic rhythms, menacing semitonal descents and a final pompous antiphony of brass (**Ex. 23.1b**) (now appearing for the last time in the oratorio) and strings, all add to the release of ruthless fury from which there is no turning back.

The palace scene having reached this pitch of evil intention, the music relaxes

Ex. 23.1a

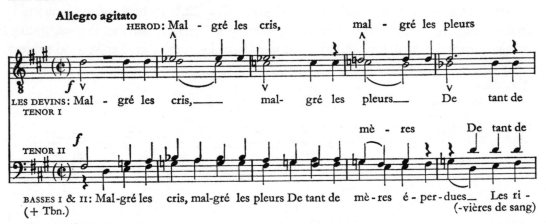

Ex. 23.1b

to deep chording and silence, to confront the Bethlehem stable. The ensuing duet develops gradually by means of two pairs of recurring phrases moulded into a curious pattern:

Ex. 24.1a	1b 1b 1a	2a 2b 2a 2b Development	1a Development
orchestra	soprano	soprano and bass	orchestra

Ex. 24.1a

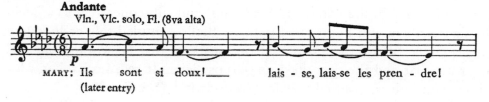

Ex. 24.1b

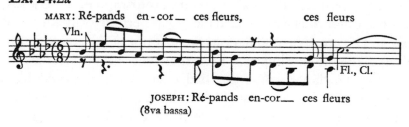

Ex. 24.2a

Ex. 24.2b

The focus is on the lambs, and **Ex. 24.**2b becomes the insistent cadential gesture. There are textural and other features besides, but the main appeal (and it is a tenuous thread) depends on the rapt delivery of the simple phrases in a measured antiphony or close imitation. Thus Herod is forgotten enough to lend point to the disruptive angelic warning from a distance, moving in a circle of tonality round **B** major, reinforced by *Hosanna* responses from invoked spectators (S.S.A.A. chorus). The exodus to Egypt, couched in succinct tokens of dispersal, forms a brief denouement, more outside the drama than in it. The manger-scene so far remains a contrasted episode in the main context of the Herod series.

In Part 2, *La Fuite*, a hieratic overture (strings, flutes and oboes) pursues a mainly fugal course with a plain, slightly modal (i.e. antiquated) subject; with relapses, in an episode in the relative major (flutes) and subsequently into a freely homophonic treatment and improvised phrases. Berlioz entitled this prelude 'the shepherds assemble before the stable' but one suspects that he worked out this stately overture first and then specified its purpose later. It remains a sober, prolonged, impersonal piece, pastoral only in its woodwind. (See **Ex. 26.**)

'Il s'en va loin de la terre' (popularly 'Thou must leave thy lowly dwelling'; but only the last verse of the French text is addressed to the child) is *known* to have acquired its three-verse text. Except for touches of woodwind punctuation in the last verse, the musical strophe is unchanged throughout. Its confidently expanding, square-cut tune of five phrases is too long for a verse of three couplets, with consequently meaningful repetitions of lines 5–6 for the harmonically striking concluding phrases; surely an undue emphasis for such simple well-wishing as 'Qu'il grandisse . . .' etc. In the two recurring verses, this underlining becomes an elegant affection. In other words, if we accept Berlioz's account of the origin of this chorus, this much treasured and spontaneous harmonized melody is perfunctorily equipped with a strophical text, and its creative modulations are just not of the type that call for strophical handling. They do not improve in instant twice-recurrence: a contrasted second verse, for which the composer had every facility, would have strengthened the resumption in the last verse. (After all, Bach never risks dulling his harmonically striking effects in a second verse in his chorale-settings in the *Christmas Oratorio*. Vaughan Williams's harmonization for his second 'chorale' in *Hodie*—as an original tune with a gratuitous second verse, a close parallel to 'Il s'en va' in method—is trenchant enough to justify the addition of its contemporary second verse.) It is apparent that in this, the first number completed, Berlioz accepted the idea of a rural song, however sophisticated, as the right thing for the shepherds, as representative worshippers. In the wider context, it can only justify its place as a focal choral item, as a quasi-communal interlude before the extended air which comprehends the realities of the escape into the desert. That it scarcely accomplishes. This comment on one of the smoothest features of the oratorio—

often, indeed, all too suave—may seem carping, but nothing is gained by an un-critical acceptance of a palpably loose structure at a significant point in the narration. A crisp tempo is essential.

The sequel is a comparatively close-knit number and full of distinctive touches. From the following starts arise two successive orchestral refrains, the first by the easy antiphony of strings and wind and a mobile tonality, the second by instant repetition, as an independent strophe, in alternating textures (**Ex. 25.1** and 2). The

Ex. 25.1

Strophe 1—Vln.   3—Vln.,Vlc. (8va bassa)   5—Vln., Ob.
         2—Ob.   4—Tenor

Ex. 25.2a

                                    Strophe 1, 4   2, 3, 5

Strophe 1—Cl., Vln. 2   3—Str. (8va bassa)   5—Vln., Fl., Cl. (trem.)
        2—Ob., Vln. 2, Vla.,   4—Tenor, Fl. (slow trem.),   (bars 2, 3—chords of
           pizz. (8va bassa)   Ob.   A major, G minor)

Ex. 25.2b

Strophe 1, 5—Vln., Fl. 3—Vln.,Cl.

Strophe 2—Ob., Fl.   4—Vln.

tenor entry duly incorporates these refrains and refers them to the narrator's plain account of the arrival at an oasis, and of Mary's thankfulness for that, leaving scope for a solemn aftermath of dedication in free arioso style (and not particularly com-plementary). One could not say whether the situation suggested the refrain, or whether the given refrains invited the tenor intervention, each valid in itself. Their compelling association ends the part firmly.

Part 3 continues the journey narrative and then dramatizes the contrast for the refugees between the initial blank rejections of their urgent pleas for shelter and their unexpected and elaborate welcome by the Ishmaelite family. An epilogue to the whole recital (narrative and chorus) strikes a concluding note of aspiration. The ceaseless wandering is retailed in a kind of air, reinforced by imitational and other turns of phrase whose cumulative recall of the overture to Part 2 (with the omission of the counter exposition of bars 1-36 and of the 45 bars of coda) may be tabulated in two cross sections, each set in the present key to show the primary reorientation of

Ex. 26

the rhythm and bar phrasing (**Ex. 26**). Such a facile transformation of rhythm, as the basis of a whole fresh number, seems an odd economy, and the absence of any connexion between the eager arrival of the shepherds and the hard trek across the desert adds to the bareness of the impact. All that can be said is that the vocal line is reinforced by imitation of which the pattern and texture are already familiar. The music thus comes at the end to an inevitable stop to enable the narrator to drop into recitative for an evocative introduction to the Saïs drama.

This final drama falls into two parts, the struggle for admission at the street doors and the various overt attentions of the Ishmaelite to the guests now in his house. For the first the composer establishes a basic **G** minor *Moderato*, with themes for a nervous Mary (echoed by the oboe) and an importunate Joseph. Against these arise various brief Allegro incidents of rejection, suspense and despair without response. The returning Moderato thus heightens the sense of crisis by a last appeal to an indifferent world. In Scene 2 the strain is suddenly lifted; amicable ariosos lead to a fugal chorus of ministrations, a trio (flutes and harp) and a goodnight chorus. The fugal chorus, response of the host family and their attendants to the summons, 'Montrez la bonté de vos coeurs', is the strongest number of this odd group. Yet instead of coming to a firm conclusion, it dissolves in a fresh and diffuse instrumental fugue, which soon draws haltingly to its cadence to make room for dialogue. The beguiling trio of flutes and harp is an accomplished and potentially transcendent piece of ensemble (if you can listen to such restricted texture for so long, in a probably unsuitable hall), but inevitably it is an interlude and a prolonged one, and the last chorus is jocund without being gripping. (No thought of the savage reprisals which the host has risked!)

The didactic epilogue concludes with a graceful piece for chorus alone. If it means more to some listeners, it must achieve this result by its spontaneous treatment of its extemporary phrases; the second, for example, which becomes a descant specially familiar to many English listeners through its apparent derivation from the end of a very old German hymn-tune treasured since *English Hymnal* days:

Ex. 27.1

Ex. 27.2

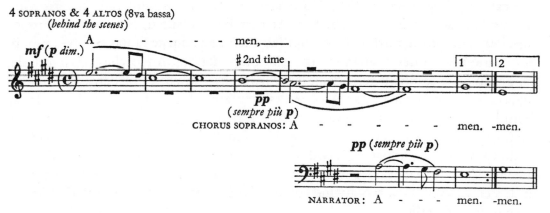

For one listener, this play on semitones (and keymanship: the key of the initial **E** oscillates, and the intrusive **B** sharp in **Ex. 27.2** is not properly treated) is too trifling to be conclusive. The rapt intent of the text is clear to all, but the absorption in musical values is not so self-evident. So far the epilogue may sound comparatively perfunctory to the mere listener. Hence the musical impact of this part, reasonably urgent up to the Ishmaelite's welcome, becomes dissipated for the remainder, and the final open appeal to the central point of reference in each listener scarcely guarantees an enhancement of depth. The hushed sweetness of a choral rendering may be persuasive, but it is not enough.

My blunt conclusion about this work is that while pursuing his usual method of fitting music to an imaginative projection of typical scenes, chosen for their variety and dramatic significance, direct or indirect, Berlioz has here been frustrated more often than not by his basic portraiture of the Holy Family. Joseph is active and concerned but hardly characteristic; Mary is maternally affectionate in Bethlehem and desperate in the search—for lodging scene, but after that her small part does little more than amplify Joseph's in mutual harmony. The Ishmaelite is a creation of social significance and compassion in any modern decade. Only Herod and the guards spring to life. It would seem that the haunting tune of what became 'Il s'en va loin' engendered a false sense of confidence. There was partial recovery, in a sense, in Part 1, composed last, but by then the rest was finished. We are left with an unequal work.

In his music-drama *Bethlehem*, incorporating the Coventry Nativity play, Rutland Boughton offers an extended sketch of Herod, as a grandiose monarch. He is made apprehensive over the fate of his son, but his 'angry look' dissolves in equivocal dialogue with the Wise Men. The stable scenes in each act, at once vernacular and prophetic in tone, contrast with Berlioz's naïve realism. In his much more penetrating cantata, *King Herod* (1964), Norman Kay dramatizes pungently the growing resentment against Herod's tyranny. At first he is assured, but the rumours of treachery and of the birth of a Saviour (an extended angelic fantasy) drives him in desperation to order (parlando) the child-liquidation. An orchestral interlude, suggesting the resultant terrorism, is followed by the voices of bereavement—an odd omission in Berlioz's narrative. A disintegrating Herod faces only bitter anger from his people. Berlioz's musical transition here is a mere relaxation of the prevailing minatory tone. On the other side, Ian Kellam's *A starre shon bright*, to medieval texts, while paying vivid tribute to Herod's part, includes a rollicking shepherds scene that at once strikes a touch of nature absent from the solemn piety of 'Il s'en va loin'. (The woodwind colour of the shepherds' song in Liszt's *Christus* has a touch of Berlioz.)

6

Latin Works

TWICE Berlioz addressed himself seriously to traditional devotional texts; those of the Requiem Mass, as commonly set, and the *Te Deum Laudamus*. In each case the occasion was a grand and civic one, calling for pomp but also gravity of sound-relationship. In the first case, Berlioz was not slow to respond to the evocation of man facing judgement in a succession of moods, quelled, fearful, intercessory, devotional. In the second, it is, arguably, the judgement theme which remains uppermost in the context of a joyful response to the ascriptive message. So far the two works reveal a more probing connexion than their attachment to an established and well-defined text, and occasion for elaborate music. Demonstrably, the *Requiem* is the bigger work; and there is no clear evidence of a more advanced method of treatment in the *Te Deum*.

No work can properly be assessed in terms of a later composition, but the foregoing survey of the musical contingencies of following a dramatic but restricted narrative, in *L'enfance*, and of the risk of diffuseness in a blend of narration and comment (to which indeed the greatest oratorios and Passions are subject, as music), may at least bring home the advantages of a concentration on a particular mood in turn, as outlined in the established divisions of the extended *Requiem* text, which since the fourteenth century has traditionally included the Offertory and (the late and disturbing break into the general tenor) the 'sequence' *Dies irae*, as well as the older features. The modern listener, who is likely to reach Berlioz through, or in spite of, Verdi's master-work, will recognize common emotional centres like *Tuba mirum*, but the pattern of treatment is quite different and may be summarized at once. (See page 93 for details.) Berlioz has ten choral numbers, with a tenor-solo part in the *Sanctus*.[1] Verdi, by a liberal use of solo-voices in contrasted but component sub-movements, has five comparable numbers. Thus *Lacrimosa*, vehemently isolated in Berlioz, becomes in Verdi a profound coda to an overwhelming *Dies irae*. From this comparison the distinctive impact of Berlioz's ten succinct choruses, each held together by broad patterns of repetition and contrast, as in Verdi, may be forecast. The upshot is that, number upon number, the *Requiem* is in Berlioz's most concentrated style of composition. This working impression may serve to dismiss at once the misleading but popular idea of a superficially emotional work that the *Requiem* may have gained from earlier misunderstandings, due partly to a lack of acquaintance with the original public occasion.

At its inception the *Requiem* was caught up in a tangled thread of interfering individuals and events. It was commissioned by the outgoing Minister of Fine Arts in March 1837 to commemorate the 'heroes' of the July 1830 revolution. Six months later, after considerable delays and opposition under a new Minister and a bland cancellation of the whole ceremony when rehearsals of the completed work were already in train—a cancellation which the Empire-minded Berlioz found inconceivable except under 'these representative governments'—the *Requiem* was commissioned a second time. It was now to be performed at the funeral of General Damrémont, who as commanding officer had been killed in the assault on Constantine in Algeria. This military feat in a foreign adventure promoted by the government called for a grand and multitudinous demonstration of the nation's support; a situation for which it would not be hard to imagine a modern parallel. The ceremony was assigned to the vast domed chapel of St. Louis at the Invalides. Berlioz's music thus gained a place, in succession to portentous civic ritual, in special acoustic conditions as well as with a packed audience. In anticipation, it may seem, he wrote for a choir of basically only three parts (SA.T.B.), besides storing some extra decibel power for special moments. (He was fascinated by the acoustics of St. Paul's during his visit to London later, and would certainly have found in the performance of the *Requiem* there, in 1964 and after, the vindication of his aural imagination.)

But the score had long been prepared, and parts distributed. It remained chiefly to determine an effective balance of numbers. Berlioz asked for 190 instrumentalists and 210 singers, with additional kettledrum and brass groups for 'Tuba mirum'. This is the 'extravagance' he insisted upon. The four separate brass groups, for which the *Requiem* is famed, were designed from the start for special intense moments in the setting. Actually, in order to meet a dateline for score delivery according to the original commission, while maintaining his concert reviewing and other commitments, Berlioz had written somewhat hurriedly. But fundamentally this was the fulfilment of a project long contemplated subconsciously. (One might assume that there could only be one conductor for the rendering of such an advanced and elaborate, and so publicly exhibited, a choral-orchestral work. But once more interfering authorities decided that, Cherubini's *Requiem* having been ignored, the veteran Habeneck (see page 30) should be asked to conduct, since he was quite incapable of mastering so novel a score.)

The tense and hazardous first occasion thus understood without undue emphasis of its material bearing, we may return to Berlioz's ten numbers, none of immoderate

Table 3

Berlioz	Mozart	Verdi
1. Requiem aeternam Kyrie	1. Requiem aeternam Kyrie	1. Requiem aeternam Kyrie
2. Dies irae Tuba mirum Liber scriptus	2. Dies irae 3. Tuba mirum	2. Dies irae Tuba mirum Liber scriptus Quid sum miser Rex tremendae Recordare
3. Quid sum miser	None	
4. Rex tremendae Recordare Confutatis	4. Rex tremendae 5. Recordare 6. Confutatis	
5. Quaerens me Ingemisco	None	Quaerens me Ingemisco Confutatis Lacrimosa
6. Lacrimosa	7. Lacrimosa	
7. Offertorium: Domine Jesu	8. Offertorium: Domine Jesu	3. Offertorium: Domine Jesu Hostias et preces Quam olim Abrahae
8. Hostias et preces Quam olim Abrahae	9. Hostias et preces Quam olim Abrahae	
9. Sanctus Hosanna	10. Sanctus Hosanna	4. Sanctus Hosanna Benedictus Hosanna
None	11. Benedictus Hosanna	
10. Agnus Dei	12. Agnus Dei Lux aeterna Cum sanctis	5. Agnus Dei 6. Lux aeterna Cum sanctis
None	None	7. Libera me

length and a few quite short. They are tabulated with the numberings of Mozart and Verdi to show where Berlioz's was arbitrary or distinctive (Table 3). It will be convenient to sort out their different kinds of appeal according to their structural organization.

Most choruses rely, in some degree, on a pivotal movement of reprise and coda after a contrast of theme or tempo or key (nos. 1, 4, 5, 6, 7; instant reprise, 9). Some depend on the working polarization of opposite or at least distinctive moods in succession (2, 9, 10). Others are broadly strophical (2, 8), or noticeably employ reiteration in shorter but consistent measure as a manner of expansion (6), sometimes in the changing voices of a fugue but in too rigid a rhythm for truly fugal development (7, 9). Number 5 presents in some degree the weave of true fugue. Number 3 seems to be the shadow of the reprise missing from Number 2, in paradoxical key (**G** sharp minor, following **A** minor—**E** flat). Thus, in some notable cases a broad structural urge is reinforced by one more specialized. These various successive patterns ensure a fresh impact for each number, and cumulatively leave a firm impression that with the exception of one or two weaker entries, the selections from the *Requiem* text have found not only characteristic music but music taken to its proper conclusion, in some cases through the unexpected touch for which a coda (i.e. final development) provides facilities. We turn now to the relation of these classical gestures to their text, with an occasional cross-reference to Mozart and, since his setting is now equally historical, to Verdi.[2]

In the opening chorus, in particular, the different absorptions of the 'Introit' text may be observed. There are three stages to handle: 'Requiem aeternam' . . . 'et lux perpetua luceat', the psalm verse 'Te decet hymnus', and 'Kyrie'. Mozart, Berlioz and Verdi all make 'Requiem'—'Te decet'—'Requiem' a compact sequence, from which Mozart and Verdi embark on fresh music for 'Kyrie'. Berlioz's equally fresh setting of 'Et lux' and 'Kyrie' is in the nature of a genuine coda to the whole movement, in which a declamatory monotone and a stark intonation, compressed to the minimum, contrast stirringly with the plenary recurring themes of Mozart and Verdi. Without any straining of rhetorical effect or of the conventional imitational process which the main 'Requiem' stretch of a descending seventh prompts, Berlioz has maintained a note of earnest pleading, augmented towards the end by a deepening sense of human insufficiency, leaving the issue in suspense. Passing stabs of perception include such semitonal slides as **Ex. 28.1** and **28.2**; the former introducing 'Lux perpetua' with a bold, unexpected approach to an established cadential chord, the Neapolitan sixth (**Ab**), before 'Te decet'; the latter progression (with symmetrical declamatory detail) returning to the same text with a similarly qualified transition to an established propulsive chord, the German sharpened

Ex. 28.1

sixth ('luceat *eis*, second time). These make typical nuances in a steadily distinctive and homogeneous texture.

Mozart and Verdi both take the intrusive 'Dies irae' (not set by Fauré) to be an invocation to devise proliferating phrases of forcible, fearful declamation. Mozart, in a concise **D** minor chorus, reserving 'Tuba mirum' for a gentle **B** flat interlude (*pace* an activist trombone); Verdi, in a pronounced, almost hysterical opening to an extended series focused on **G** minor up to 'Lacrimosa', with 'Tuba mirum' a brief but thrilling **A** flat minor outburst, to follow and then to be displaced. Berlioz begins very soberly in **A** minor, with a plain and essentially bass intonation framed to support counter-theme or rhythmic monotone, not least while the key slides to **B** flat and **D** minor. On this orderly intensification of the familiar idea of conscience-burdened man facing judgement there bursts the more sensational fancy of the warning trumpet call from the supreme court. (This is in **E** flat, a candid repudiation of the pious concern of **A** minor; a jerk from the bowed head to a cosmic vision.) What will measure the universal summons? Will four trumpets suffice? No, nothing

Ex. 28.2

less than four brass consorts of 8–12 players each, placed at the four corners of production, so that their antiphonal fanfare fills in all gaps in the continuum. (In fact the placing of the bands on the fringes of the platform but together, as was done, for example, in the Royal Albert Hall in June 1951, has the advantage of evoking a more homogeneous harmony.) The normal orchestra also contains eight pairs of kettledrums, each forming a different concord or discord.

A broad and entire stanza of brass pomp and choral declamation absorbs 'Tuba mirum'. It is repeated with reinforcements and rejoinders for 'Liber scriptus', but the end is subdued: *mors stupebat et natura*. The main music is as triumphant as Handel's trumpet music in the relevant and flamboyant solo in *Messiah*. An explanation is that 'Tuba mirum' is closely based on the setting in 'Et resurrexit'—the surviving portion of the early Mass music (see page 40)—of 'Et iterum venturus . . . iudicare . . . Tuba mirum spargens sonum coget omnes . . . [*sic*].' There the 16-bar declamation forms a prelude to a mysterious Allegro couched in **E** flat minor. Here it is left to organize itself in its grandeur. While, therefore, it would be a gross error of judgement to ignore the originality of this complex 'Dies irae' music, the symmetrical strophical declamation is disarming, and it is no surprise to learn that it reproduces an earlier formula.

For 'Quid sum miser' (primarily for tenors and oboes) Berlioz reverts to the initial material of 'Dies irae', but in a restricted texture and in **G** sharp minor; echoing the previous movement (and that implausibly) but in no sense rounding it off. No long-range sense of key is needed to convey this tone of irrelevance, but Berlioz's choice of a remote key confirms his structural intentions.

'Rex tremendae'—reserving the bands and drums for 'libera me ne cadam', the climax of the more animated middle section—uses a convenient 'arch' pattern (A-B-C-B-A) to connect bursts of declamation with succinct imitation, in a mood of intense appeal, which is noticeably differentiated in the contrast between the sudden urgency of 'Salva me', leading straight to the middle *animato*, and the halting suspended phrase of the final setting. A chorus hard to remember but well knit. Incidentally, it absorbs midway 'Recordare', which has already appeared, out of order, in 'Quid sum miser'; a contrast to the extended, tender solo cantabile of Mozart and Verdi. Berlioz reserves the associate 'Quaerens me', however, for a brief piece of unaccompanied fugue in symmetrical stages. An insipid interlude. The nugatory 'subject' might be tolerable as a background for other melodic or contrapuntal features. As it is, it soon palls, and its final entry in the basses is tautologous, and a worthy setting, indeed, of the text ('inter oves locum praesta'), of which one questions not the method but the bare inclusion. The rhetorical point of this tranquil movement is obvious, but it betrays the lack of any true grasp of fugue per Reicha. (When did Bach ever write an entire vocal fugue on one subject? So exceptionally as to prove the point.)

Suddenly, then, in 'Lacrimosa' Berlioz presents his finest and most over-whelming movement. Its order of impact is unmistakable. The insistence of a recurring and strenuous minor-key intonation of 3-4-4 bars is followed up by a contrasted, beseeching setting of the same text in a relative major (**Ex. 29.2**); answering bands punctuate an otherwise literal return to the minor (**Ex. 29.1**); the sequent and equally predictable major (a conventional tonic major) is polarized, after six bars of cliffhanging between a major and a minor finish, by a final and superlative delivery of the now riveting intonation with the Bands no longer just textural but melodically affirmative. In an escape from this burden a slide into utterly irrelevant keys releases an unexpectedly permanent close in the major. So much may be put down as a necessary preliminary to intelligent response. It may then appear that the exactness of the recapitulation of the two main sections, each in themselves repetitive and symmetrical, is surprising, and the stiff use of the established pattern of sonata-form decidedly unclassical in a derogatory sense. Only in the coda is there a somewhat greater freedom of rhythm. It may be argued that the rigidity increases the feeling of the inevitability of man's trial. As it was ordained, it will come upon him. It is nevertheless the conductor's problem to express this without allowing the successive reverberations of this not too hard wearing theme to sound automatic. It remains to secure a properly rehearsed synchronization. The two main elements may be illustrated. The second is clearly subsidiary, or at least secondary in its hold on the ear, and correspondingly vulnerable to any stress of repetition.

Ex. 29.1

Reprise: init.

Ex. 29.2

The Offertorium chorus, 'Domine Deus', is a subtly knit movement in **D** minor, restrained but tense. The proliferation of a long theme, at first in more or less fugal style but later in a brief and more adaptable version, expands, with auxiliary matter, an almost self-sufficient orchestral piece. Through this broad assertion of theme the chorus haltingly deliver the text (a kind of litany of souls) in a steady monotone of response, as traditionally attached to the fifth degree and in a receding articulation of speech, until 'quam olim Abrahae et semini eius . . .' is reached in an apparently conclusive fade-out. Then, in a visionary flash, which seems to justify the whole repression of vocal melody, the six-part chorus begin to spell out major key harmony for 'promisisti' and a serene close. The pinning down of each vocal entry by a coincidence of plucked strings sets its seal on this affirmation. (Those who, surveying the record of the present century, find the ancient promise of delivery from the pains of hell, with the assistance of the archangel Michael, rather more than they can swallow, can vent their indignation and disbelief in the rollicking satire of the Britten version of 'Quam olim', in the context of the Owen parable of Abraham and Isaac, A. D. 1918).

In the brief impressive 'Hostias' a progression for male chorus, marked by changing key, is flecked with a strange, challenging sonority or counter-sonority of flutes and trombones, which Berlioz must have meant. He wanted a minimal, barely cohesive chord to envelop the stage without any cover of open pockets of sound. Berlioz contemplated the immense gulf between earth and heaven, as implied in the continuation omitted by Berlioz: *fac eas, Domine, de morte transire vitam*. The whole bold petition twice, to silence doubters.

For any informed listener, the hearing of the 'Sanctus—Hosanna' setting arouses, afterwards, recollections of the art not only of Verdi but of Bach (amongst others) on the same ground. Reversing the order of comparison, it may be felt that beside Bach's tremendous setting of the 'Sanctus' and exceedingly resourceful and fugal 'Pleni sunt coeli', or Verdi's energetic, overwhelming and partly fugal dance of the sons of the morning (conflating 'Sanctus' 'Benedictus' and 'Hosanna' in one movement), Berlioz's succinct 'Sanctus' of patterned phrases in a subdued tone and a sequent 'Hosanna' fugue of no particular character, are remarkably uneventful, and do not call for the total reprise that succeeds with slight extensions. The tenor solo, moving through a high arch of solo-violin harmony and supported by tremulous violas, lends, indeed, an individual touch. But if the text is to be sung, reverend awe is not enough. Nor is this relaxation of tension a soft interlude before a final creative effort. The 'Agnus Dei' proves to be no more than a revised version of the 'Hostias' strophes, linked to a steady repeat of the initial 'Requiem' chorus, starting with the sadly solitary middle section, 'Te decet hymnus', and adding a perfunctory close in the major. This customary reprise of the 'Requiem' start is no more persuasive in the event than the many facile parallels.

The *Requiem* thus rises above the established *planctus* for a person of eminence, or for a nation-wide loss, to the patterned pleading and consuming sense of urgency invoked by the liturgy from men of sensibility, of whatever sect. At the same time, as in Beethoven's *Masses*, the traditional framework is being permeated by a new concept of grief-struck commemoration, springing less from a pious and pathetic concern for 'rest' and 'light' for the dead than from an uprush of humanity stung to the quick with visions of judgement to come, as stressed in the imported sequence, 'Dies irae', but also in the Offertory. This trail was consistently pursued by Britten in a historical double-thinking *Requiem*, instantly placing all thoughts of a continuing liturgy in the context of an unfolding exposure of man preparing for death as Wilfred Owen, poet and serving officer of 1914–18, recorded them doing, in a nervous swing from liturgical chorus to solo-arioso (and chorus) and back. In the line of *Requiem* settings which made the *War Requiem* for a new Coventry Cathedral conceivable, Berlioz still stands pre-eminent with Verdi, each pacing the other on his own scheme. If in Berlioz's work there are some slighter numbers and very little shape in the order of musical events, it retains a pioneer quality in its less thematic style.

As a monument of compression, Stravinsky's nine-part *Requiem Canticles*, each of under two minutes, form a stimulating comparison with Berlioz's mainly conventional proportions. Each brief moment is cogent and compact, from the dramatic 'Dies irae', the vigorously contrapuntal 'Rex tremendae', the partly spoken 'Libera me', and the contralto line in 'Lacrimosa', to the passionate string counterpoint of the prélude and the arresting chordal sequences of the interlude and postlude, a kind of perpetual rehearsal of things to come. The work seems to select the kind of impression at which Berlioz often aims, in the distancing of a wider context.

After the failure of *Faust* to attract adequate audiences in Paris, Berlioz, seeing no chance of a recovery in later concerts, went concert-giving, with no little success, in St. Petersburg (Leningrad), Moscow, Berlin and subsequently London. He returned to the Paris of the 1848 revolution vaguely hoping for some eventual gain of freedom of activity for the artist. It soon became clear that the general benefit of the new government in being 'strong' (i.e. ruthless) towards the rebels amounted to an indifference to all popular social aspirations, including dispossessed artists. However, with the aid of Baron Taylor, a devoted patron of the concert schemes needed to avoid placing the entire risk on an impresario's shoulders, Berlioz organized a concert for the benefit of the Musicians' Association. This, given in the theatre at Versailles in unaristocratic dress and at unaristocratic prices, and at the same time ranging from Rossini to Beethoven, was intended to win substantial favour for the arts from the new masters. Actually this popular gesture was mistimed. Louis Napoleon's star was rising in the elections. However, thanks to the loyal republican leader, Cavaignac, Berlioz was now retained as librarian to the Conservatoire with arrears of salary made up and a bonus of five hundred francs 'to encourage him as a composer'. Fortified by this allowance and undaunted either by the reduced wages from the *Journal des Débats* and the weekly *Gazette musicale* (whose payment by the line now meant that one contributor could no longer afford to be concise), or by the splendid appearance of *Le Prophète*, his qualified commendation of which in the *Gazette* could leave no discerning readers in doubt about his contempt for Meyerbeer's surrender to the public standard of taste, Berlioz pressed on with his creative work.

Having finished an orchestral version of *La Captive* for a London concert and a funeral march for *Hamlet* (in aid of what?), he turned in 1849 to the project of a *Te Deum* as a sequel to *Requiem*. Sequel, we say, rather than companion-piece, for what was the connexion? It is true that a long time before, in a notebook of 1832 (confirmed in a letter of 1835), Berlioz had formulated the conception of celebrating the nation's great men in a spreading symphony of seven movements, which had eventually materialized in part in the *Funeral and Triumphal Symphony* of 1840. Now, arguably, there was an opportunity for a 'religious and military fresco . . . closely related to the revolutionary era of which 1848 had revived certain aspects—war, grief and the terror of divine justice' (Barzun), although the composer had no intention of intervening personally in politics. But *Te Deum* is not the text of a whole church service, still less part of a commemorative one; and no special occasion was in view when Berlioz finished his setting in 1849. Undismayed, he proceeded to found and direct a Philharmonic Society which gave twelve well-rehearsed concerts and became the obvious vehicle for introducing this grand new work, having revived the *Requiem* in aid of the families of the Angiers bridge disaster, 1850. But while this was laying foundations for later schemes, after eighteen months the society collapsed in the hands of its now weary director. Sharing out the profits amongst nearly 200 performers left a trail of dissatisfaction, which was augmented by bad feeling between singers and players.

Te Deum received its first public performance in 1855—at St. Eustache's, as the first of seven concerts planned in connexion with the Great Exhibition, of which Berlioz was put in charge of three. The critics' warm reception of the public rehearsal ensured a smooth performance in a packed church two days later. Berlioz's many-pronged communicativeness (composer, conductor, acoustic controller, business executive) served him well; and apparently the attested distonation of a low-pitched organ and a concert-pitched wind band did not jar unduly. The work was accepted as non-liturgical church music with some military features but fundamentally for all occasions, and as such it will be treated here.

101

There are six choral movements and a final march for the presentation of the colours, which must be considered superfluous where, as on most occasions, there are no troops to march. Roughly there are two triumphal movements, 'Te Deum' (1) and 'Christe rex gloriae' (4), and one of growing exuberance, 'Tibi omnes angeli' (2), linked by a mild 'Dignare, Domine' (3) and countered by an intimately appealing 'Ergo quae sumus' (5). On this restrained confidence, moving from minor to major, bursts 'Iudex crederis esse venturus' (6), after which the March has to protest very hard to seem in the slightest degree relevant. The *Requiem* reveals a clear unity of principal mood, as well as the associations of its traditional text. *Te Deum* remains unpredictable. While the maintenance of two three-part choirs quickens a sense of working contrast, as between repartee, polyphony pulling against a homophonic background, and a fully harmonic progression, and while the addition of a third choir of boys' voices in unison in choruses 1, 2 and 6 introduces a communal touch, these textural coincidences do not, of course, commit a given movement to particular music. This *Te Deum* is also peculiar (but quite intelligible) in its sudden transposition of verses after the second movement (vv. 3–13 in the *Book of Common Prayer*); the remaining associations being: (3) 26, 21, 27; (4) 14, 15, 17; 16; 18; (5) 20, 28; (6) 19, 29; 22, 24, 25—with repetitions as convenient. The final connexion of verses 19 and 29 is cogent in the context. We must take the composer's arrangement as it comes.

'Te Deum laudamus', then, flows easily along from the soprano lead in an imitational but not studiously fugal style. The characteristic feature of the exuberant counterpoint proves to be, not one of the cross-rhythms but a slowly descending figure announced by the organ and declaimed later to the words '*Te aeternum Patrem omnis terra veneratur*', with the boys augmenting the other voices. As this permeates the texture, the original subject begins to sound a point of ancillary detail, as in many a chorale prelude; but such a recurrent combination of ideas (no more), does not justify the popular description of 'double fugue'. It is merely a classical device for renewing by counter-metre the impact of the main subject, here by adding a touch of solemnity (*veneratur*) which eventually draws to no agile fugal close but a surprise modulation to a remote key. Thus in or, as it proves, after this Allegro in **F** it is suddenly **B** major for a leisurely organ prelude, of minimal significance, to an ascription of glory transcendent that is eloquently serene, ecstatic and joyful by turns—the enhancement of 'Sanctus' by wind and later string arpeggio figures is noteworthy—and then vindicates the organ prelude (somewhat) orchestrally. Why the sequent *Dignare Domine . . . nos custodire* should be furnished with a prelude designed for a military celebration to be omitted otherwise, I cannot fathom; it is omitted in most vocal scores. The musical reverberation of 'Te Deum' also seems pointless. But in any case 'Dignare' is on the dull and rambling side, without any noticeable structural assertion to sharpen its edges. 'Christe rex gloriae' begins firmly enough with an elate descent from the third degree, apt, as we discover, for a triumphant finish, but it is superseded by the second theme, to *Tu ad dexteram Dei sedes*, taken from the corresponding setting in the 1825 Mass, with its infectious trochaic 'Gloria', prompted by vigorous pizzicato arpeggios. A simple chorus to hear. 'Ergo quaesumus' (**G** minor) introduces a tenor solo, more compulsively than in the *Requiem*, to find words for the prevailing concise strophe of urgent appeal, countered by the strained monotone of the sopranos' 'Fiat super nos misericordia'. This latter is delivered rather confusingly against a hieratic brass background, but it converges nicely (ascending strings) in a serene major, whose cadence, with the strophical theme in the bass, holds the ear before the next chorus assails it.

For at whatever level the foregoing movements grip the listener—and there is a certain self-conscious straining after a portentous effect, exultant or abased—it is 'Iudex crederis esse venturus' that lifts the work to a point of utter absorption in its

Ex. 30.1

Ex. 30.2

103

material. Citation of the starts of the two main themes shows how Berlioz has projected Verses 19–29 and 22 into a working contrast. The first theme quickly spreads from voice to voice imitationally, not in the usual order of balanced repartee but in ascending *semitones* from **E** flat minor. With this start and further capricious deviations of key in a brief climax of tone, a drop into **B** flat minor (a near key) for the second theme appears as a coincidence. Here the initial bar *y* (**Ex. 30.2**) soon shapes an insistent and richly scored orchestral rhythm to carry along the formal, antiphonal declamation of Verses 24–25 by tenors and basses in **D** flat. If, today, one stops to think of all the peoples of the world who, troubled by war, dissensions or poverty, seek 'preservation', one begins to enter into the significance of those monotonous rhythms. The return of **Ex. 30.1** is thus unmistakable.

This reprise is steadily developmental. The first entries of the subject, confined to a monotonous phrase *x* (**Ex. 30.1**), now rise in steps of *three* semitones, and are countered by impressive tutti in strange keys.[3] Recovering its original shape and semitonal ascent (up to **E** flat minor) in a firm, reinforced delivery, the subject appears in a striking unison in a rich orchestral setting of pulsating wind, tremulous strings and tense brass rejoinder. After further restless exploration of key, it implements a unanimous and trenchant outburst of choral-orchestral-organ harmony. For a conventional grand release of this tension, Berlioz draws upon **B** flat major, *y* (**Ex. 30.2**), doubled in length, and finally an orchestral *z* (**Ex. 30.2**), lit by brass fireworks. So to an 'optimistic' conclusion, musically just acceptable, but somewhat weakened by anticipation 17 bars earlier. Also, the return to *y* (**Ex. 30.2**), as associated with the joyful Verses 24–25, seems a confusing echo of extraneous matter.

Compared, then, with the 'Lacrimosa' of the *Requiem*, whose mood may well be recalled here, this chorus, while providing a slighter second section than 'Lacrimosa', shows a much more interesting thematic growth and the more its corroborative detail is observed, the more the creative shaping makes its effect. There is none of the 'free-wheeling' that marks each stage of 'Lacrimosa'. This incisive mode matches the inward judicial message of the text, and, indeed, expresses it, as of one possessed. While the previous numbers range from adequate treatment to fine choralism, this in particular, given the new collocation of verse, sounds right for the occasion. After which the dignified march for ceremonial use seems almost surrealistic. Can one reconcile an image of man at the seat of judgement, trusting to be vindicated, but never sure, with a conventional ceremonial of dedicated Forces? The categories do not blend.

Te Deum is scarcely a compulsive whole, apart from the varied succession of recognizable projections of the common text, but its composition suggests a final or penultimate fit of concentration in 'Iudex'. It is an evident sequel, but not a true companion piece, to the *Requiem*. The elaborately assembled forces of the *Te Deum laudamus* of Tony Hewitt Jones (1965) moves forward to a like climax at 'In te, Domine, speravi' by means of a convergence of multiple counterpoint.

From these two large works we may turn to *Redentore e nato*, the brief 'chorus of the Magi' which Berlioz sent from Rome to the Institute in 1832. Influenced, surely, by the Easter hymn in *Eight Scenes from 'Faust'*, it suffers, if anything, from an excess of material—declamatory, harmonic, imitational, semitonal—but its celebration of a festival, with an agile orchestra, has a spontaneous air, and it is a pity that the vocal score is out of print. Why is this outburst put into the mouth of the Magi? One is reminded somehow of a famous over-secular picture whose titular provenance was changed from 'The Last Supper' to 'Supper in the house of Simon'. 'Popoli contento'? Better make this an academic feast of reason! In any case one might at first have expected it to appear in the first part of *L'enfance*; but after all the Herod music it would not have fitted.

NOTES

1. Berlioz drafted the vocal part of a setting of the *Sanctus* bringing in a soprano as well as a tenor, but obviously found the repartee ineffective in addition to the chorus.

2. In his *Requiem* (1967) Mr Alec Robertson has eloquently distinguished the established settings of the *Requiem* text, combining a special insight into the long history of the text with an unfaltering demand for musical standards as the crucial test of the quality of the setting. He is thus illuminating about what he calls the unpredictables in the Berlioz *Requiem*, including the end of the 'Offertory' and the commonly misunderstood 'Hostias'. Robertson attributes the perfunctory conclusion of 'Agnus Dei' to hurried composition to meet a dateline.

3. How much Berlioz has exploited overt key-relationship in this chorus to keep up the tension, both in the fugal incidents and in the episodes which intervene or augment, may be seen in the following synopsis, which also shows the considerable proportion of imitational texture to improvized harmonic progressions, apart from the *Salvum fac* interlude and the virtual coda after the unison reprise. The figures refer to the examples. Non-capital key-entry indicates a minor key.

Table 4

Fugal Entries		30.1: e flat, e, f		30.2: b flat, D flat
Episodes	30.1		D flat, f sharp, D	
Number of Bars	7	24	25	16

Fugal Entries		30.1 (x): e flat, g flat, a, f
Episodes	30.2(y): A flat, D flat, e flat	
Number of Bars	41	20

Fugal Entries	e flat, e flat	**30.1**: c sharp, d, e flat	
Episodes	**30.2** (z): E, D flat, A flat		
Number of Bars	11	25	

Fugal Entries	**30.1** (x): b flat		**30.1** (x): g
Episodes	e, D, c sharp, C sharp, (D flat), b flat	**30.2** (y): B flat	
Number of Bars	25	11	6

Fugal Entries			
Episodes	**30.2**: B flat		
Number of Bars	21	Total: 232 Bars	

7

Songs

APART from early pieces, Berlioz wrote some thirty-six songs for voice or voices and piano, to a wide variety of texts. He subsequently set sixteen of these orchestrally at intervals from the original song ranging from one to sixteen years. Spasmodic as it always was, this accumulation formed a genre in itself. Although most of the songs are thoroughly strophical in musical as well as in literary measure, they open up a distinctive way of communication and in certain cases approach the condition of a succinct tone-poem, such is Berlioz's control of texture. They represent the composer's obvious métier, as the piano settings do not. They will be taken here to be his best setting in each case, superseding an earlier draft for a more workaday context. In this version will these songs most be publicized in the foreseeable future. They are generally neglected, apart from the set, *Nuits d'été*.

The first song to emerge in this way, in 1834, was 'La belle voyageuse', the fourth of the collection, *Neuf mélodies* or *Irlande* (mezzo soprano, strings and woodwind). Here Thomas Gounet has rendered Thomas Moore's 'Rich and rare' (*Irish melodies*) into his own light-footed stanzas, in which 'L'honneur en cet asile est le souverain Dieu' is conveyed without Moore's didactic touch. There are four verses, with a frisky 'burden' at the end of Verses 1 and 4. The strings supply a supple, uniform lilt of arpeggio and off-beat ictus, with some woodwind counter-phrases and support for the voice in the even verses. The setting makes a nice pulsating background for a typical Berlioz melody. It swings easily from two 8-bar phrases to two which are not, with a pronounced but facile modulation in the second phrase and recovery in the third. All this soon shapes itself in the ear, in aid of a portrait of this solitary, dazzling girl, originally scheduled to appear with that of swinging Sara, as features in a concert intended to prepare the ground for the première of the *Harold* symphony.

Ten years later came orchestral versions of two other songs from the Gounet set, 'Hélène, and 'Chant sacré'. The first of these is the ballad of humble Ellen who wooed the lord of a castle (Rosna Hall). It is set (vv. 1, 2, 3, 6) for two voices, with strings and drums to mark the beats, to a perky strophe that weakens in repetition. The second song is an expansion of Herminia's 'Dieu tout puissant' (see page 49) by the addition of choral parts and a midway recitative and coda. A superfluous task: what had been an individual turn in a dramatic air has been sentimentalized as a devotional exercise.[1] 'Le jeune pâtre Breton (*c.* 1834) is a setting of four verses of 'Le chanson de Loic', a poem from the *Marie* of the Brittany poet, A. Brizeux, who drew his fanciful tale of a shepherd and his receding lover from a local encounter with Loic and Anna, an engaged couple. The song is based on a cheerful, somewhat commonplace, though asymmetrical, strophe, with a horn obbligato in Verse 2 and, at a distance, Verse 4, and special suppressed and tremulous tones for 4. This naïve song is soon forgotten, while the resigned shepherd of Schubert's 'Shepherd's lament' leaves a trenchant impression of nonchalant retreat from a discouraging event.

It is thus something of a revelation to encounter, as audiences of 1848 must have done, the wistful melancholy of 'La captive', projected into the orchestral version of a recently revised song first composed (a tone higher) in 1832, with these starting and finishing basic phrases (**Ex. 31.1, 31.2**). As usual, the second phrase goes

Ex. 31.1

Ex. 31.2

Ex. 31.3

further out of key, the third meanders back and the fourth (**Ex. 31.2**) supplies the reassuring, symmetrical rejoinder to the initial *cri de coeur*, a modish invocation. In the 1832 setting, this sufficed for the four verses selected (vv. 1–3, 9) from Hugo's poem (found like 'Sara' in *Les Orientales*), and it captivated the senses of all who heard it. A version with a slight violoncello obbligato followed, with the piano echoing

Ex. 31.2 after Verse 4. In the final and orchestral version (the piano version is lost), the setting, augmented by an extra penultimate verse (v. 8) and by free composition in Verses 2, 4, and 5, takes on a new life. The orchestra specified consists of ten wood and horns and forty-two strings, with an optional second string group for the last Verse. For Verse 1 the 'mer plaintive' is matched with undulating violins and a slow undertone below, while wind figures maintain rhythmic connexion. In Verse 2 the tune is compressed into hustled vocal phrases (**Ex. 31.**3), prompted by the woodwind and some apt string guitarring. In Verse 3 the tune regains its measure with woodwind harmony in rival possession. In Verse 4 an 'air espagnol' or bolero for strings takes charge, with a dashing vocal part, while a 'burden' in the bass sounds strangely familiar. For the final dream the voice, in a retarded metre (quaver-beats specified), haltingly recovers the tune against tremulous muted strings—the second orchestra should enhance a true pianissimo here—and a final touch of pitchless percussion. A graceful coda of lingering allusion to Verse 1 (**Ex. 31.**1), with the phrase of **Ex. 31.**2 in the violins, sustains the last flickering fantasy of being free, converging in a normal suspended cadence. So the sad but vivid wishful-thinking of the homesick slave girl, skilfully adumbrated in the opening slide into **B** minor, reaches musical fulfilment in a succinct set of variations, calling liberationists of all periods, whatever Hugo intended. It is astonishing that the song has never yet been effectively revived.

It is diverting in every sense to compare Charles Wood's setting of Whitman's 'Ethiopia saluting the colours', a dialogue between a humane conqueror and an old captured slave at the wayside of his triumphant march onward and upward. The robustness might have amused Berlioz, as Berlioz's skilful economy and inventive detail would have impressed Wood.

Three other pieces completed the output of separate orchestral solo songs. 'Zaïde', celebrating home in exile, is an infectious bolero with an all too recurrent refrain, spiced by modulation to the third-degree major, a potential coloratura finish and the inevitable castanets. Plain and subdued interludes, sweetly sad, receive different types of accompaniment in the orchestral version. To avoid a direct plunge, a harmonically diversionary opening was added in a second piano version, and this was kept in the orchestral version. The song was encored at its introduction, in a Vienna concert in 1845, part of a Berlioz season. 'Le chausseur danois' (bass and orchestra) is negligible and trite. 'La mort d'Ophélie', rendered from Shakespeare by Legouvé—Delacroix's fine 'Ophélie' (1844) affords a parallel of 'literary' art—is a somewhat laboured projection of the Queen's tense, compassionate narrative, written for soprano or tenor and then for S.C. chorus. Four balanced and melodious strophes, linked by a twisting lamenting figure, reflect

Ophelia's fatal flower-play and gradual extinction, singing to herself. The orchestral version, which is of the duet arrangement, is almost a document in bowed and fingered string tremolo, the woodwind garlanding these vibrations and marking the fatal branch with percussion effects. Berlioz published this with the *Méditation religieuse* (see page 56) and a funeral march for *Hamlet* in a set that he misnamed *Tristia* (for he was not in exile), and he subtitled the song with a quotation from the first of Ovid's *Tristia*—qui viderit illas lituras [blots] de lacrimis factas sentiet esse meis—to set the compassionate tone. But manifestly *Ophélie* has no real connexion with the *Hamlet* epilogue. Its pathetic tone hardly stands up to the fourfold statement.

In 1856 Berlioz published in orchestral form his best-known set, the six songs of *Nuits d'été*, having published the piano setting in 1841 and the orchestral version of 'Absence' in 1843. The poems (1835–8) were taken from the *Poésies diverses* of Théophile Gautier. The chance adjacency there of Songs 2–3 and 5–6 might account for two pairs, and thus for the surprising inclusion of *two* laments, 3 and 5. The common theme is, literally, love unrequited or lost, symbolizing, arguably, an ache for vanished or unattainable beauty, but the musical order appears to be fortuitous, and forms a working, not a compulsive, association. Moreover, while the soloist in modern performances, actual and recorded, has normally been a soprano, Berlioz specified a mezzo or tenor for Songs 1, 4, and 6, contralto for 2, baritone, contralto or mezzo for 3, and tenor for 5. Baritone and tenor for the two laments seem particularly essential, once heard. It does not look as if Berlioz thought of the set as a cycle. Whatever the practical difficulty of securing three soloists, a coherent conveyance of the songs in instant succession calls for the utmost empathy, song by song. It may not be necessary or judicious to make a 'Scene' of each song to the degree sometimes employed—distance can lead a superior intimacy—but an acoustically soaring cantabile is certainly not enough.

The differences of character are brought out by the varied impact of the three musical strophes which broadly reflect the symmetry of the three verses of text of Songs 1–4, or the three pairs of verses in 5 and 6. In 'Villanelle' (1) a consistent strophe finds its spontaneous reverberations. 'Absence' (4) concentrates on the first verse, repeated twice with Verses 2 and 3 intervening in arioso counter-phrases. 'Le spectre de la rose' (2) adroitly balances a cantabile start with a fanciful arioso in three dimensions. 'Sur les lagunes' (3) tempers the prevailing quasi-rustic mood of Verses 1 and 3 with a visionary cantabile interlude in another key (in both senses). 'Sur le cimetière' (5) cultivates a solemn solitude on the same pattern in reverse styles, the initial cantabile being broken up in Verse 2 by capricious declamation. In contrast, 'L'île inconnu' (6) approaches in miniature the condition of a

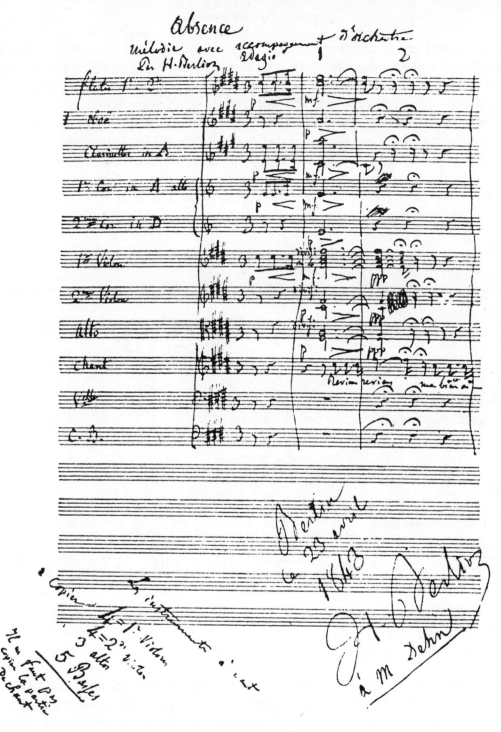

The first page of Berlioz's fullscore, *Absence*.

sonata-movement of different phrases in development and reprise under a common impulse, to embrace the pithy dialogue. The tripartite formula set by the first song thus returns in a shifting surface of recurring and divergent trends, and of cantabile and arioso, to ensure a recognizable but flexible sense of structure.

To come to details of this fascinating chamber-orchestra score. In the ardent 'Villanelle' a graceful but quickly travelling tune (**Ex. 32.2**), shapely but never dully symmetrical, and lightly propelled by throbbing upper harmony, recurs with witty canons in the bass, a mobile bassoon and refreshing string sallies. Incidentally, this song exposes the meagre stanzaic rhythm, here as elsewhere, of the opera composer, F. X. Boisselot, to whom Gautier gave the poem to set (**Ex. 32.1**). In 'Le Spectre

Ex. 32.1

Ex. 32.2

de la Rose' the precious imagery is matched by a piquant blend of cantabile and recitative, while the instrumental background veers from a decorative viola arpeggio to variously devised tremors (strings, woodwind and harp) and dubious semitonal lapses. A forced climax of tone prompts a pacifying final verse. What, with the down-to-earth appearance of the poet, threatens to be a raw ending to the dream, can in practice, at a duly measured pace, become a whispered half-tone to remember. So far a haunting passion piece. The composer lowered the original piano version from **D** to **B**, and added an integral anticipation of the basic melody; an expedient anacrusis for a vocal entry with orchestra which, while blunting the harmonic impact by prediction, neatly rehearses the viola figure in violin fragments. 'Sur les lagunes' is a graveyard lament. The dull melancholy of the theme, haunting the opening stanza, while thematically supported with a rich economy of harmonic nuance, is somewhat mannered. In a rapt middle verse in the fourth-degree major, marked by tremulous figures (woodwind), a forsaken dove becomes a focus of desolation. The third verse, increasingly tremulous and capricious at first (strings), recovers shape as 'Que mon sort est amer!' strikes its note of recurring punctuation. The song wins on empathy plus harmonic interest, at first glance. Fauré's early *Bar* setting of the poem shows two symmetrical verses and an after-verse, with a piquant refrain for 'Que mon sort' and piano-arpeggio links. A formally organized 'reading', in Norman Suckling's estimate unusually declamatory. In the equally compact version for chamber orchestra, while a harp accounts for the piano part, fresh repeated counter-phrases appear in the viola and woodwind, and in the third verse an intensified background and final *niente* drive home the sense of desolation. The formal vocal line remains.

'Absence', a favourite concert-song in England early in this century, is still the most commonly admired in the series. An unutterable sense of longing lies in the stretched melodic line of the recurring verses. The intervening verses afford rhythmic contrast and their own intensity. The song occupies the central place in a cyclic performance. How essential succinctness of style is may appear from a comparison of Bizet's setting. There a conflation of verses in pairs (vv. 1–2, 4–5, 7–8) becomes a passionate and vibrating but elongated musical stanza, whose dubious coherence wavers in repetition. After the rapture of 'Absence', Berlioz's return to gloom and glumness with the tenor 'Sur le cimetière' is rather unexpected. It is a more introvert and absorbed lament than 'Sur les lagunes', ostensibly on the misery of being forgotten (again the dove!) and the dread of returning to a certain tomb. No theme, only texture. (The semitonal fall from the sixth degree, stressed by Dr. Noske, is not a motive.) A solemn, hieratic style (strings), maintained to take two verses in tandem, is disclosed. It is broken up midway by the dry-eyed pathos of monotonous or tortuous declamation and vibrant string arpeggios. Night and dread frame a reprise of fresh colouring, resulting in a lyrical impression of considerable poignancy. Here Duparc unites Verses 1, 3 and 6 as a *Bar* of declamatory periods, linked by a piano motive but noticeably fragmentary. Again, a reading.

After songs 2–5, or even without them, the resounding surge of 'L'ile inconnue' (Gautier's original 'Mirage' is preferable) is a congenial surrender to a more conventional and absorbing rhythm, for the romantic, garrulous, quizzical voyage to the unattainable. ('Barcarolle' (subtitle) is presumably ironic.) A free expansion of the initial two-verse period releases many salient phrases. In the third strophe, 1a and 1b coalesce in reverse order, and a final evanescence of theme leaves no doubt

Ex. 33.1a

Ex. 33.1b

about the abiding disillusion as the upshot of the nostalgic quizzing and counter-quizzing and the resultant diversions of violin counterpoint (v. 2), wind syncopation (v. 4), easy vocal climax (v. 6) and a tonality open to the minor key. Whether the text-bound details fall into place at the first or the tenth hearing, this is a most satisfying little tone-poem. Unless you favour Gounod's early, jaunty and once popular setting, a hundred-per-cent Barcarolle. Massé's version advances persuasively from its recurring two-verse strophe to an arresting minor-key 'menez moi' (v. 6), but the continuation to the same tune as in Verse 2 and Verse 4 is a lapse. At every comparable point Berlioz's musical insight in this set is not challenged by that of his successors, or his resourceful treatment of the text. These miniatures fasten circumstantially on to the inner ear as much as the larger vocal-orchestral works do in their more cumulative fashion. The opportunity to hear all at one go, orchestrally, will naturally not be refused, but it is not essential, in my judgement. Each song is attached to its own poem, and in their chosen styles the first and last songs excel respectively in spontaneity and abiding song-melody, to borrow a term from Schumann.

114

Four other solo-voice arrangements for orchestra require special mention: 'Le Pêcheur', 'La chant du bonheur', 'Premiers transports' and 'Le roi des aulnes'. The first two are found in *Lélio*, the third in *Romeo and Juliet*, and the last by itself. In three cases, there is little or no doubt that each arrangement succeeded its published voice and piano version. The music of 'Le Pêcheur', with some improvement of its rhythmic-harmonic scheme, appears in *Lélio* as in its piano version, except that Verse 3 is dropped and replaced by the intrusion of the *idée fixe* of *Symphonie Fantastique* (violins), and the setting is, of course, theatrical. In that context, the piano is an orchestral instrument! 'Le chant du bonheur', as published for voice and piano, corresponds exactly to the orchestral version in *Lélio* except for its vocal cadenza, omitted in *Lélio*, and some trifling textual differences. It sounds more like a transcription than an original; no more authentic, in fact, than Scharwenka's skilful piano part for the later vocal score of the melodrama (1903). Here, then, the orchestral version seems to be the earlier one, and the piano version preserved for extra-*Lélio* occasions. *Premiers transports* for voice and piano, with violoncello part, is, as far as it goes, a valid composition, but its transcription for harp and violoncelli, with occasional wood harmony, in the pregnant context of dramatic narrative turning to symphony via lyric, comes near to a transformation.

What Paris came to know as 'Le roi des aulnes', for voice and piano, some time after its publication in 1837, was orchestrated by Berlioz in 1860 to a text by Edouard Bouscatel. It will fall for review in Chapter 10. Meanwhile, we may witness Berlioz's belief in orchestral song, reaching the pitch (in aid of providing a concert item for his tenor friend, Roger) of setting for his own medium the most dynamic voice-and-piano piece known to him.

Berlioz wrote or arranged a number of choral songs with orchestra. In some of these he indulged his inclination towards popular harmonized melody. The aspiring 'Hymne à la France' (A. Barbier) has each choral section (T.S.B.) in turn melodizing in 3/4, answered by a devotional phrase in full harmony in 4/4. The fourth and last verse ('Et toi, grand Dieu') begins at once in 4/4, in a powerful unison, energetically accompanied. The resulting coincidence for two bars with Vaughan Williams's hymn tune *Sine nomine* (1907) may serve to expose for some listeners the conventional modulations on which Berlioz's tune hinges, unconcealed by the orchestral development. It is doubtful if a less flamboyant text could rescue so stilted a song. The proud and energetic 'La menace des Francs', later published with the 'Hymne' as *Vox populi*, is at least a structural contrast: one long verse of rebellion, somewhat marred by a heavy repeat of the central portion ('Malgré ta couronne') and followed by a brief grand exit. The grateful vocal writing does much to conceal the artificial quality of the composition, but it is a spirited tune. The 'Chant de chemins de fer'

115

(tenor, chorus and orchestra) celebrates the opening at Lille of the completed Northern Railway. Orchestral pomp, stimulating key-manipulation and total variations of phrase, metre and key in the second part of the middle verses (2–5) attend a jaunty 6/8 melody of basically 43-25 bars, in the generous mood of 'Soldats de la paix, c'est votre victoire', with a devotional touch in Verse 5, in which women's voices join the men's for the first time. The piece would be worth a revival with a modern substitute for Jules Janin's long schedule of heroics. A special verse for shop stewards, perhaps. Still, a less comradely refrain and more characterization of speed and noise, such as the composer was well capable of devising, might have made an effective challenge in advance to *Pacific 231*, which remains in circulation.

Berlioz added *Le cinq Mai* to the *32 Mélodies* which he published around 1860, but the work is essentially an occasional cantata, and has been so treated in Chapter 3. The final setting of *Sara la baigneuse* for chorus and chamber orchestra belongs to its own genre, being neither a choral song nor remotely a cantata. Its reliance on a basic melodic refrain links it formally with the songs of this chapter, but as a work of much wider orbit on its slender scale it has been relegated to Chapter 3.

NOTES

1. Later, Berlioz cheerfully arranged the six-part chorus for clarinets, bugles, trumpet and—saxophone—thus ennobling the pioneer work of Adolph Saxe at a historical concert (Barzun).

8

Voices and Piano

WE now turn to the forty or so songs written, solely or originally, for voice or voices and piano. They may be divided into five groups, chronologically only in part: (1) early songs (2) *Irlande* (3) *Nuits d'été* (4) the miscellaneous songs eventually collected in *Fleurs de landes* and *Feuillets*, with a few in no group (5) choral pieces.

(1) Do songs for the private musician (singer and pianist) matter? If the question be thrown back to 1820, a relevant round date for the present inquiry, the answer depends on the range of survey. Is the connoisseur aware that, to mention nothing earlier, that year represents an interval between Schubert's astounding and prolific progress from "Meine Ruh' ist hin' (no. 30) to 'Erlkönig' (no. 178) and beyond, on one side, and a limitless continuation and expansion, through the 'Millmaid' and 'Winter journey' cycles, on the other side? Is he aware, too, that this prodigious output in a new genre, served but not established by the Reichardts and Zumsteegs, administered to the developing environment of the solo-singer and pianist in the private concerts of sympathetic patrons, soon to become a foundation feature of German middle-class homes, along with sonata and quartet? With such a magisterial glance into wider musical history, informed of events to come, the recognition of this new flow of intimate song is merely concerned with source-names and song-titles. The stream is indisputable.

For Berlioz song initially signified something very different from this masterful absorption of verse in a voice-and-piano ensemble. It meant the stilted vocalization of a representative verse in the 'romance' style typical of the preceding half century of French song (F. Noske, *La mélodie française*, ch. 1). Stilted not only in its strophical pattern but also in its rhythmic phrasing, melodic shape and harmonic movement, with the accompaniment interest confined to the occasional underlining of a textual point. Such were the first published songs, 'La dépit de la bergère', 'Toi qui l'aimas, verse des pleurs' and 'Le Maure jaloux' for solo-voice. Only the jealous anger of the Moor (v. 3) shows a flicker of expression, in the use of tonic-minor inflexions. Hence it is surprising to find the piano prelude to the first song, containing the opening and closing phrases, reappearing in the minor as a start to the welcoming

117

dance for the conqueror in *Béatrice et Bénédict*. Of the early songs for two or three voices, *Amitié, reprends ton empire*, a soprano ditty with trio 'invocation' to end each verse and a piano right hand in flowing thirds, is almost negligible, and the suave duet, *Pleure, pauvre Colette*, is equally nugatory. Of the other duets, *Le montagnard exilé* exudes bitter nostalgia with a jejune contrast of rhythm, especially the tedious 6/8 midway. *Canon libre* lives up to its title. It exhibits successive canons at the fifth in graceful succession and fetching cross-rhythm, with a free bass to ensure unrestricted harmonic movement. In the canon part the contentious **F** sharp is flattened where it clashes with **C**. The jeu d'esprit comes off as an application of method to musical uses, to voice the welcome oncoming of night and a prayer to Phoebus to stay hid. It may be added to this tabulation of non-events that Tiersot's ingenuous reconstruction from the beginning of *Symphonie Fantastique* of the tune for the very early and lost 'Je vais donc quitter pour jamais mon doux pays' from Florian's 'Estelle et Némorin', on the literal acceptance of the composer's reminiscent word in *Mémoires* (vol. 1, ch. 4), is not credible. Such a delicately sprung melodic line was simply not on at this stage.

None of these early songs was included in the comprehensive *32/33 Mélodies* which the composer brought out in 1863 (see page 116). Slight confirmation of an utterly preliminary group of trial and recognized error.

(2) The *Neuf mélodies* published in 1830 and re-entitled *Irlande* in 1850 are so included, and so far command our first attention. The composer's friend in art, Thomas Gounet, had aroused Berlioz's interest with his free translations of pieces in Thomas Moore's *Irish Melodies*, that extraordinary Anglo-Irish compilation of mock-graceful aphorisms of patriotic intent. (The composer's attraction towards the Irish girl who had made such a hit as Ophelia in the first Paris *Hamlet*, Harriet Smithson of Ennis, may have augmented his bias, as well as the Irish revolt.) 'How dear to me the hour', 'Rich and rare' and other effusions were thus conditioned to assume the vernacular of 'Mélodies françaises', as it may seem today. At the time Berlioz's method defeated the 'critics'. Writing, for instance, in the *Gazette musicale* of 1834, François Stoepel confessed his inability to explain in words so extraordinary a style. Evidently it was altogether too asymmetrical and unpredictable, although all the songs but the last are basically strophical.

Three songs have already been considered in their orchestral versions; 'Hélène', 'Chant sacré' and 'La belle voyageuse'. The last was the first to be thus re-set. This legend of the lovely bejewelled girl who travelled fearlessly through the land of masculine honour is recited to a spontaneous and extended melody. Its four verses expose the dull piano accompaniment, but its central impulse deserved more, and soon Berlioz saw his opportunity. The other two songs are not worth further consideration. Two more songs are for chorus and will be reviewed in their place. This leaves four for solo-voice and piano (Songs 1 and 7–9).

The first, 'Le coucher du soleil' ('How dear to me the hour'), is at least distinctive. The initial burst of semitonal modulation precludes a conventional reverie in **A** flat, and the restless harmonic scheme of the basic strophe stiffens the balance of phrase in an extended melodic line. The balance is poetic, if anything; no two phrases are alike. The dying falls are persuasive and grateful to the performers, but in total repetition the lush nostalgia cloys, for my ears. 'L'origine de la harpe' (in **G**) is painfully trite, fourfold. 'Adieu, Bessy' ('Sweetest love, I'll not forget thee') was revised, with some rhythmic adjustments, a fresh start for Verse 4 and a change of key from **A** flat to **G** (which surely rules out any idea of a cycle), but the song remains worthless. The 'Elégie' for the patriot and martyr, Robert Emmet, was a latecomer into the set. First written, instantly and exceptionally, to Moore's 'When he who adores thee'—according to Berlioz's later recollection (*Memoirs*, 1848)— it was apparently then adapted to Gounet's prose. The song remains an unparalleled piece of free declamation and pianistic excursion. Certainly not for Stoepel's ears. Today the music may strike the listener as advanced in method (as was 'Hagar's lament', Schubert's first 'song') but barely coherent, in spite of a recurrence of phrase ('Car le ciel ... La plus chère faveur'), and ultimately forced in musical expression. On the whole *Irlande* shows little advance in a grasp of the medium as we now understand it, or in revelation of the composer's calibre as declared in the *Faust* scenes.

(3) Berlioz's Gautier settings date from 1840; an age after *Irlande*, with the gap scarcely bridged by 'La captive' and a few other songs. Here was no pursuit of a chosen métier, in spite of the stimulating example of Schubert, whose *Six mélodies celèbres* to the egregious Bélanger's text were published by Richault in 1833, including 'La poste' and 'La jeune fille et la mort', with 'Le roi des aulnes' to follow. There were no *Berlioziens* to counter the Schubertiads of an earlier decade, in default of any testing concert performance. It was a vicious circle of non-communication. Hence the free movement of musical thought in the several songs of *Nuits* is remarkable. Helped by the composer's sale of his revised edition of *Freischütz*, this set went well for a time in the shops. Those who tried or promoted it with enough resolution not to be deterred by the various idiosyncrasies cannot have failed to discern the projection of moods of more or less passionate longing in musical vignettes without precedent in any song by Niedermeyer or Monpou. The songs were also independent of the calculated and piano-aided contrasts which were

marking the contemporary output of another novice in song-writing, Schumann of Leipzig, though his songs were not actually introduced into France until 1855 (Noske, *op. cit.* p. 24 *n.*).

Yet even a Francophil must have admitted the meagre contribution of the piano, in *Nuits*, to delineation, harmonic nuance or even its own enjoyment, except in the last song. The piano part sounds too often like a transcription or a realized bass. Thus apart from 'Absence', orchestrated 1843, Berlioz's most distinguished song-set faced audiences, if any, in a confined, black-and-white framework for its first fifteen years of communication. Somehow this reduction of expressive intention, which the revision of 'Absence' and 'La captive' (1848) must surely have brought home to him, did not irk Berlioz, or he had lost touch. 'Zaïde' (1845) and the rest showed that he continued to regard the piano as the normal medium of accompaniment, as composers tended, indeed, to think for the next hundred years, apart from opera and cantata. What he eventually did with *Nuits* has been told in the previous chapter. Obviously the piano version still available is a useful approach for performers and listeners besides being less expensive than the full score, when it is republished.

(4) Of the eleven songs, dating from 1831 to 1850, distributed at random in the late collections, *Fleurs de landes* and *Feuillets* (augmented from three to six songs in the second edition)—neither of which have ever been republished as yet—four have similarly been discussed in their orchestral versions: 'Le jeune pâtre' (*Fleurs*), 'Zaïde', 'Chant des chemins de fer', 'Chausseur danois' (*Feuillets*). Of these 'Zaïde', intensely vocal and at the same time an infectious pianistic bolero, is most worth reviving as originally conceived. The boisterous hunting song needs an orchestra without deserving the heavy forces which it received. The railway song began with an orchestra and requires its glamour. One can just imagine it sung to the club piano, given a deft pair of hands, equal to bringing off Stephen Heller's nimble transcription, including the arpeggios of Verse 4 (a ripple of woodwind).

Of the remaining songs, *Fleurs de landes* (a metaphysical wasteland?) opens oddly with two separate minor-key settings of 'Pour chanter le retour du jour', the second omitting Verse 3, the first treating it freshly. 'Le matin', with its facile turn to the major at the verse-ends, is commonplace. 'Petit oiseau' is a pleasant diversion of no consequence. The 'Chant des Bretons' is for chorus, and 'Le trebuchet' will be reserved for separate comment. *Feuillets* contains two contrasted songs. 'Les champs' (1834) began as a cheerful, ill-wearing strophe for seven verses. For *Feuillets* Verses 3–5 were dropped, and the resultant 3rd and 4th verses set to fresh music in free style, thematically capricious and eventful, up to the returning 'Viens aux champs'. Yet this half confident, half hectic appeal of the 'lion romantique' to his adored scarcely 'raises the temperature values' of assignation, to borrow a term from a weather report. 'La belle Isabeau' (1844) is a little stronger but confused. In this absolutely didactic ballad about a girl in a double storm, nature and hers, the strophe begins promisingly, but soon declines into devotional admonitions.[1] (The second verse defies reason by setting 'L'ouragan faisait rage etc.' to what had been 'Elle était de votre âge etc.') The third verse, again, begins arrestingly but then becomes hysterical and admonitory in turn. One cannot but recall a no less improving monument of a similar conflict between a present storm and a novice's pious recollections of her passionate past. There each side struggles thrillingly for attention, to the greater glory of musical invention, the art of Schubert and incidentally, as usual, the pianoforte, but nothing can be more penetrating and symbolic of inner control than the final major 'Allelluja'.

A late duet in *Fleurs*, 'Le trebuchet', trifling as it may seem, is of distinctly more consequence. It is intended for two sopranos or tenor and baritone. The text is a queer conflation of a verse by A. Bertin and two in a different vein by E. Deschamps, Berlioz having lost his copy of the Bertin poem. (For details, see the Berlioz Society's Bulletin 54, April 1966.) Pertinent changes of detail and texture bear out the simple A-B-A pattern of the three verses, which frames this tale of two who fall in and out of love.

Three songs are in no group. 'Je crois en vous' (1834) was intended for the journal, *La Protée*. With an initial melodic anticipation of the (non-Institute) Prize Song, it has a fervency of its own, rendered nugatory in sheer repetition (6 vv.; or even with 3 vv.). Its exclusion from *33 Mélodies* is perhaps due to the brevity of the basic strophe but more probably to its complete recall as the outline of Harlequin's lovely florid arietta (i.e. the oboe's) in *Cellini*, forecast obscurely by the jaunty theme in the overture. 'La captive' and 'La mort d'Ophélie' have already been introduced (pages 108, 109). 'La captive', in its third version, enlisting Verse 8 for corybantic service, is sufficiently vocal to take the guitarring, undulating and tremulous figures, on the piano, in its stride. It deserves more revival than it receives, as such. Hugo fans can find a pencilled sketch for the setting of another poem, 'Dans l' alcove sombre'; a melodic line in 3/4 for Verse 1 (**C** minor to major) and another in 6/8 for Verses 3 and 4 in **G**. (Quoted by Tiersot in *Le Ménestrel*, Nov. 1905).

'La mort d'Ophélie' is set to a fantastic paraphrase of Queen Gertrude's impeccable narrative, but in this solo-song Berlioz's pathetic stanzas give it new life. The piano can suggest both the flux of Ophelia's free and spasmodic movements, on land and as she is dragged into the depths, and the recurrent lamenting figure (**Ex. 34**). As a two-part chorus the song would lose in intensity what it may gain in resonance

121

Ex. 34

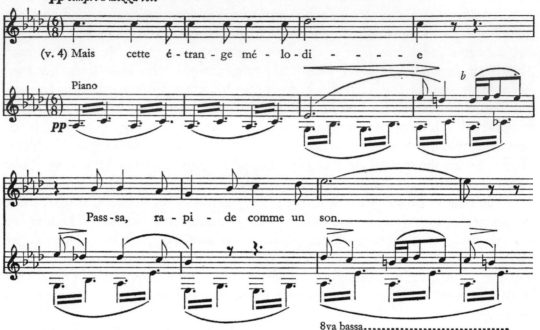

and a slightly richer vocal texture of thirds and sixths. *Sara la baigneuse*, on the other hand, cut down to a duet of S.C., T.B. 'or even S.B.' timbres and a piano reduction by A. Bouscatel (as in *33 Mélodies* and a separate republication in 1905), can only retain a token of the multiple choral texture, a minimum of imitational writing, and a grey diminution of the orchestral sparkle. Even so, it could give a lot of musical pleasure to a well-matched pair and their audience.

(5) Berlioz wrote seven songs for chorus and piano. The 'Ballet des ombres' (1829) is a curiosity which Berlioz withdrew. Its supply of scherzando phrases to the order 'Formez vos rangs', with a noticeable type of cadence, matches the initial 'witching time' impulse, but three verses more than exhaust it. A passing falling-fifths phrase survives as a familiar gap-filling motive in the coda of the 'Queen Mab' scherzo. Of the two songs for male chorus in *Irlande*, 'Chant guerrier' is a translation of 'Forget not the field', a forerunner to Rupert Brooke's 'The soldier'. The last stanza must be quoted to show that it is not just a war-song. It is, indeed, remarkably pertinent to the half emancipated, half ruthlessly restrained, world of a century and a quarter later.

Far dearer the grave or the prison
Illumed by one patriot name,
Than the trophies of all who have risen
On Liberty's ruins to fame!

The song ('N'oublions pas ce champs') was taken up by liberationists in 1830. It has a rousing refrain in **C** and mutually contrasted interludes; the first two tense (tenor solo, move to **A** flat), the third blandly aphoristic (bass, **G**). 'Chanson à boire', too, sharpens conviviality with sad memories (tenor solo). The 'Chant des Bretons' in *Fleurs* has another text from J. A. P. Brizeux, explorer of Brittany's Celtic origins (*Les Bretons*, 1845). A buoyant, dedicated 'Oui' answers the call of the local motherland, for which Berlioz bothered to re-write Verse 2 later. (The extant orchestral version, copied by Weckerlin and printed in *Werke* 16, may or may not be by Berlioz.) The song could be a non-combative demonstration piece today for any restive Department or once independent region. 'L'Apothéose' is an arrangement of the finale of the 'Symphonie funèbre et triomphale' for six-part chorus, soloist and piano, in the higher key required for a chorus which is in command, instead of being a mere reinforcement, as will appear in the next chapter. An inevitable offshoot, it was serviceable in its time; but 'palmes immortelles' etc. are scarcely acceptable today. A vainglorious text balks a grand tune. 'Le temple universel', for male chorus (1860, 1868) was written first for double choir and organ. Later, it was re-written for single choir, with the first episode ('Salut aux peuples') omitted. Moving from a stalwart **F** major to a gentler **A** flat and back, it seeks to raise the standard of freedom over a dictator-ridden world; a gesture towards a human rights charter, as we may think. The piece maintains a cool dignity, but gesturing is not enough for art any more than for politics. As 'The star of liberty' the song took root in England for a time. Today it would seem altogether too undemonstrative to cut any ice.

It is impossible to write at all exhaustively of Berlioz's songs without becoming encrusted with detail of dubious importance—in which I do not include purely informative comment, if it concerns a composition—or even an occasional sense of going slumming with the composer as he potters around in unfamiliar terrains. Certainly there is, apart from *Nuits*, little sign of a fresh grip of a text or of a growing method of organizing material to reinforce routine vocalization. The vibrating elements of natural surroundings or even of the human psyche did not somehow attract Berlioz towards an expert selection of the many rhythms and harmonic progressions at which the piano is so adept. The upshot was a more cantabile style. But the duller the wider impact of the more extended song and of the songs as a whole. In no other genre does one have to make allowances for Berlioz's period.[2]

We shall turn now to Berlioz's accomplishments with the orchestra itself, beginning with the largest schemes, the symphonies.

NOTE

1. Mr. Hopkinson has recently come upon a copy of an earlier printed version of 'La belle Isabeau', without the choral endings (*Brio.* 7.2).

2. In the course of a critical statement about Berlioz's tempi (p. 175) T. S. Wotton refers to an adjustment of his original metronomic marks in the *33 Mélodies*, 'a fact ignored by the editors of the German edition'. I can find little evidence of this. In the 'Hymne à la France' the brief opening and recurring Andante maestoso, marked 60 for the crotchet-beat in *Vox populi* (and the Collected Edition), is slowed down to 48 in *33 Mélodies*, but the prevailing Moderato remains at 76 in all editions. The *Méditation religieuse*, put at 54 in *Tristia*, comes up to 66 in the *33 Mélodies*. The other thirty-one songs show no variations of tempo-mark from edition to edition. In 'Le spectre de la rose' (in **B**) *33 Mélodies* specifies contralto for the voice intended, not mezzo or tenor.

9

Symphonies

IT is not easy to arrive at a balanced appraisal of Berlioz's art. On the larger scale of performance Mozart remains outstanding as a progressive exponent of Italian opera, symphony and symphonic piano concerto, each output independent and yet with plenty of musical material in common, and each a small history in itself. Beethoven by the same standards offers symphony, concerto up to a mid-point, one German opera, some overtures to stage music or plays, and one late-period Mass. Schubert offers select symphony and an operatic medley. Each of these is reinforced by unquestionable achievement in string quartet and piano-ensembles, and in Schubert's case by the foundation of intimate song with piano on an un-paralleled scale. On the basis of these classifications, the different shape of the work of each composer in symphony or quartet, and the component stages of Mozart opera (Italian and German) and of Schubert song, fall into their place for subjective consideration, with the controversial Mass work of Mozart and Schubert on the fringe. The output of Richard Wagner is still simpler to write up, in its various categories of music-drama.

We have now put a ring round all Berlioz's works with voices except the operas and the Dramatic Symphony (no. 3), resulting in the emergence of semi-dramatic cantata, a number-work[1] to a devotional text, and orchestral song-setting, as notable genres. It is difficult to specify what distinct method of composition is involved in each case. Nevertheless, without repeating details it can be assumed that writing to a text for concert-performance, without stage accessory, became one of the composer's most persistent and far-reaching approaches to composition; but also that the text was used as a stimulus or guide-point to creative activity, not a determinant of its shaping. Accordingly the designs of the many various numbers or parts involved show few trends, other than a convenient strophe, some balance of exposition and varied reprise, and an active *genre instrumental expressif*. While complete instrumental interludes occasionally appear, and a few postludes, as in the ends of three of the Rome prize cantatas, suggestions of a purely musical urge that tends to carry all before it occur too spasmodically to convey that symphony is a personal imperative, as surely happens, sooner or later, in all Viennese opera cited. So far, in turning to the Berlioz symphonies, we have not only to go back to 1830 but to consider a new genre. Yet this previous extensive acquaintance with his principles of associating music with a text will not be an unilluminating approach to Berlioz's symphonic work. It will bring home that a stir to the imagination through some literary image could tap his musical invention without depending on any further outside reference. While such a recourse, inevitable in absorbing a continuing overt text, would not embarrass him artistically if it seemed expedient for communication, it remained optional.

In this context of a wider than contemporary experience of Berlioz's art we may turn to his best known concert work, a symphony whose final programme is as familiar as its five-movement plan. Following on public performances of the Rome-prize cantata, *Sardanapale* (now rendered with concluding 'conflagration' without mishap), and of the *The Tempest* fantasia, which the composer later used in *Lélio*, in December of the politically disturbed year of 1830 Berlioz introduced a symphony in **C** minor and major, which he entitled *Symphonie Fantastique* and served with a programme of which the straightforward thread is as follows. In a fit of amorous despair a young musician has tried to poison himself with opium; but the drug that he takes only plunges him into a heavy sleep, haunted with weird visions. His recollections and sensations pass through his sick brain in the form of musical ideas and images. The beloved one becomes a melody, a haunting *idée fixe*. So to projections of (1) melancholy, volcanic love, tenderness, religious consolations; (2) the beloved discovered at a brilliant ball; (3) infectious rural tranquillity (duet of shepherds), eventually thunder-clouded with dark suspicions; (4) nightmare of being led to execution for murdering the girl; (5) the final dream: a diabolical orgy of witches gathered for his funeral. Into the centre of this mockery steps the beloved, utterly downgraded and haggish, as P. Magnette stresses in his enthusiastic book on the symphony. A monstrous funeral knell is incorporated in the general dance. The scenario of this 'Episode in an artistic life' presupposes a 'dramatic' performance [*sic*] to be followed (years later) by *Lélio*, a 'Return to life' explained and expanded in a spoken part, with an orchestra behind the curtain. Other programme notes on these lines were prepared. But for a performance of the symphony only, Berlioz demanded a simple statement of the five titles: (1) Reveries, Passions. (2) A ball. (3) In the country. (4) March to the scaffold. (5) Dream of a witches' sabbath.

Actually, the audience found the symphony to their liking, as *Le Corsaire* (12 December, 1832, 4 January, 1833) later testified and d'Ortigue had anticipated (*Revue de Paris*, 30 December, 1830, reproduced in *Le balcon de l'Opéra*). Programme notes and programmes were a tolerably customary part of music 'for the people', and Berlioz's account of his work was coherent, suggestive and original. The later bizarre elements, which seemed to justify the main title, were relished after a period (for Paris) of pallid trends, and the programme filled in gaps in credibility regarding the connexion between movements, for the' scarcely, advanced concert audiences. But it is more important now to decide what the composer intended with such an elaborate programme in the first instance. Various motives can be suggested besides the dubious example of Beethoven's use of the synopsis of Knecht's *Musical portrait of nature* for his Pastoral Symphony, which he later found necessary to play down in his declaration of intent, 'expression, not painting'. The psychological narrative of *Symphonie Fantastique* (*idée fixe* is a psychiatric term) is a useful analogy for the mood-sequences of the symphony, and the note for the last movement is more than relevant in suggesting what kind of close it is. Berlioz was as yet an unknown composer; and this was his first major musical production.

But Barzun is surely right in considering that for Berlioz the main problem was to convey the unity of a multiple work at a time when this quality was still a chance concern of most Paris audiences and not an obvious concern for composers. Even in the hands of Haydn and Mozart a prevailing pattern of four or three movements in a clear key order—each equipped with individually suitable material for sonata form, variation, minuet etc.—went a long way towards the amplification of an initial impulse to affirm in orchestral terms. Beethoven was the first composer to impose his personality sufficiently on a movement to make each resultant symphony a succession of utterly non-transferable pieces. When Habeneck produced the fifth symphony, to Berlioz's astonishment, with the *Allegretto* (not even the scherzo) of the seventh as 'the' third movement—presumably because it had proved a hit— he not only ignored a truly fabulous double-movement finale, and the polarizing significance of **C** minor and major, but also the 'fantastic thinking' of movements, which Hoffman had already noted in his perceptive review of 1810.

Berlioz accordingly set himself to organize movements round an emotional centre. Ostensibly, as implied in a letter (April 1830) to his lifelong friend Ferrand, Berlioz planned the sequence of movements and then drafted a life-story to fit them together. In all probability, some of the movements were already in being. The 'Witches' Sabbath', in the *Faust* ballet partly set in 1828 for the Opera to a three-act scenario by a manager–dramatist, Victor Bohain; probably also the Waltz; and the March, commonly though implausibly attributed to a 'marche des gardes' at an undefined point in the musically fragmentary opera, *Les Francs Juges*, a tale of the overthrow of a terrorist regime. Moreover, Berlioz contemplated a 'Faust' symphony in 1828–9. So far, *Symphonie Fantastique* as published is not programme music in the ordinary sense. It is music and a music-programme. Nor, broadly, is it auto-

127

biographical; that is, a serial portrait of the composer's vacillating relations with the Irish actress, Harriet Smithson, who in 1827 had made a dazzling brief appearance on the Paris stage as Juliet and Ophelia, but enough to captivate his affections to a degree that his serious friend Ferdinand Hiller, for example, believed to be partly based on fictitious qualities. Hector did not ever contemplate killing Harriet, as he did at least plan to liquidate her successor, Camille Moke, in the following year. At the same time, this is not the whole life-and-art story of the preceding twelve months and after.

In 1828, advised of the English company's return to London, and most quixotically determined to bring himself to Harriet's attention by a public appearance, Berlioz arranged a concert of his works, to be given at the Conservatoire, incidentally invoking the assent of the Superintendent of Fine Arts to defeat the opposition of the reactionary director, Cherubini, intolerant of this Beethovenite upstart who defied all the rules. He wrote letters to the press to make sure of their attendance. He gave the *Waverley* and *Francs Juges* overtures, *Scène Heroïque* and *Resurrexit*, and by and large triumphed. *Post hoc* and rather hypothetically *propter hoc*, Harriet made enough response to these remarkable 'overtures' to make him associate his thoughts of her, during her absence in London throughout 1829, with the connecting thread of his proposed symphony, which would glorify his passion for all Paris to learn about. But by April, 1830, he was crediting a kind friend's insinuations about Harriet's relations with her manager as 'awful truths'. On her return to Paris she was relegated to walking-on parts in spite of long experience on the English boards, which may have softened his anger. But he turned against her, and it is difficult to dissociate her later role in his do-it-yourself drama from the witch part in the Sabbath Round, though he told Ferrand he did not feel vindictive.

It was not long before he fell for an even more bewitching piano-teacher, 'Camille' Moke, whose designing mother appears to have agreed to an engagement after the success of the Fantastic Symphony on top of the Rome prize. (Or she was confident that absence would *not* make one heart grow fonder.) Subsequently Berlioz heard in Florence that Camille had accepted the proposal of Camille Pleyel, head of the famous piano firm (1788–1855). His elaborate plans to go, disguised, and shoot her and her mother having miscarried, principally owing to visa difficulties, he proceeded to Part 3, and threw himself into the sea at Genoa. Rescued instantly without any awkward questioning, in 1832 he wrote *The return to life* (*Lélio*) to be performed as the second part of the Episode [*Symphonie Fantastique*]. In this remarkable supplement, after the 'Chant du bonheur' Lélio exclaims, 'Could I but find her, this Juliet, this Ophelia, whom my heart is ever seeking'. Berlioz imagined (he declares in his *Memoirs*) that everyone would recognize the reference to Harriet who was back in Paris. (And the witch of the earlier musical event? Let them sort that one out.)

A short while before the performance at the Conservatoire, Berlioz managed to contact an intermediary, through whom Harriet was persuaded to attend. She received a box 'in front of the stage', the cynosure of curious eyes. Habeneck was conducting but Hector appeared and, as she recalled later, was identified by Harriet as the Berlioz whom she had known. In the interval between *Symphonie Fantastique* and *Lélio*, the intermediary went into her box and twanged the lyre about the heart-broken composer. Complete that scenario as you will! A year later he married her. God had joined an ambitious creative musician to a failing actress of a different category, whose personal inadequacy soon became a burden to both. The rest was more sadness than joy, and, for music, silence. One duly notes that the disturbing attraction–repulsion—in common terms, love–hate—which initially stirred the composer's pen in one way and another, soon changed to something like indif-ference–compassion, once it was formally resolved. The next woman to be involved in symphony was not this Juliet, but Juliet Capulet of Verona herself.

So much needs to be said to convey that while *Symphonie Fantastique* was ulti-mately the completion of a musical experience, its processing contained elements that must be referred to external emotional stirs to explain their intrusion in an otherwise classical pattern. That the composer, nearly two decades after the event, professed to have gone out of his way to link the work and its nominal complement with the audience of a particular woman might be attributed to a habit of dashing the purple ink around when he felt inclined, but the mere suggestion strengthens the association of the *Episode* and its recurrent theme with the composer's wavering obsession. *Symphonie Fantastique*, as performed, is the first renunciation (after the *Waverley* overture) of a supporting 'text', and so far pivotal, but the renunciation is qualified. It would not be inappropriate to enter the concert hall with the motto: *Music, wake her. Strike!* echoing in the mind.

A symphony is not a set of moulds. It is a method of composition, of which the main principle is that a motive or a movement raises an issue larger than itself. On these lines the orchestral pioneers at the Vienna and Mannheim courts began to show that suite and concerto were not the only way of extending a movement in and beyond itself. The contrasts of orchestral *tutti*, strings, wind-solo with strings and more subtle combinations, were handy material for the formulation of com-plementary themes or groups. The more characteristic an opening theme, the greater the demand for something different and then, sooner or later, for a return of the first. The more self-contained a theme, the more exclusive its impact, so that a sequel would have to be a break-through. So with movements. In his use of

129

symphony Mozart tended to set up coherent thematic groups, whose statement and restatement were separated or joined by bridge-passages, propelled by such thematic material as might lend itself to extemporary treatment. Alternatively, there could be divisive episodes. The abiding impression is a sense of fitness, movement by movement. In Beethoven there is from the first a greater concentration of melodic or rhythmic force, in development or episode no less than in plenary statement. To say that each movement is 'firmly *knit*' is often a bland understatement. Succinct as they are, the Beethoven symphonies are arrestingly exhaustive and expansive. Yet they too are riveted by a wider mastery of structure and texture, which calls for no material link between movements. The recollections of the previous movements in the Ninth Symphony finale are exceptional strokes of rhetorical preliminary, and they are there to be forgotten in the new transcendental theme.

Berlioz, starting a symphony with one or more *soi-disant* middle and later movements in hand, may have been roused to devise linking factors by an acute sense of accidental association in what lay on his table. Or he may have decided independently that a recurrent motive was a good policy for him. Or he wrote the first movement, and then decided to push his luck further with the main theme of the Allegro. Or, of course, he may have had the artist-hero in mind. The point is argued to hinder a too cut-and-dried rationalization of Berlioz's adoption of what is usually called the cyclic type of symphony; that is, one which is marked by the recurrence of some theme or feature in all or most movements, disturbing by its incursion the normal balance of interest in each movement concerned. The method was re-applied (unconsciously) by Schumann to a more casual overlapping thematic system in his **D** minor symphony, and the examples of Liszt, Franck and Tchaikovsky have since made the surprises and defiances of the emergent or disguised linking theme familiar concert experience, but Berlioz first tried it out creatively.

A fifth motive for going cyclic may now be suggested. Casting round, as he was wont to do, for material that might be considered serviceable but so far confined to a private occasion, Berlioz recalled the opening of *Herminie* and the dramatic use to which he had put the theme in a relenting episode of the second aria ('J'exhale en vain ma plainte fugitive'). However that may be, this melodic line was what he wanted, cut down to four bars (omitting bar 5) to make a square eight with a responsive phrase (now written as eight, sixteen, bars). It is a shapely but plain theme, and the symphonic Allegro that opens as transparently is hard to find; the comparable opening of Schubert's Eighth is at least in the bass. Hence Berlioz addresses his pervasive-to-be motive to the ear as an escape from a Largo in the minor. The composer has diverted many readers by declaring that the succinct strophe (of 12 bars and extensions) around which he rather surprisingly constructs this Largo

Ex. 13

was derived from a youthful setting of verses in J.-P.-C. de Florian's sugar-sweet pastoral, *Estelle et Némorin*, beginning 'Je vais donc quitter pour jamais mon doux pays, ma douce amie'; for which Tiersot obliged with fitting these lines and the remainder of the first verse plausibly to the *Symphonie Fantastique* melody. (Quoted by Noske, *op. cit.* p. 88). Barzun comments on the 'new *melos*' of which Berlioz was thus capable at twelve. I can only repeat my previous observations that Berlioz's 'just as it was' need not be taken literally, and that the present melody has no precedent in kind in the early songs. Its compulsive quality is only paralleled so far by Margaret's song in *Eight Scenes*. Here it is completely in place as an opening. Its subsequent repeat by the violins is maintained by astringent harmony and an advanced coloratura in the woodwind that assures the listener at once of no routine execution.

So to the *Allegro agitato e appassionato* and to **Ex. 13** in **C** with complementary phrases. It soon becomes clear that the bridge-passages are informal. However, the signals for the second-subject group become clear, namely key-establishment (**G**)

Ex. 35

and here is the start. An alert listener would perhaps identify the hint of **Ex. 13**, as an overlapping feature in matter usually kept studiously apart, but the violin re-partee is what most catches the ear and persists later in this context. Actually the new subject peters out almost immediately in favour of re-exposition (a procedure now returning to favour in recordings) and in any case of development. It barely retains its status symbol. The phrase marked *y* (**Ex. 35**) soon returns, however, still in **G** as a corrective repartee to harmonically erratic first-subject exercises in the bass. A nervous, impromptu semitonal ascent, rising in set sequence, heralds fresh development, one thinks, but the whole fabric collapses on to a single cadential note, **D**, on the horn, signalizing an ample reprise in the provocative or at least puzzling key of **G** again, with the second subject twisted into **E** minor, to be different. But is this perhaps all a diversion? No. This due arrival of the second subject after some skirmishing confirms the formal reprise. Hence a long coda, expanding independently and somewhat nonchalantly various components of the first subject, with new ideas such as the oboe's entry, now converges in a masterful, compressed cornet *et al.* return of the first subject, at double speed but in **C** at last, before melting into afterthoughts and a lingering cadence marked *Religiosamente*.

This movement never hesitates about its direction, but it leaves an impression of orchestral effects strung together on a conventional overall pattern, rather than of an association of ideas finding its implications within that pattern. Any one whose *idée fixe* about first movements happens to be Beethoven's symphony No. 1 in **C** will realize that Berlioz's ideas about a coda are informal, and lack the Beethoven combination of a *tightening* control of thematic impact with a final *concentration* of orchestral antiphony, distilling unanimity. Also while the temporary drift into **G** en route for a full restatement in **C** is positively refreshing and quite unequivocal in the overture, *Leonora* No. 3, where the spacious second subject has been in **E** and the trumpet calls in **B** flat and beyond, in *Symphonie Fantastique* the tumble into **G** for restatement so soon after this has been registered as the second subject key is almost a repudiation of all the logic of tonal distribution so ardently pursued by Beethoven on the Mozart trail. If this analysis leaves any listener thankful he has not such a precise sense of key, he will lose his confidence as he improves his acquaintance and can, in fact, identify **C** with **C**, and **G** with **G**, as primary pitch-centres, in different places. The upshot must be a harmony of textures rather than a balanced thematic display.

After this there came originally the slow movement, the pastoral scene, with the waltz following as the scherzo movement, and then the march as an extra. In revision the waltz came first here, as an early dance-movement, leaving the slow movement as central and then diverted by the march. As it is now, ballet breaks in early, where in Tchaikovsky's No. 5 the Waltz enters acceptably in the normal place reserved for minuet, scherzo or whatever, after a strenuous slow movement. Here, however, a waltz and a march in succession would have been too much music for movement.

There seems no reason why this waltz-tune (bars 39–56 *et seq.*) should not start at once, and one may attribute the preliminary Lisztian diversion, establishing two harps as concerted soloists, more to a ballet programme than to any inclination to link **C** major with **A** major via an **A** minor start. Once begun, the voluble and symmetrical expansion of the tune by the violins, with the initial plain string *oompah* replaced by a piquant harp-wind dissipation in the repeat at the end, is a delight to hear and expect again. (See **Ex. 69**, page 255). The self-contained tune and line accepted, what interlude will not seem contrived? Here the *idée fixe*, with its 8-bar unit conveniently tailored to suit the triple metre, comes in neatly, with its original accessories, led by the wood; a familiar outline but no more, and (as Herminia had demonstrated in her second aria) decidedly vocal, where the main tune has been made for violin **A** and **E** string texture; so, here for flute with oboe/clarinet support. It remains to add fresh life to a full return of the Waltz in its compulsive pattern, mainly by giving the wood new rhythmic features, some phrase entries and a bit of canon. This makes inducement enough for a coda half as long again, in the course of which the clarinet again proves its capacity for vocal impersonation. In a later version Berlioz added a heartening part for cornets. But the waltz can be made to sound chilling, as one recording shows. Intoxication has a sinister side.

From the dance-hall to the fields. Not to 'nature immense' but at least nature unruffled, typified by herdmen piping *ex tempore* in simple communication, namely leader and follower (at the octave), but still, it may be suggested, in a rough correspondence, not too precisely phrased. The second theme may be quoted, less for itself than for its somewhat ambiguous treatment. At first it is the start of the top

Ex. 36

line of a continuing paragraph in Beethoven style. Then it briefly forms the flowing bass of a decorative texture, in **C**, implying a second subject. But it returns later in **C**, as a top line in a more elaborate combination. Thus it serves in turn as primary theme and transition in a fixed key in an arch pattern (*a1 a2 b c b a1*), where *b* takes its theme from *a2*. Midway the *idée*, exploiting its changed metre and attended with fresh repartee, informs a convenient digression, as the terminus of the transition and the point of return; and further brief and scattered suggestions can be heard after the next recurrence of **Ex. 36**. So back to the pipers for a kind of dissolution of the movement in canonical recitative? But what is good for a mannered prelude will be a pathetic ending. Hence the 'leader' receives no predictable response but the nearest thing to *musique concrète* viable: the roll of four kettledrums in discordant harmony, leaving to the piper and strings to frame the cadence, somewhat as in the end of Margaret's last air in *Faust* (1846).

Musically, then, the problem of an arch pattern which starts, not with a principal theme or mood, but with a colourful dialogue in near-plainsong style, is met by the release of a normal theme which flows over into a further transitional stage and reappears penultimately; and the dialogue takes a piquant, almost horrific, turn, the texture being the essential, not the canon. In short, the shape of this mainly delicate movement is determined by musical considerations, and has no need of any picture to explain its unusual feature. It remains a wayward piece in my ears, and the recurrence of the *idée* is diversionary, not a linking feature.

Three movements now disposed, with the traditional dance-movement placed second without true precedent (for the scherzo movement of the Ninth Symphony is a tremendous part-continuation of the first movement, manifestly designed to be an exercise of agility before the absorption of the Adagio), the normal expectation would be a finale amply furnished with energetic material. But on the usually accepted hypothesis a death-march, already to hand, claimed consideration. Whether or not it had been written as a 'marche des gardes' for the terrorist instruments of the nefarious Vehmic court in whose shadow the liberators of *Les Francs Juges* work—a source question to be considered in Chapter 11—the piece is clearly a thing of stiff ceremony, with its constant succession of repeated or symmetrical 8-bar phrases in each of the main sections; the stark descent, step by step, of two octaves as a kind of ground-bass, and the fine martial tune for full wind, good enough for any presentation of colours, if it were a trifle more extended. Certainly a march, and possibly planned for operatic marching, though in the reprise the rhythm is elaborately scored. Certainly, also, a minatory, not a triumphant march, and one of brilliant individuality. Noticeable features include: the low thud of drums and double-basses at the outset; the subsequent bassoon counter-role; the pungent broken scoring, later, of the descending theme, paralleled in the close of the 'Dies irae' movement of Britten's *Sinfonia da Requiem*; the sweeping figurations of the strings in the repeat of the martial tune; and the reserve of energy in the reprise and coda. This may be said about the general quality of the expression of this familiar movement before observing that near the end the *idée* is dragged in unmercifully and almost without point before the orchestral force is gathered for a final blast and tremor; as if so trifling an entry could make the movement more integral.

Otherwise, the march, thrilling as it is, plays a quite enigmatic symphonic role, both as the extra middle movement, which it purports to be, and as a sequel to the Adagio. Hence, it seems, Berlioz tries to bridge any gap in credibility by positing a nightmare for the 'artist' whose experience the symphony unfolds. The intrusive *idée* symbolizes, in this fanciful context, the melancholy spectacle of the dreamer as he appears (to himself) the moment before annihilation. As such, a crude stroke of communication. What is more relevant, the Terror still haunted men's minds at the

134

time, as Barzun argues. In particular, the death in 1794 of the poet André Chenier, poignantly recalled by Chateaubriand, Hugo and others, had taken hold of Berlioz's attention, as the doom of youth in remembered history. The present generation needs no Wilfred Owen to prompt the resurgence of a like sense of grief and guilt over wasted lives. So far this movement might be taken as a stroke of romantic realism; as a passing projection in art of a standing burden of the time, even if it originated in a sinister march of ruthless authority. The music is thus enriched by this conception without actually needing it to motivate its course. It is *reduced* by any conscious thought of Paris in the seventeen-nineties or of contemporary parallels, however unforgettable.

Forward, then, from this baleful piece to a finale that resumes without duplication the emergent ardour of the first movement? Perhaps, but not without reference to the *idée* on which that passionate Allegro depended for its main turns, and subsequent movements have relied for interludes of integration. The frailty of this theme has been acknowledged, in the starting Allegro, in its sparse occurrence in its original melodic shape and its efficient compression to half size for the coda. It cannot be used so plainly again. Hence the conception of a scherzo-like version, such as Vaughan Williams carried out on the scale of a whole movement (as the first part of a composite finale) with the tightly sprung coil of an initial 'theme', in his fourth symphony. Here two more or less perfunctory entries were thought to be as much as the new 'dance' version was good for; so they arise in a crude folksy setting, from a touch of the mysterious or loudly impetuous, the second (high clarinet) being swept into a pungent semitonal *tutti*. Rather similarly the main theme in **C** major emerges from a preliminary bout in the minor, in which, against the ominous pealing of two bells (not for Evening Prayer, as they sometimes sound), a traditional church Tone takes over from an attempt at thematic statement. Each phrase of the Tone is announced ponderously (ophicleides) and then lightly reverberates at doubled speed in set harmony (brass, woodwind-pizzicato). For the informed, the succession of phrases corresponds unmistakably with the text of two verses of the sequence in the Mass for the dead, as set in plainsong, for lines 1–2, 7, 8–9:

(1) Dies irae, dies illa.
(2) Solvet saeclum in favilla.
(7) Tuba mirum spargens sonum.
(8) Per sepulcra regionum.
(9) Coget omnes ante thronum.

To any one able to identify the text from its Tone, and to almost any one else, it would be apparent that the brass-wood echoes are in the nature of a cynical demonstration. The basic tune, with its genuine antique, modal flavour and primary integrity is receiving 'the treatment', like the *idée* before it, and one may be sure that the last has not been heard of this intrusive plainsong. From this characteristic, almost joyous confusion the main movement arises confidently, at first unfolding in the answering manner of rising entries (B.T.A.S. in orchestral terms) on the surface of a fugue on a stiffly patterned subject (bars 4-3), even with an oncoming counter-exposition to shape a climax. Further excursions, which include both stretching the basic steps of bars 1–2 into a piquant, wayward harmonic unit and a more consistent reduction of interval to bare semitonal limits, are terminated by a reprise which invites counterpoint of a sort. It comes amply enough in the 'answer',

Ex. 37

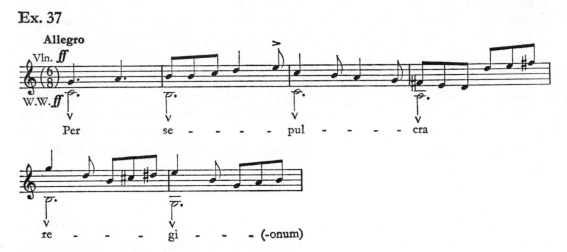

in a heavy gait, spreading its ungainly length in a way to command early absorption in a flowing accompaniment, rather than to form an organic figure. Against a rattle of violin sticks, the main theme returns in the woodwind with a flamboyant half-speed entry in the minor, but development having served its turn, orchestral energy and harmonic invention ensure a triumphant close and the repudiation of the cyclic process in a whole symphony.

The usual purpose of a contrapuntal combination is to induce either a fresh harmonic slant or a new sense of metre. On the first count, the placing of the Tone in **A** minor with the subject in **G** might seem positively exciting, but in fact the only result is that the Tone grudgingly fits into a **G** major progression. On the second count, the virtually 2-bar sense of the Tone's 8-bar phrase broadens the sweep of the subject from 16 beats to 4. But that is all: the fugal 'round-dance' has been extended and taken a new turn with its slower tread, but this is not the climax. That is achieved by a pressurized orchestral rejoinder more easily experienced than described, with a sense of ample harmonic margin enhanced by the tight fit of the earlier combination. It is necessary to make this comment to prevent any easy acceptance of the combination as a conclusive entry.

It will be clear to most readers that the object of the foregoing survey is to justify the symphony, especially the finale, as a musical composition. Apart from the interposition of the March, the course is clear for four movements. The composite finale is more problematical. It obviously owes something to the Ninth Symphony finale-opening for its method of approach, but the component preludial sections make no pretence to Beethoven's inner grip.

The initial Larghetto is frankly sensational and inconsequential. The development of the *idée* into one false start, and a second attempt that soon peters out in a solemn unspoken cadence for basses in unison, do nothing to promote a sense of direction. Yet the subsequent polarization of a quasi-popular movement in the minor and an exultant dance-tune in the major bears, in a fresh accentuation of the first part, an obvious relation to the opening movement through its tonality and its buoyant **C** major mood. There is no urgent call to refer to any external mood-patterns, as the composer's titles and published programme tempt the listener, and much more the half-listener, to do. The hypothesis that the composer conceived the symphony as a dream of sensational experience, including a fantasy of threatening destruction and horrific witchery, need not concern the listener.

Barzun, indeed has argued that the confluence in Berlioz's mind of de Quincey's report on the fruits of opium eating, of Hugo's description of a *Ronde du Sabbat* (*Odes et Ballades*, Ballade 14), and, above all, of the Brocken scene and cathedral scene in *Faust*, where the guilt-haunted Margaret hears 'Dies irae' chanted, pressed on the composer as he worked. Moreover, the scenario of Bohain's projected *Faust* ballet may have been suggestive of a Witch Dance, and this could account for the fantastic final opening. But this is not to accept the idea of oncoming death (the march), succeeded by a horrible confrontation with the powers of darkness, as a tangible explanation of the last two movements. The treatment of 'Dies irae' is decidedly on the insouciant side and and the dance is steadily creative, not destructive, and not in the least deterred by the return of 'Dies irae'. Accordingly, it is best to forget not only the twisted Harriet-relationship, already outlined, but also the demonic influences and overflowing unconscious, and to sit back with alert ears; prepared for the unclassical juxtapositions which a romanticist may see fit to insert into a pursuit of symphonic tradition, however intensely and exclusively admired in its greatest exponent, but assured that the sonorities are for the total musical effect until proved otherwise.

In the same spirit one may attend to *Lélio*, negligibly attached to the symphony, as explained earlier, and musically significant as an independent choral-orchestral suite to its own volatile text, spoken and sung. The 'return to life' being an entertaining *point d'appui*, but quite irrelevant to the fisher-fable or the reconstruction of Hamlet's father's message to his son. The symphony needs, of course, no after-song. If it implies a wider interest than it states, its symphonic character is enhanced.

The *Symphonie Fantastique* is thus, as many recordings and concert performances confirm, a work variously interpreted as an extravaganza, as a suite with sinister, menacing intentions (in the coda of the first movement as well as in a horrifically deliberate March), and as a classical structure, disposed with a difference of attitude to shape. That difference can only be pinpointed as an inventive spirit. The success of Beecham's art in the conversion of a then sceptical public lay in his penetration to the nervous centre, not least through his perception of texture. With all its blemishes and non-sequiturs, the work remains a thing of extraordinary originality. One cannot otherwise explain its undiminished and excelling popularity at the present time, in the concertroom and in the disc world. Even in Liszt's piano transcription (recently experienced in a fabulous London performance in 1969)—balder, starker and more capricious and hazardous than the full orchestral gamut has it— the work apparently went home, in default of an orchestral rendering, to audiences still scratching their heads over middle Beethoven, and to the more sophisticated Beethovenite of today the challenge to convention still appeals.

For a rising composer who had only just gained the Institute's Rome prize with the usual three-number cantata (with explosive material buried in the cadence), the *Symphonie Fantastique* was a prodigious achievement, and must have encouraged Berlioz to go on. After the 1832 revival of the work, revised and followed by *Lélio*, the critic D'Ortigue, in *La Quotidienne* (4 January, 1833) emphasized the pioneer qualities of the symphonic writing in a French (i.e. Paris) concert-hall, particularly the power of dramatic expression. He warned those in power, 'Do not let this burning gift cool down.' Meanwhile, however, Berlioz was bound to proceed to Rome, where he found the operatic atmosphere repellent and anti-musical, but the country folk of the Abruzzi, near Subiaco, were friendly and responsive to his guitarring and a walking repertoire of folk-tunes of a sort. They included bandits, who were then romantic figures, good enough for a place in *Lélio*. Eventually he wrote the *King Lear*, *The Tower of Nice* (renamed *Le Corsaire*) and *Rob Roy* overtures, besides *Lélio*. He sent some of these to the Institute. They would be sufficient to convince the authorities of his creative talent, industry and, what they most insisted on, his improvement on earlier work? They proved so, grudgingly enough as regards the award for a Ministry grant. To make further progress in the Paris world, Berlioz needed, as Barzun points out, promotion in the press, and for some time he was fortunate to receive the support of Jules Janin in the *Journal des Débats*, as a representative of the French school with a high potential, if his 'legend' could be developed. An understanding of this effort to secure public interest is needed for a realistic grasp of Berlioz's inner creative struggle.

Meanwhile he was due to proceed to Germany for further Rome-prize rehabilitation. He found it necessary to abandon this journey. In 1833 the 'improbable romance' with timid (and at the same time carelessly ill-reputed) Harriet Smithson was sufficiently developed and undeveloped to make departure out of the question. After many incredible vicissitudes of broken communication and pleas for delay (Harriet's), the two were married at the British Embassy on 3 October. A new financial struggle began, for Harriet's debts were considerable and her assets as a stage personality in decline. At this point Berlioz was fortunate to become a protagonist in the new periodical *La Gazette Musicale*, founded by his publisher, Maurice Schlesinger, with a brother in Berlin to pursue equal aims of cementing French and German musical thought *vis-à-vis* the unthinking Italians. Actually, the German market for publication was a security against the risks of publishing anything advanced in Paris.

About the same time came the announcement of a request from Paganini for a concerto for viola and orchestra to display his new Stradivarius acquisition. If this was true—and it seems much more credible that Berlioz contrived to associate Paganini's name committally with a viola work of some description—it was a curious commission. Paganini was no practising Tertis, to fill Berlioz's imagination with fresh ideas of solo or concerted-solo texture. Nor is it conceivable that Paganini's notions of structure were cast in terms of the advanced symphonic design by means of which Beethoven had lifted the genre to a new plane of coherent expression while affording the soloist a range of outstanding entries; for to this day most violinists are as proud to make this range their own as any later example, with the arguable exception of Brahms's concerto. In the event, Berlioz wrote no viola concerto as we now understand the term, and not surprisingly Paganini declined to appear in a work in which the soloist was so sparsely involved and scarcely stretched at all.

Berlioz did not, in short, make any attempt either to go on where Beethoven had left off, or to re-orientate his classical scheme by introducing the soloist as the focal point from the start, as Mendelssohn was to effect in the next decade. He was content to allot the violist a kind of stage role, part announcer, part elaborator. One cannot call it lyric merely because the soloist repeats a short refrain. The latter is conspicuously absent in the finale, after the preliminary reminiscences. It seems that once more, with various musical ideas surging in his mind—not least the matter of the *Rob Roy* overture, some of which plainly reappears here—Berlioz sought to secure a working connexion by means of some chorus part (text never disclosed), but abandoned this in favour of a solo-viola at turning points, complete with *idée fixe*, both musically and psychologically. Thus a 'symphony with viola' grew from two movements to a normal four. To define the fixed mood proposed by the recurring *idée*, the composer recalled his past provenance and, going one better, hit on the title 'Harold in Italy', indubitably in reference to a Byronic Childe Harold. We shall return to this sobriquet later.

Berlioz's second symphony, then, presents four normal movements, with some linking features: the viola's naïve tune in the preludial adagio, reflected in the coda of the main Allegro, forms an inner counterpoint in a developing phrase in the March, and, more insistently, in the second section (Allegretto) of the buoyant Serenade that serves as Scherzo; and the final *Orgy* only settles into its Allegro frenetico after brief token recollections of the Adagio, March and Allegretto, Allegro and viola tune, between a series of false starts, which (the opposite of what happens in the Ninth Symphony) prove to be desultory moves in the right direction, lacking only in commitment and in resistance to the succeeding diversions. Apart from these transparent overflows of theme, to which the first symphony has attuned the ready listener, the course of each movement is confident and clear. The first is much the most closely put together. On the whole—that is, in an intelligently controlled performance—its palindrome form is effective. From an obscure opening the viola motto-theme suddenly emerges as a figure of clarity in a delicately conceived texture, as a preliminary to a developed Allegro of capricious shape. The primary theme passes from the orchestra to the soloist in an apparently classic style, but followed closely by a second orchestral theme in now quick repartee. A repeat from the solo-entry confirms the association of ideas but repudiates an established concerto principle; and an exploitation of concerto-rejoinder terminates in the formal return in **G** of **Ex. 38.2**, as a route to **Ex. 38.1** and further, witty celebration

Ex. 38.1

Allegro

Solo Viola

Ex. 38.2

p Vla., Vlc. & Bsn. (repeated by Solo Viola, in D)

of the motto-theme and the motive of **Ex. 38.1**.[2] Hence the palindrome effect (sometimes called 'arch'). The resourceful variants of **Ex. 38.1** accentuate the steady textural interest of this retracing process. This pronounced pattern does not bear out the programme suggestion of *Scenes* of melancholy, happiness and joy; its steady revelation of widening interest in development and reprise is valid in itself.

Berlioz once attributed the second movement to a boyhood experience of isolation, followed by the sight of a procession passing. But no explanation is needed for the solemn **E** major March with its suave succession of symmetrical elongated phrases, bell-reiterations (*Benvenuto Cellini*), and, except for the violist's arpeggios (which Tertis was to make so revealing to audiences of a century later), the bland simplicity of the interlude in **C** for intoning a quasi-traditional church melody, from a Rouen psalter perhaps. Is it more compelling for purporting to be a march of the pious and committed, protestants pressing forward to some focus of devotion or significant peaceful demonstration? In fact, it gained at once the popularity for which Berlioz hoped, and duly passed into Liszt's carefully promotional repertory, but it cannot be considered a strong movement, with its proliferation of straggling phrases and scarcely spontaneous tune midway. The coda (last 52 bars) is the most striking feature: its dry, automatic, straying bass deftly makes harmonic sense of the opposing pivots of **B** and **C** until, as the bass reaches vanishing point, **B** remains—as the top of **E** major. (The basses, at first in unison with the violoncello, were in revision dropped to their bottom octave, from 22 bars before the end.)

The 'Serenade' is tuneful in a more rhythmic sense and the combinations of the oboe theme in the Allegretto (the second tempo) with the motto, duly spread over the counterpoint in three-bar units, keep the stimulus taut; the effect being, as usual, that the oboe theme takes on an attendant role, and that its entries (on other instruments) are flexible. In the first Allegretto, the tune in the viola, supported by strings, is propelled by a simple harp progression and violoncello oscillations. (This replaced bassoon support, with the strings (1) in a low tremolando (2) in a blunt pizzicato at the start of the bar; only the violoncello tremor was retained.) In the second Allegretto, the solo-viola with the oboe theme chases the motto on the flute and harp, while the violas, by way of harmony, maintain the reiterations of the first tempo, which inevitably continue until exhausted. It is all rather loosely combined. But the opening folksy piping (34 bars) is hardly more than a prelude to the Allegretto, which is no interlude, but the main movement, as is soon apparent. The whole movement is thus a slight break before the finale, and it stretches the motto to a sticking-point which it can scarcely hold.

The finale yields its guiding and tumultuous theme after a contrived struggle with rival recollections, already sketched. This point gained, a fresh turn of key

(**B** flat) completes a conventional sonata-exposition whose extraordinarily literal recurrence in the reprise, **B** flat and all, remains a baffling non-event. A move into **G**, the tonic major of the basic **G** minor, for the return of the second subject releases further orchestral energy. This light finale is vigorous and arguably aggressive, but impossible to take as seriously minatory, in spite of the vivid dismissal (conceivably) of the forces of light. The Allegro frenetico is surely not insistent enough, especially in the absence of any development or re-pointed restatement of theme (up to **G** major ending, an unmistakable relaxing of tension), to reach a crisis point.

Nor does Berlioz justify the implied invocation of Byron's *Childe Harold's Pilgrimage* for the definition of the 'culture hero' of his Italian symphony. *Childe Harold* is a document in the melancholy, despair and cynicism that haunt the search for a perfection unattainable in the real world; in the unsatiable longing that drives the Pilgrim on, sustained by distant visions which fade on closer approach; in the Weltschmerz of a disillusioned era. (Conrad in *The Corsair*, 'warped by the world in Disappointment's school', bears an obvious affinity with Harold, as we shall observe later.) Berlioz's symphony betrays no sign of a projection of this then universal Harold in its radiant opening, lyrical-ceremonial march and blithe serenade, or even in its impatient finale. The Byronic Harold was just one more person or role which Berlioz saw as his own without considering any detail involved. (Some years before, a music teacher had saluted him as the Byron of music and the *Francs Juges* overture as its 'Childe Harold', not inappropriately. The sobriquet was cherished!) It is a convenient title for those who hanker after literary labels, but for musicians 'symphony No. 2 in **G**' will prompt them much more readily to receive a successor to the Fantastic. It is still equipped (in announcement and score) with fanciful titles to movements, but offering, in the event, four movements in a loose but reasonably compulsive succession. A rather rigid motto-theme connects them with a recurrent image of a dreamer, who has not yet lost his simple illusions, even if the 'real' threatens them in the Allegro frenetico. (The original associations of the motto appear to have been a lament for the absconding Camille Moke, as found in the *Rob Roy* overture composed after that débacle, but the tender passion remained operative in the tune.)

Harold offered, too, a symphony with a limited opportunity for a solo-viola; without any exploitation of the virtuosity of Paganini or any one else, or even of a new relationship between the orchestra and the soloist (although, as reported, Lionel Tertis's performance in 1935 proved revealing in certain aspects of effective communication), but relying frequently on the viola for a fresh one. Yet it was still a symphony, following up its predecessor with a new train of associations and schedules for movements, similar only in a certain indulgence in a controlled defiance of precedent in the finale, and in an unfaltering pursuit of textural rightness. I judge the first movement to be the strongest of the four, but I know of no reason to be apprehensive that the second symphony will disappoint the vast audience for whom there has been only one Berlioz symphony, the romanticist's dream. It is a question of gaining the familiarity which the engagement of a soloist tends to restrict, and also of not expecting at all another *Faust* symphony in disguise, with Harold as the guiding spirit, nor of demanding a succession of tremendous sub-structures, or solo-virtuosity, but rather letting Berlioz's still new orchestra take charge in his fanciful, scene-minded way.

In 1845 Berlioz visited St. Petersburg, where he was welcomed by the ardent crusading essayist and, in modern terms, socialist realist, V.V. Stasov, the composer Cui, and others. Welcomed both as a creator of progressive (i.e. programme) music and as a supporter of the Russian hopefuls, Glinka in particular. (In the *Journal des débats* he had recognized both the 'national' distinction of *A Life for the Tsar* and the greater musical maturity and German traits of *Ruslan and Ludmila*.) In 1867 he finally returned for something like a festival week's programme of his works, conducted with acclamation. Amongst other works *Harold* made a great impression. A friend of Balakirev, the didactic doyen of the rising group of composers and now a firm Berliozien, furnished him the programme for a comparable symphony on Byron's *Manfred*. Characteristically, Balakirev dithered, but in 1881 he pestered Tchaikovsky with a proposal (key-scheme supplied) for a *Manfred* symphony. Reluctantly Tchaikovsky set to. In the event, the more Tchaikovsky he. But coincidence's long arm may be suggested as the aftermath of the genuine earlier influence which Berlioz's creative aims had on some of the Russian pioneers, along with Liszt and Schumann.

After *Harold* came the long and disappointing struggle to mount a *Cellini* opera at the Opera, which ended with four not over-successful complete performances, pending a revival at Weimar in 1852. To convert public taste from its frivolous, mischievous, barbarously unmusical attitude was still a major reform, and the Cellini, a recently arisen singer named Duprez, was a master of cantabile but not of dramatic situation, still less capable of quelling a rocking audience. Critics were not missing who pointed out the revealing nature of Berlioz's handling, or the difference between his creative touch and Meyerbeer's fatal eclecticism. But they did not carry the day. Nor did Berlioz. His first attack on the citadel had been thwarted. It was a bitter reverse to a man who knew his worth and the infinitely wider range of his dramatic art, compared with any one else's. Where he had taken the greatest step forward, he was balked.

It was in this contest that he made his third symphony a Shakespeare symphony, and set to work almost at once. Under pressure which has been variously explained (for he was reputed to be mean), Paganini had sent him 20,000 francs to make it possible. After hearing the second symphony at a concert, he had come forward and knelt before Berlioz, whispering 'Beethoven's successor'. It was a more prophetic salute than he realized. The new symphony was to be a choral symphony after *Romeo and Juliet*, the chorus being both narrator and occasional participant and thus augmenting the orchestra from the start. The only soloist in the drama is Father Lawrence in a concluding part of Berlioz's own making. He had no intention of reproducing Shakespeare's dramatis personae, or indeed of setting a single line of the play verbatim.

The writing of more than incidental music under the stimulus of a play by Shakespeare in the way of operas, overtures and symphonic works, is now a familiar side-line of musical history since 1800. The progressive translation of his stage works, from Schlegel and Tieck earlier to Letourneur and Guizot in the eighteen-twenties, brought his art in contact with other national cultures, as the symbol of a liberating spirit, breaking down emotional fences in startling con-frontations of scene and character. For a composer an established theatre version of an accepted story was a useful thread to bend or stretch in a translation of medium. In this craft of re-creation Berlioz became a pioneer, with two main Shakespearean works, *Romeo and Juliet* and *Béatrice et Bénédict*. The first of these revealed, once and for all, his method of selecting scenes from familiar ground as working definitions of the terrain in which he was moving, not as ready made dramatic sequences to be set to music. (The reader is now familiar with such a treatment of *Faust*.) In this way he could project the chosen features of the established saga on to a musical screen with his own characteristic colouring and shaping without depending on a vocal text. Wagner, who was genuinely struck with *Romeo and Juliet*, was baffled by the lack of running clues to the developing phraseology.

On these lines Berlioz was able to continue the 'experiment' which he had recognized in the finale of the Ninth Symphony as a turning point. To make the chorus organic (i.e. dramatically participant or involved) from the start was an obvious advantage to ensure, for Beethoven's sudden and contrived introduction of Schiller's radiant stanzas was a hazardous and unrepeatable precedent. But a scenario was necessary, and here a project which Berlioz had broached in 1828 with Émile Deschamps, a translator of *Romeo and Juliet*, sprang into line: to make a symphony out of the play. He knew now that he had within him the invention and means to match on his own terms the basic blend of frustrated and declared passion, grief and didactic appeal, and for scherzo a somewhat far fetched invocation of fairy influences. It remained to plan in as symphonic terms as possible.

144

Berlioz eventually composed seven main movements. The odd numbers are choral, amounting to nearly half the work, but the full chorus does not sing for the first hour. Moreover, the two prologue soloists (contralto, tenor) and the finale baritone appear only in one movement; awkward facts of presentation. The even numbers and most of the third movement are purely orchestral. The second, third and fourth movements are thus, in the main, Allegro (with grave preface), Adagio and Scherzo, while declaring a clear enough intent to justify the pioneer title, 'dramatic symphony', without a confusion of means. The ensuing lament and its distracted sequel, however, need to lean on that title to explain their unprecedented accretion, and the final large reconciliation scene is an outright piece of didactic music-drama, more oratorio than not. It may have been influenced by the Ninth Symphony, with its absorption of Schiller's missionary ode to 'release', calling overtly for audience-involvement in the simple reverberating stanzas, whose diversionary setting shapes the climax of the whole symphony. It remains a departure from symphony as then understood. On the dramatic side, a message of reconciliation implies an established state of conflict. This the prelude retails, but not till the fifth movement is there any sign of the tragic consequences there adumbrated.

In the prelude Berlioz set out to convey to the uninformed (in swift leaps) his appraisal of the situation: the tragic, violent conflict of two Verona houses; the passionate exchanges, instant transports and dangerous relationship between Capulet Juliet and Montagu Romeo; the gay Mercutio's flamboyant description of Romeo's frenzied reverie as a visitation of the fairy queen; and, in an obscure allusion, the fatal consequences of the imbroglio, and the challenge to the two houses to make it up once and for all. This (to us) somewhat Victorian forecast is a provocative concert-proposition. However, to make a virtue of all this explaining, Berlioz provides an overture blending contentious fugue with imperious quasi-parlando trombones, and then, after Shakespeare but not repeating him, he summarizes his version of the saga in solemn choral recitative; indeed it can sound a mock-up, like the (recorded) chanting of the traffic code. Moreover, this narration is waywardly interspersed with illustrative and in fact guiding themes to establish a convention of dramatic motives taking musical shape for purposes of later development. (In revision, a reference to Tybalt was cut out, and also, and more essentially, a final and otiose appeal to the audience for their interest.) This prologue arguably offers necessary clues to an audience not quite aware what they are in for, and at the same time the sober narrative arouses expectation. The remaining six movements meet it with a call on the chorus as prompted by a closer dramatic contact, and, in varying distance from the titular scene of a movement, with a spontaneous release

145

of the orchestra with or without the chorus. The documentary start is to be justified by symphony, and balanced at the end by a didactic gesture.

So involved a symphony challenges criticism from many angles. First, the underlying drama: apart from the too long feud between two houses, whose casualties cry out for the madness to stop, the twisted, incredible plot of *Romeo and Juliet* exposes 'the obsession of sudden, gratified, youthful love' (Masefield). To convert this encounter into an operatic situation, or the suggestion of it, would have been fatal. Berlioz therefore devised, with a choral prelude, an extended orchestral sequence, containing passionate, incandescent music without any frenetic crescendo. The defect here, if anything, is the static character of the motives, calling for nuances in performance *faute de mieux*. Earlier, Romeo, gazing inwardly at the ball he cannot attend, has *his* love music. In his case any illusion for the listener that the oboe theme is his longing for the unattainable is rudely engulfed later in a whirl of orchestral bombast. Mercutio's mockeries of his dreaming friend have been disgorged in the prologue. The essence of his diagnosis is reserved for a splendid piece of fleeting, ubiquitous imagery, the 'Queen Mab' scherzo. But the upshot is that the solo appearances are mainly for narrative purposes. The band of Capulet revellers (preluding the love-scene), and even the mourners at Juliet's funeral rehearsal, are fringe-figures. Only Father Lawrence confronting the two Houses involves a leap into direct, person-to-person speech and argument. Hence the bolstering of the prologue with anticipatory themes (especially the love-scene motive) is most injudicious. These details absorbed, the prologue forms an acceptable introduction in its solemnly didactic-announcer fashion. This leaves a coherent succession of prepared Allegro, prepared Adagio, Scherzo, Andante, and prepared Allegro vivace in a somewhat telegraphic, disjointed idiom absorbed, as one critic has suggested, from the late Beethoven quartets. After that, the finale is admittedly not the masterful assertion by the orchestra, presumably reinforced by voices, which the rich foregoing conglomeration, and the unforgettable Beethoven precedent, lead one to expect. Here the composer makes capital of the bespoken and fatal catastrophe into which Verona is plunging deeper and deeper, in order to strike a substantive didactic note, in a prophetic and oratorio manner alien to pre-Mahler symphony (nos. 2, 8).

Let us recognize these potential inequalities and iniquities of style and design before attending to Berlioz's inventive compromise, the music as it occurs in sound and word, the first programme symphony of importance, paper programmes being discounted. So to the seven movements.

The prelude in **B** minor must be regarded as the witty blend of a very permissive fugue (the full four-bar subject is altered after two entries, and the final reprise is soon reduced to the 'false entry' of an automatic reverberation of the fourth bar) with what can only be called rodomontade on the trombones, first as counterpoint, then as solo-declamation, which sounds rather like a forecast of dire retribution, viz. the prince's early threat to users of violence. In the recital of the plot four themes, developed in varying degree in stated contexts, are for better or worse significant trailers of later appearances. (1) The noisy festivities in the castle as observed by Romeo (*x*, **Ex. 40**), presumably with cynical disdain. Appearing fleetingly on the violins in an earlier sketch to underline 'L'enivrement fatal' before introducing the angry Tybalt, it is now a sizeable entry for woodwind, in **A**. (2) The ball over, the thought turns to the departing revellers' regard for Romeo, torn from Juliet. This vignette of Romeo sighing, confined originally to a harmonic touch in recitative, receives special treatment, with a phrase on the traditional 'aching' string of the violoncello. (3) From the sighs to declaration, after a

Ex. 39.1

Ex. 39.2

Ex. 39.3

leap over the wall (**Ex. 39.2**). Here the knowing listener will compare a motive in *Tristan* (**Ex. 39.3**), ignoring both Berlioz's extempory touch and on the contrary the cutting rhythmic impetus of Wagner's final image of lovers driven ecstatically along their fatal adulterous course. More relevant, the phrase *y* (**Ex. 39.2**) figures in the final melody of the love scene to come. In fact, the anticipation of that melody here is most questionable. The subsequent whole song, 'Premiers Transports', derived from a song with piano in hand (see page 115), balances the fragmentary pattern by an independent, somewhat intrusive, strophe in a rather stilted style, more motivated in Verse 2. Mercutio's riotous arioso in tribute to Queen Mab defies packaging, and is also not heard further. (4) The end of the action suddenly in focus, the orchestra pay tribute to 'sovereign death' in hieratic monotone, recalled later in the 'funeral march'.

In this moody fashion, veering between choral recitation and engagement with theme, the symphony rises above the ground and promises further insight with the aid of the symbols accrued. The first three movements of the symphony proper, then, are readily recognizable as such. The first ('Roméo seul') takes up two of the self-styled Romeo motives, with a new theme to go with the second. An *andante malinconico* in **F** moves from an eloquent violin soliloquy to an extension of **Ex. 39.1** and so to an oboe theme (cf. top part of **Ex. 40**), marked by harp-like accompani-

Ex. 40

ment (violoncelli), with tambourine shakes. On this mood of distracted reverie there bursts the main Allegro with an expanded version of *x* (**Ex. 40**), already heard briefly in the prelude, in measured phrases; here dangerously melodic and self-contained for a symphonic movement. An apparent move to a new subject relaxes to further play with *x* (**Ex. 40**), and then instant and decorative reprise. Three fresh 'furnishings' in quick succession (for alert ears) qualify repetition. The initial delivery of the woodwind with light pizzicato (replacing strings with woodwind) is bound together by a silky violin figure; minatory wind-string antiphony breaks the thread; and, most important or rather most obvious, the main subject is pitted against the oboe theme as typified in **Ex. 40**. One may ask how the 3-bar metre of the wind can fit into the main subject which firmly keeps up its normally 4-bar harmonic rhythm. (Thus 15-12 is equated with 16-7-4.) My answer is that of course it does not and cannot fit, and the combination is only audible as a rhythmic dissonance. Moreover, the delivery of the once plaintive oboe tune by a battery of trombones, as if it were for a band of exultant pilgrims, is a crude stroke, and, as may appear, a derivative one. In a coda as long as the rest of the Allegro, the reverberation of a plain descending bass figure related to x (**Ex. 40**), acts as a common denominator for a series of extemporary happenings. Thus the movement eventually shapes into a drifting **A** (slow) and an organized **B** (quick) into which **A** is laboriously integrated; a plain subordination of structural balance to mood-portraiture.

It may now be revealed that both parts of **Ex. 40** are derived from the Rome-prize cantata, *La mort de Sardanapale*, in the preserved coda of which they make distracted but unmistakable entries (see page 52). Consultation of the available *text* makes it evident that the upper part was the setting of 'étoile du matin, Nehale, prends ta lyre', the desperate king's address (aria 1) to his favourite concubine; harp-conditioned, literally or in a pizzicato version. Phrase x must be referred to the dancing-girls, ordered to dance in the same context and now in a terrified state; so in frenzied bitterness Romeo might have exclaimed 'Dance away!' to the Capulets. In this way tokens of a grim situation (see Delacroix's picture) have been absorbed in the trials of a romantic passion par excellence and brought to a brilliant orchestral climax (after the combination). In this way, too, a once formal and gracious cantabile finds a fresh place in a prolonged slow introduction, and has then to justify itself. Not quite a vicious circle, but the awkward consequence of re-using material from a different genre and scene. Of course, Berlioz would not have agreed; but is that release of the oboe tune necessary? Moreover, it has been suggested that the opening of this movement is more suited to Romeo's solitary walks in dark humour (as related by Benvolio) when he is in love with Rosaline; but the transference to Juliet (act 2 prologue) has already been established in the prologue here.

The series of interlinked sections which make up the Adagio to follow is one of the best known Berlioz movements and by his own testimony his most treasured piece. The choral introduction conjured up by the spectacle of the young Capulet sparks proceeding audibly home with convivial, answering adieux (the most operatic feature of the symphony) provides a neat identification of them with the phrase *x* (**Ex. 40**), now couched in a more lilting rhythm, usefully inserts the male double-chorus as participants, and altogether makes a rare, convincing prelude to the main movement. A well-blended chamber orchestra of over sixty players now matches Romeo's here unspoken discovery with throbbing, articulate and

> How silver sweet sound lovers' tongues
> Like softest music to attending ears!

dynamically uninhibited expression, the stronger for being shaped in tranquillity! Successive ideas, including an odd passing mention of **Ex. 39.2** (horns, violoncelli), converge in a memorable string melody, with the phrase *y* (**Ex. 39.2**) as a kind of instant refrain.

Ex. 41

It does not need an advanced literary grasp to recall the 'Et de son coeur les feux éclatent' of the prologue. It does not actually need a text at all to explain what or whose ineffable exchanges the music (more down to earth in the dialogue of oboe and viola in the brief Allegro agitato) is about; whether a moment of truth, snatched from adversity, or (as in a modern stage context) the self-indulgence of angry teenagers. The rapt quality of the music, whether insistent or, as Harty made it, a matter of hush and suspense, leaves such questions behind. The nearest precedent in Berlioz's own work is the brief epilogue of the early *Orpheus* cantata. For a full movement one has to turn to Beethoven; to the Adagio of the second symphony, perhaps, also in **A**. Comparison with that still potent and firmly structured musical thought may expose to some degree the steady dependence of 'Scène d'amour' on textural control. So far admiration has often been too highly pitched. The movement remains a prototype of many since.

Romantic lovers may be vivacious but not, in that age, humorous. To fill the gap Berlioz astutely fastens his imagination upon Mercutio's jaunty picture of the fairy queen in her tiny horse-drawn car, attended by buzzing insects (*Romeo and Juliet*

Act 1, scene 4). This brilliant translation of Mercutio's rendering of Romeo's state of mind dismisses all dreamers with fugitive and repetitive but never quite predictable material, its wanton antiphony repudiating in advance the symmetrical orderliness of Mendelssohn's *Dream* scherzo. In the main scherzo here there is so much recovery of theme linked by varying diversions, as to impede any sense of comprehensive pattern, but in repeated hearings three rounds of scherzo make themselves felt. (1) 28 bars, repeated; (2) a pattern of 13-80-32-28 (**B** minor) bars, repeated as 0-44-36-28; (3) 24 bars. Then an interlude in slower tempo, followed by a reprise that is nearly all development. A recurrent figure of descending fifths in declining sequence, exploited by the clarinets as starter to the coda, must have been suggested by a phrase in *Ballet des ombres* (chorus and piano), there set to 'Entrez en danse' (also to 'Pressons la danse' in an early version of the carnival scene in *Cellini*). The flickering connexion of image is obvious, and the fitful sequence lends itself to capricious turns of semitone. Some of the quick modulations suggest Schubert. A free but truly symphonic sequel, then, to the Allegro in **F**, but without heavy brass.

Dark shadows now fall suddenly over the dramatic background, in two curious movements. Berlioz had a weakness for marches, as has been observed earlier. The spectacle of the drugged Juliet, believed dead, invited a processional dirge. For the egregious Garrick version of 1750, which was reprinted several times and continued well into the next century, went on in British theatres and was used by Kemble at Paris. In this revision the singing of a dirge for Juliet's funeral procession (originally with music by Boyce) makes the first scene of Act 5. Here the lament stretches out imitationally in two set stages. In the first, the orchestra of strings and wind take up a melodious fugal theme in traditional four-entry sequence, with eloquent free counterpoint, episode and compressed entries. Meanwhile, the mixed soprano and tenor chorus of Capulets, whose entry approaches the oratorio genre, haunt the counterpoint with a dragging ritual monotone ('Jettez les fleurs!'). Then, more briefly, the two forces change round. The chorus, now complemented by a bass section, declare their aptitude for imitational rejoinder as they fit the text to the fugal subject, the strings know their ritual place, and the wind draw a decorative thread into the polyphony. **E** minor becomes **E** major, with a characteristic coda slipping back to the minor. Obviously not the main slow movement, this Andante is an impressive interlude from the symphonic point of view. It invokes some depiction of scene and ceremony without surrendering musical considerations, which, indeed, grow with closer hearing.

But since the normal scherzo has already taken its place, the dirge is utterly polarized by the distracted portmanteau sequel. A compound of agitato, lugubrious tenor melody (woodwind) in measured twelve-beat metre, and secretive and pathetic clarinet interlude terminates in a riotous Allegro, in which racy parodies of the love-scene motives (phrase *y* in **Ex. 39**.2) can be picked out in a carnival of scoring and counter-scoring. Juliet's death assumed, it needs little prompting from the movement's title ('Romeo at the tomb of the Capulets') to take it as a final outburst of the Romeo ego, caught up in a whirlpool of deprivation and delirious memories of possession. In Shakespeare's plot, Romeo, not having received any intimation from Father Lawrence of his plan, hears without question from Balthazar the news of Juliet's death and entombment. Equipped with poison, he hurries to her tomb, where he encounters and in a fight kills Paris. The sudden soft chords in the trombones, emerging from the Allegro desperato, thus suggest the discovery of Juliet's body, and the sequent lament (tenor woodwind against throbbing lower strings) Romeo's invocation, after laying Paris in the tomb, of Juliet ('beauty's ensign yet is crimson in thy lips' etc.). The clarinet sequel is less certainly Romeo's last look at Juliet as he takes the poison. But the delirious orchestral outburst is theatrically non-significant, and Berlioz's specific subtitle, 'Invocation—reveil de Juliette. Joie delirante, désespoir, dernières angoises, et mort des deux amants' (as if they had died together) manifestly presupposes another text.

Such a text is found in the Garrick version at this stage. Here Romeo does not die instantly after taking poison. Juliet meanwhile awakens slowly, and there is a dialogue of over sixty lines. With this respite, Romeo plunges into a frenzied expression of his love ('It is thy Romeo, love; rais'd from despair/To joys unutterable!') and he 'brings her from the tomb'. Soon he collapses, dead, and after a contentious dialogue with the entering friar Juliet makes away with herself. In this context the clarinet conveys a picture of Juliet awakening to a disturbed Romeo, and the orchestral outburst, parodying the love-scene motives in the same manner as in the 'Ronde du Sabbat', typifies Romeo's 'joie delirante' clearly enough. On the same parallel lines, Romeo's collapse (fragmentation of texture) and Juliet's suicide (reckless harmonic wrench, tutti) converge in a point of no return, as falling intonation is compressed to the semitonal limit (oboe), sealed by a truly basic cadence. If a passing comment in his *Memoirs* of ten years later (ch. 16) is to be believed, Berlioz was far from deploring Garrick's pathetic dénouement, finding in it the exception to his usually rigid rules on adaptations.

So far the source-incidents of this musically confused movement, with its *avant garde* juxtaposition of blocks of unrelated texture, are identifiable. Any normal linking of penultimate and last movements is waived in favour of a brash token of conflicting purposes, a new type of joy unconfined and dramatic suspense, before a finale is conceivable. The binding spell of the foregoing prelude and four symphonic movements has been broken, in subservience to a spurious theatrical sequence. But let us not doubt the validity of Berlioz's intentions. He intuited the need for a break-up of the set moods of the middle movements, remembering Beethoven's prelude to reconciliation. Romeo's desperation gave him a jog, but it was not enough. The Garrick twist, prolonging the agony, provided a cue for a round of raw ecstasy and dissolution and the ironic moment. Berlioz decided to hazard the impact of this spasmodic music, as an acceptable entity by reason of its analogy with its psychic counterpart, each of the four sections being self-contained. No hasty dismissal will make any sense of his plan. It has been necessary to probe into this movement, in the light of its at first baffling subtitle, because it has been widely criticized, as excessively representational, from Jullien onwards.

Such an explosion called for a firmly based finale. Finding no possible stimulus in the prince's concluding reproaches (*Romeo and Juliet*, Act 5, scene 3), Berlioz had recourse to the positive emergence of Father Lawrence as the transforming spirit who will reverse as far as possible a situation that should never have arisen; an issue of wider application than the feuds of two ancient houses of Verona, as world-wide events perpetually remind a modern audience. Lawrence confronts the senseless guerilla of the opposing family groups, each bent on further violence but shocked to find Romeo and Juliet dead and declared by the priest to be man and wife. By bringing home the shame of it all, he is enabled to obtain an oath of perpetual reconciliation. Instead of Beethoven's plunge into ecstatic but universal celebration in flowing lyrical stanzas, made for strophe and variation and altogether a workable expansive finale, Berlioz returns to *Scene* in its most substantive form, in the coherent incidences of concert-drama or oratorio as laid down firmly by Handel, for Berlioz by Lesueur or whoever it might be. There is no attempt to answer the opening narrative by its conclusion, or to bring salient themes of the symphony to completion. The dramatic symphony has folded up into a cantata, combining choral dialogue, bass arioso and aria, and a truly swinging 'song in the heart' for bass and chorus in **B** major. The barrier between concert-music and an art that consciously invites the audience to be involved in the issues of conflict has been surmounted, and the symphonist is left to make the best of the anomaly.

What makes this departure heavy-going at early hearings is the extensive dialogue between priest and people. Having come forward to aid them in their mystified state, Lawrence explains how his plan to make a drugged Juliet appear dead fatally miscarried. This long-drawn declamatory melody in **C** minor, with sinuous violin motive, continues in a short, compassionate 'air' in **A** flat. Lawrence proceeds to a lengthy hortatory arioso, answered fiercely by a volubly antiphonal double-chorus, reinforced by the orchestra with a recall of the opening fugue of the symphony (confirming its contentious impression). The torrent of mutual recrimination and

153

offensive intent is all too credible today. This bilateral declaration of a right to continue armed (in defiance of the prince's order) is met by Lawrence with a prayer to God (short strophe), which in further compression is greeted with infectious signs of a change of heart in the opposing houses. Only then can he pass on to administer the binding oath of friendship and kindliness. This expansive melody

Ex. 42

(**Ex. 42**), unfolding in three 10 bar stretches with a pronounced slip of tonality to accentuate the last, is taken up by the male chorus with incisive orchestral support, which acquires a brilliant sense of punctuation for a condensed third verse. Thus for the orderly juxtapositions of the conventional finale Berlioz has come out with a dramatic struggle for mastery in conference, which finds late resolution in a reverberating strophe to lend substance to Lawrence's faith in humanity under an auspicious influence.

There is no need to cite a contemporary parallel for the human condition in actuality; gross and scandalous examples overflow from the surface of national life from west to east. So far the romantic probe (in the sense of tested personal involvement) sharpens the impact of this theatrical music. The finale remains in a genre of its own, a question to be resolved by the conductor as best he may. Many audiences seem to find no flaw in the arbitrary course into which Berlioz has steered choral symphony from his Shakesperean résumé, spasmodic glosses and settings, and didactic conclusion. Yet one retains a haunting conjecture that he was formulating the next best thing to the further opera which he was eager to compose. Subsequently, indeed, he became resigned to concert-drama. He took up *Faust* in the freer pattern of a cantata, and eventually his own text for a Christmas oratorio. But opera was still his true métier.

In 1832 Berlioz sent the *Revue Européenne* (March–May) a report on music in Italy, entitled 'Lettrc d'un enthousiaste'. He begins by declaring how eagerly he anticipated a performance of Bellini's *I Montecchi ed i Capelli* at Florence. 'What a subject! made for music; first, the dazzling ball at the Capulets', where in the centre of a whirling crowd of lovelies, young Montagu observed for the first time the *sweetest Juliet* . . . that inexpressible scene on the balcony . . . the piquant railleries of Mercutio . . . the monk . . . finally the solemn oath of the two hostile families . . .' The writer proceeded to tear in pieces the Italian travesty of Shakespeare's scenario, with its female Romeo etc. But the chief interest for us is the sketch of a programme (more than was used for any future musical work on the play). Evidently it was in Berlioz's mind for some time before he decided on such a symphony; before *Harold*, for a start.

A fourth work was given the title of symphony: the symphonie militaire commissioned by the minister of the interior for the tenth anniversary of the 'July Revolution' in 1840, and given six instant performances under the baton of the composer (walking backwards) during the procession from the church of St.-Germain-l'Auxerrois to the Place de la Bastille, where the new column was inaugurated and the slow movement played (exclusively). For a performance in 1842 string parts were added, and later in the year a chorus part for the last movement, to a text by Antony Deschamps. Of the original titles of movements—'marche funèbre', 'hymne d'adieu' and 'apothéose'—the second became 'Oraison funèbre', and the work was renamed 'symphonie funèbre et triomphale'. Berlioz had thought of a choral symphony on a victorious Napoleon in 1832, when he was crossing the Bridge of Lodi. He jotted down 'farewell to the fallen heroes', 'triumphal entry into Paris', with a text, but the accompanying musical notes relate to *Harold*. In 1835 he told Ferrand that he was starting on a 'Fête musicale funèbre à la memoire des hommes illustres de la France', in seven movements (why seven?), on the grand scale of a festival work. Two of these may well have become the outer movements of the completed symphony.

The upshot is an eminently occasional composition, designed for a long march, a short ceremony, and another march, all in the open air and with each march tolerably repeatable ad lib.; so far misrepresented in the conventional confines of a concert-hall. It is scored primarily for full wind band, the strings being chiefly later additions for the last movement, and that in literal support of wind parts. The first movement, alien as it may appear to the blossoming-Allegro-minded, shows some constructive interest in its pompous, repetitive style. The fine first theme (**Ex. 43.1**) is formal but thematically adaptable. The second theme (**Ex. 43.2**) (woodwind cantabile) is slight but massively prepared by a contrived suspense-period, and the almost instant reprise reasonably varied and pointed. The finale has a vigorous mobile main tune (**Ex. 43.3**), an inventive middle section and a concise return, with a chorus to support but never to control the swelling phrases.

155

Ex. 43.1

Ex. 43.2

Ex. 43.3

The middle movement is bluntly histrionic and fragmentary. It is conceived as a recitative and aria for tenor trombone (with optional alternatives). The *parlando* effect is presumably intended to arise from the explosive opening chords, like the string basses in the finale of the Ninth Symphony. Doubtful, but let that pass. The trombone then assumes a more cantabile style, in a brief stanza and an extended mellifluous sostenuto, resourcefully accompanied but with the extemporary phrase-development of a verbal setting, quite unsymphonic. A close scrutiny of the fragments that survive from torn-out pages (see p. 178) in one scene of the un-finished opera, *Les francs juges*, makes it clear that the melodic line of each of the three sub-movements owes something to this scene. (To be precise, bars 40–43, 46, 55–56 and more coherently the opening of the sostenuto, show their derivation from the opera.) The 'Oraison' so far developed from a poignant operatic situation: Arnold, a heroic resistance-man bent on destroying the murderous usurper-power in the region by a concerted break-in, while waiting for his contact-man calls upon sleep to come and calm his nerves. Thus in some degree the trombone solo sprang from a *vocal* solo composed for a tense moment in a thrilling narrative. Why Berlioz went back to this scene at all is obscure. We are left with this trombone thing, freely derived from a tender tenor solo and originally offered to the memory of the men of 1830 but later promoted as a prelude to the triumphal finale (the funeral march being dropped) and today posing as an interlude between march and march. It remains a curiosity, and whatever symphony the funeral march suggested to Berlioz's imagination, the 'Oraison' and 'Apothéose' do not fulfil the expectation of the basic title. No entire symphony, indeed, can recognize the limitations of being played on the march. The misnamed symphony is a band suite; a Berlioz suite, each component unmistakable. (Wagenseil's admirable Concerto in E flat (recorded) had long vindicated the trombone as soloist.)

We have, then, three symphonies: two orchestral with programme but no singing and one choral-orchestral and 'dramatic' in its admission of narrative, participation and imaginative translation of aspects from *Romeo and Juliet*. We turn to the titled overtures as to further potential translations of dramatic situations in independent music.

NOTES

1. I.e. a work divided into separate or clearly defined numbers and occasional subdivisions.

2. Originally the tonal digression of **Ex. 38.2** was slightly extended by solo bravura into a sequence, moving to **A** minor and **G** minor, before the viola makes its entry in **D** (min. sc. 38, 3–6), which also was twice repeated with an anticipation of the **D** minor of the following bars.

IO

Overtures, Marches and Arrangements

OF Berlioz's eight orchestral overtures, five are concert-pieces and three, although each intended for an opera, are not so established in the concert room as to need only a footnote to explain their original contexts. Moreover, it is scarcely a co-incidence that these overtures project whatever literary or dramatic image was in the composer's mind into a developed Allegro, arising out of a slow movement in seven cases, and recognizing the balance of sonata-form in seven cases with a variant in the eighth. The same may be said of Beethoven's dramatic overtures, each composed as a prelude to a play or an opera. But the obvious general inference is that, as *Coriolan* and *Egmont* portray very different mood sequences by their common methods of thematic appeal, much more may Berlioz suit his more flexible recurring patterns to his imagination. This, at least, is the cumulative effect of listening to these eight essentially separate pieces in conjunction, considered as the background of the symphonies.

Waverley, then, supplies the working rule. From a pondering Larghetto, soon neatly settling down to an expressive violoncello melody that obtains drum protection, the music breaks into an insistent Allegro on almost conventional lines of subject-groups, disposed by key, slight development and succinct reprise (with a queer change of order in the second subject), augmented by the select thematic emphasis of a coda. (Just before the final tutti the strings appear to be starting up a new theme. It is in fact a piece of the woodwind tune in the second subject, com-pressed to half its rhythmic length.) It is a comparatively glib composition in black and white—no theme is noticeable except the woodwind refrain and the loud wind entry midway—but the orchestral colouring is distinctive in its open-air style. The motto couplet from Scott's *Mirkwood Mere* suggests a forsaking of dreams of love for 'honour and arms'. The Larghetto mood is certainly shaken off as in many a Haydn Allegro, but there is nothing in the Allegro of the barrack square or war's destructiveness or even the buccaneer. It is just a resolute, collected statement, full of promise as a major orchestral item in the composer's first public concert, given to a small audience in 1828 and including *Et resurrexit* and *Scène héroïque* (see page 41).

The other orchestral item was the overture to the opera then in progress, *Les*

159

francs juges, written before *Waverley*. After a tentative start, the minor-key Adagio in **F** strikes a pompous aggressive note (brass unison in **D** flat), from which an agitated Allegro motive escapes, soon to give place to the quiet violin theme whose square and repetitious phrasing might forecast a short shrift. Meanwhile for its repeat it secures not only a plain antiphony of woodwind melodists but also a counter-theme (first motive). The theme is no more persuasive because it is referred (in the composer's inventive *Memoirs*) to a youthful quintet than because it is remembered today as a signature-tune for a television series. For the present it unpretentiously slots in and out. Yet it would be inhuman not to quote its salient curves. No further development being possible, the arbitrary appearance of a dour new tune (woodwind), treated strophe-wise and drama-wise, provides—without

Ex. 44.1

Ex. 44.2

parallel in the other overtures—a point of remoteness from which to recover. (The violin-entry mark, *poco f*, agrees with the composer's 'Mettez une certaine rudesse' in his piano duet arrangement.) The return of **Ex. 44** in full is confusing but in due course it is displaced by fragments of agitation. Reprise spells renewal in the streamlining of the first motive and eventually of **Ex. 44**. The latter, now in **F**, is first reduced to a fussy dactyl muttering in the bass, like the start of Schubert's March in **D**, and later to the equivocation of **Ex. 44.1** in rising sequence, before it recovers its true melodic élan in the brilliance of a high octave. To avoid an anti-climax, the aggressive brass statement returns, spread out in the main tempo, while acrobatic figures and minor expletives fill in gaps. This provides enough 'in-fighting' to invoke a quick burst of tutti, with cymbals. It is notable that Berlioz put so much structural energy into this early piece.

In the known context of the operatic scenario, one might expect the brass theme to anticipate some appearance of the ruthless tribunal through which the dreaded arch-tyrant liquidates his enemies, the midway tune to forecast something *triste* but resolute (Berlioz told Hoffmeister it is a prayer), and **Ex. 44** to comfort the honourable resisters and inspire the attested 'peculiar conspirators' gaiety'—say, of a von Trott (July, 1944). But there is no trace of these themes in any of the surviving scenes. One is left with an obvious struggle between two emotional forces, of which the decisive issue is near-ecstatic but never in doubt. There is far more sustained conflict in the not dissimilarly conditioned *Egmont* overture, in which the break into the daylight major (**F**) is pointedly held back till the coda, anticipating Egmont's vision of victory in his condemned cell. *Les Francs Juges* remains a memorable and heartening overture, for what that may be worth at any time.

The *Intrata di Rob Roy MacGregor* of 1832, one of the composer's Rome works, was 'so badly received by the public that I burnt it the night of the concert'—Paris, 1833. Actually (as usual) he kept a score, but he did not publish it, and it was soon forgotten. It has been little played since its publication (as *Rob Roy* overture) this century, presumably because some of its material was used in the second symphony, but it remains an independent overture in a racy, rural style, arising from, as it concludes with, a horn motive (bar 10) in **D**. The overflowing content of its sonata form includes an oboe phrase that today catches the ear because, with a trochee neatly changed to a spondee, it became **Ex. 38.2** (see page 140), and in a central Larghetto an oboe introduces with harp accompaniment a melody later familiar as the viola motive of the second symphony (the Adagio, from *quasi niente*. Confirmation that this was not intended for viola.) Here the absorbed melody, so apt for the cor anglais with its **D'–A"** compass (sounds), as also when repeated for the same with clarinet-bassoon doubling in the lower octave, provides an acceptable diversion from the jiggety rhythm of the main tempo. It is heard no more. Yet after it the resumption of the horn motive is piquantly tentative. The rest of the reprise restores the balance and the final mock-solemn entry of the horn motive at half speed (earlier anticipated by a casual trumpet entry) makes an effective parting salute to the supposed hero. If the overture is a tribute to R. R. MacGregor, it dwells on his roving side. A pleasantly insouciant opening for any concert, far better than many chosen.

Listening, however, to the *King Lear* overture, written about the same time, one is aware of a wider range of feeling. Echoing the repartee in the Ninth Symphony (finale), the opening *maestoso* at once strikes a grave and solitary note, pursued in an almost ritual succession of three *quasi parlando* phrases in the order: 1 1 2 3 2 3– X–1 2 3, interspersed with a deceptively simple melody (X). An Allegro of brisk string themes, bustling tuttis and wayward second group follows, with a short

161

Ex. 45.1

Andante non troppo lento, ma maestoso

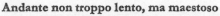
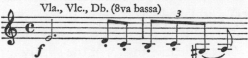

Ex. 45.2

Allegro disparato ed agitato assai

Ex. 45.3

Ex. 45.4

poco riten.

Ex. 45.5

but busily discursive development to prompt a reprise. In this reprise the second group (**Ex. 45.4, 45.5**) is held up by a full incursion of **Ex. 45.1** and companion phrases, each duly spread across the Allegro bars (but still moving 4/3 faster) against sustained harmony. The coda, on the other hand, made up of rhythmically compressed versions of **Ex. 45.2** etc., is all verve. The music is as triumphant as it is grave. Any attempt to discern a built-in panorama of Lear, King of England as universally known, has soon to admit defeat or maintain preposterous associations.

In his note on the overture in *Shakespeare in Music* (ed. P. Hartnoll), Mr Roger Fiske, while declaring it 'not a successful translation', offers a portrait (maestoso) of Lear announcing his will to a rustle of courtier comment (wind), of his three daughters replying severally in similar terms (oboe theme), and Lear's angry reaction

162

to Cordelia's silence. Then, in the Allegro disperato, Lear emerges, more energetic than desperate but battling with the storm winds, more especially in the intrusion of the maestoso motive in the reprise, and then breaking up, as signalled by a shattering pizzicato (see page 173). Meanwhile, the compassionate start to the second subject (**Ex. 45.4**), for oboe, allegedly the romantic heroine's signature-instrument, must be Cordelia, continuing presumably in **Ex. 45.5**, confronted with Lear in rising temper but returning none the less, compassionate as ever. The correspondence does not work, and it is inconceivable that Berlioz should try to force into sonata form a complicated pattern of character and scene. It may be assumed that Berlioz started with an image of the deserted king-father of the first act, and from there proceeded musically, retaining an intention to use the king theme later as a rebarbative component, and possibly to derive a second subject from the character of Cordelia. But at no point does the musical working-out falter, and in the concert-hall it is far better to forget *Lear* and listen, remembering the name as a convenient distinction from the other overture in **C**, *Le Corsaire*.

'Magnificent!' thought Balakirev in 1858, doubtless welcoming the 'symphonic poem' in some sense. A year later (the play being on in St. Petersburg) he wrote his own overture, also couched maestoso—allegro, but making the former ominous and preparatory, and the Allegro stormy and passionate and tense, and in **B** flat minor, with a second subject in a remote **D** major, pointing to Cordelia, and destructive elements that suggest Goneril and Regan; all contained in a firm musical structure, yet without the consuming interest that keeps a work in circulation. Balakirev went on to write some concert-worthy preludes for the various acts. Obviously *Le roi Lear* had sparked him off.

In the overture to his opera, *Benvenuto Cellini*, which must surely owe its concert popularity to its title, Berlioz seems to claim operatic licence to stir together matter for a conventional curtain-raiser with one unsubtle gesture of anticipation, prefiguring the cardinal's solemn air of pardoning. Let us consider some details. The main Allegro proceeds after a false start and a Larghetto adumbrating the cardinal theme and developing Harlequin's little song in advance. In the Allegro itself complementary opening motives in **G** appear, and the arrival of a sprawling second-subject in the conventional second-key is signalled by colourful gestures of devious transition. (A slightly different bridge in an earlier script, marked by an otiose oboe anticipation of the typical semitonal start, was replaced; and an episode separating the two statements of second subject was removed.) A rambling development of both subjects (originally with a combination of themes 9 bars before the reprise, replaced by the present harmonic phrase) merges casually into a bare recapitulation. Here the first subject is quickly interrupted by a 'brilliant transition', in order to be

163

resumed later in attendance on the cardinal-theme, now a majestic bass. The latter being in three-bar units and the counter-phrase in four, they do not fit, as in the 'Romeo' movement of the third symphony. So to a quick climax. The second subject, having secured attention (in **G** minor and, oddly, in **G** major) in the development, is, after all, expendable, not a necessary complement. Altogether one discerns so loose a construction as to sound a non-construction, and dull at that. It may seem tedious to analyze a relationship of events that offers so few pretensions to a symmetrical pattern, but such an assertion of musical ideas may be presumed to amount to something more compulsive than a dominating rhythm, as an ear-opener before the singing commences. Much more does a concert-appearance arouse expectations of a total musical satisfaction.

The fine concert overture which Berlioz wrote six years later *à propos* of his opera was in the nature of a nostalgic encore, of the kind that Berlioz sometimes gave to parts of works regarded as beyond public recall. *Le Carnaval Romain* can be analyzed as an orchestral conflation of the not very distinguished love-duet (act 1) between Cellini and Teresa, torn between mutual passion and agitation over contrary parental plans, and the exhilarating chorus for the show people and crowd in the carnival finale of Act 2. (It appears that Berlioz was especially anxious to show the public how this saltarello should go, Habeneck having ruined it in the opera by taking it too slowly.) The extension of the carnival number with a long coda provides a very plausible Allegro, with a preliminary sostenuto from the duet. Thus accidentally this overture in **A** conforms to the general pattern.

In the *sostenuto*, which shoulders the burden of carrying through a conventional melodic line three times *per se*, changes of key (**G-E-A**) and a resourceful handling of texture serve to minimize any sense of verse-routine. All the same, it is a relief to reach the Allegro. Those who remember the carnival chorus well would identify the salient phrases by their texts, and these may be quoted here. The texture scheme, by which these vocal intonations (with **Ex. 46**.3 dominating) find a new appeal in

Ex. 46.1

(Ve-nez, ve-nez, peu-ple de Ro-me)

Ex. 46.2

(Mais dé-ja la fou-le Dans l'om-bre et la nuit.)

Ex. 46.3

symmetrical statement and re-statement, offers a rewarding test of Berlioz's control of precise sound-effects. One may tabulate a few of the typical devices for shaping and re-shaping the top line. The carnival chorus breaks off with an entry

Table 5

Theme	Statement	Reprise
Ex. 46.1	muted violins/woodwind	ff strings/woodwind, more abruptly
Ex. 46.2	ppp violins (mutes now off)	violins and woodwind in flute clarinet counter-phrase (ppp percussion cue) violins/woodwind abruptly
Ex. 46.3 (in **E**)	violins and woodwind (brass-percussion starter)	repeat (still in **E**)

of trombones in a flat key. The overture dissolves in a rush of flickering phrases, promoting a sense of vacuum. The *Sostenuto* (opening) fills it, spreading its three-beats over the bare Allegro rhythm maintained and here taking undisputed possession, as it slides from **F** to **A**, until the tumultuous second subject is recovered, with more besides, but ultimately and decisively just that. This carnival is ended unpredictably and with no whimper. It is, of course, post-*Cellini*, and to play it before the second act of the opera, as has been done, is absurd.

Berlioz called his next overture 'The tower of Nice', having twice worked at it in that ruin (1831, 1844). Performed in 1845, it did not satisfy him. A revised version (London, 1851–52) was re-named 'Le corsaire rouge', after *The Red Rover* of Fenimore Cooper, whose death in 1851 may have brought Berlioz back to the novel (Barzun, vol. 2, p. 50). But fearing the title was obscure or misleading, he cut out 'rouge', leaving the broad suggestion of a bluff Byronic rover for music already fully designed. Here is no monument to a fugitive on the seven seas.

In shape this concert piece follows the last two overtures in beginning with a false Allegro start and then a move to Adagio, here a succinct piece of somewhat

165

precious melody and semitonal harmony. In the main Allegro the impulsive opening is balanced by a symmetrical and convivial tune in the bass, an embarrassing phenomenon at this juncture, especially when it provides the start of the otherwise esoteric second subject. It is left to the woodwind to strike a different note by the development of two-bar phrases, in no particular key, and providing no more special linking feature than rising thirds (as in Romeo's sighs in **Ex. 39.1**, see page 147) or falling thirds, string-brass chords of punctuation, and garrulous but sturdy bassoons. This extension of a short formula in **A** minor (**Ex. 47.1**, see page 173) was an entire after-thought.[1] In the reprise the second subject is soon despatched, its two divisions appearing as complementary phrases of one melody. Once more the second theme replaces a different episode. In the ensuing *tutti* some of the brass gain the big bass tune, the remaining wind reverently holding on to the harmony, but the strings' scalic excursions and rejoinders keep the basic progressions vibrant. Penultimately there is room at the top for the melodic line. String and brass groups, maintaining a harmonic rally on alternate beats, shake the forward rush in their turn, and Berlioz needs no ghost-writer to continue the rhetoric. Finally the upward scale of the opening comes into its own: a *coup d'oeil* before the arresting cadence. Not obviously Berlioz's latest or most mature overture, but an interesting composition for an alert listener, and by chance one in which the process of gestation is on record at several crucial points.

The overture to the opera *Béatrice et Bénédict* proceeds on familiar lines, with a preliminary Allegro and Andante before the main Allegro, whose first subject obviously straightens out the opening theme (with four beats for three) without being committed to anything but a general curve of descent and twist back. A cantabile complement 'entrusted' to the woodwind for four bars and then left to the violins and violas completes the stock in hand, but the almost instant recapitulation succeeds in raising the wind, and not only in the coda. For English listeners, at least, the playfulness of the main theme cannot but suggest 'lively coquetry' (Barzun) in an overture so titled, and conceivably the hesitant semitonal fall of the woodwind-string cantabile distils sensations of 'gentle melancholy', and no need to ask whose coquetting or moaning, or storming about (between themes) in the reprise. In fact, the opening 26 bars also begin the final scherzo between Benedict and Beatrice, and continue in effect throughout the duet. The first 25 bars of the transitional Andante form the basic section of the Andante portion of Beatrice's air, 'Il m'en souvient'. But as an 'overture to a comedy' this piece would work its passage well enough in the concert-hall, without any probing into Shakespeare or the opera that Berlioz drew from *Much ado*. Indeed, with the possible exception of the *Cellini* overture, all the overtures are acceptable as 'characteristic overtures' without reference to their titles. They form a secure wall behind the symphonic works. They may even represent a surer touch, on their narrower scale, than those wider-aiming achievements.

It is noticeable, for what it may be worth, that three of Berlioz's symphonies—1, 2 and 4—include marches of sorts. The most pronounced march-music is, inevitably, the opening movement of the fourth. It seems likely that it remained in the composer's mind when he decided to write a march for the end of *Hamlet*, the last nine lines of which he quotes in English, and in French prose, at the top of the score. The very quotation suggests that the music is not intended for a stage performance (where it is inconceivable) but as a concert-hall tribute to that scene and man. Even so, a ponderous entry, most likely of revival on radio or disc. It is none the less a fine composition, fully orchestral (64 strings minimum), with no extra brass and only six side drums and a gong in addition to the usual full percussion, and that in moderation. A burst of fire behind the scenes marks the climax. A unison chorus (of underground revisionists?) add intermittently their bare sighs, mainly of conventional lament but twice in loud protest.

The march is economically constructed from three phrases; the first melodically

Ex. 48.1

Ex. 48.2

Ex. 48.3

evocative, the second explosively cadential (in one key or another), the third a set phrase apt for a rejoinder or serial development at fresh pitches. The expansion of **Ex. 48.**1 and 2 reaches a point of tension supported by the full force of the orchestra, including the percussion. The succinct reprise which resolves the tension avoids any 'processional' monotony by means of fresh accompanying figures and a restlessness of key, while being haunted by the pitchless drums. The climax of tone (with 'concrete' noise from the firing squad) is, once more, disruptive. The answer this time is a subdued and mysterious and, in plain words, extemporary lead back to a point of equilibrium. Some organic link is required. The listener is left to decide which is most apt for prolonging the coda. The deep entry of the chorus on the third of **A** minor (not the more elementary first or fifth) maintains gravity to the end. The march thus combines an inventive and balanced development of melodic line with the sweep forward of a march-past. It was published as the last of *Tristia*, following 'La mort d'Ophélie' (see page 110), but it bears no musical relationship with the song-setting. Nor does it owe anything to *Hamlet* except an occasion for the commemoration of a character and drama well known to Paris audiences, and possibly of the kinship which Berlioz habitually felt for the prince's struggles with discordant times, a motive now familiar in some modern productions. Lekeu apparently established a further connexion with his *Marche d'Ophélie* (1883), but this was not published. Walton's short march for a *Hamlet* film, extracted by Muir Mathieson for concert use (1963), remains just a competent functional piece.

Berlioz also arranged three marches for orchestra. In his *Memoirs* he recalls that in July, 1830, when the French Institute, with music prize contestants contained within, had come under insurrectionist fire, he dashed out at the first opportunity with a pistol in his pocket and (having made certain that Camille Moke and her mother were safe) joined the 'sacred rabble', where he found, to his secret pride, a handful of young men giving tongue to his 'Chant guerrier'. Later, a much larger crowd broke into 'La Marseillaise'. This reminded Berlioz (he relates) that he had just made his own arrangement of the song, possibly as a double thrust for art-music, which was being pushed out of concert existence by patriotic songs of low quality. The song already had a history. An amateur musician, Captain Rouget de Lisle, stationed with the Engineers at Strasbourg, had written in a night of 1792 the words and tune of his second patriotic song, 'Allons, enfants de la patrie'. Anonymously scored at once for a performance by the Garde Nationale band, it struck fire when delivered by a singer at Marseilles, and this 'Hymne des Marseillais' was produced at the Opera as a scene, arranged by Gossec and Gardel. Presumably it was Gossec who altered certain details of melodic shape to what we know now. Berlioz conforms closely to this, with certain adherences to de Lisle, of which the most noticeable is the intonation of 'Marchez, marchez' with the third syllable *not* going up a step. (The original tune is in *Grove's Dictionary*, and all four versions are quoted by Wotton in a letter to *The Musical Times*, September 1915.) The tune, it may soberly be said, is magnificent in spite of a somewhat laboured middle phrase of 8 bars. Berlioz gave it new life, not only by his dynamic orchestration but also by a simple scheme of vocal contrasts. Four stanzas are to be sung in unison by all present. The fifth is for (?) solo-voice and strings until 'Aux armes!' restores the full orchestra. The last verse proceeds similarly from an unaccompanied start, T.T.B., with a stirring crescendo and brilliant semitonalism in the background. The setting remains unofficial ('Marchons marchons' has the middle notes the same, as in de Lisle), and so unused. But it surely gave Berlioz an idea for a **B** flat march tune of his own composition, no less patriotic or assertive in its dramatic context, and compact enough to stand repetition on an epic scale (see **Ex. 54.**1, page 215).

In 1844 Berlioz returned to Paris from resting at Nice to find his services required by an entertainment manager named Franconi to conduct a four-day festival at the Cirque Olympique. At the first concert, *Tuba mirum*, *Hymne à la France* (see page 115) and the *Tour de Nice* overture were given. The second concert (1845) was devoted to the work of Félicien David, a popular exponent of the quasi-oriental, and the pianist Leopold de Meyer, who played a new Moroccan march of his own. A year later Berlioz orchestrated this, adding a coda. The main tune, which is chiefly entrusted to the wind band, harps too much on the third degree, and the middle theme (strings) is artificial, squirmy and prolonged. A short recap soon becomes involved in a coda typified by trombone bass excursions off-key. A facile work which somehow it interested Berlioz to project orchestrally. A little later, it seems, he orchestrated another of de Meyer's marches, the *D'Isly* (dedicated to the duke d'Isly). This piece of 265 bars, the orchestral version of which may one day be publicized and will in due course be published, is a more interesting construction. Uniform in key and without a formal interlude, it presents the appearance of a succession of excursions from the gradually extending symmetrical and slightly Schumannesque melody which occupies the first hundred-odd bars. In place of a middle section, a series of fresh snatches of tune and episode jostle each other for attention in an obviously extemporary style. The first is loud but soon abandoned, but a later one, starting (unlike the rest) *on* the beat, proves more important and repeatable. A slight afterthought reinforces a perfunctory return of the opening curve. The repetitions and deviations invite colourization, and if the polka stamp and rather fussy vibrations can be controlled, one can imagine a Changing Guard marching off to the strains of the *D'Isly*, and in wind-arrangement actually doing so.[3]

Two other arrangements are a great deal more important. In 1841 Berlioz was engaged to revive *Freischütz*, which involved writing recitatives (in Weber's style) to replace the spoken dialogue not countenanced at the Opera, and also ballet-music where there had been none. For the latter purpose he arranged *Invitation to the*

169

dance for orchestra. Here the substance was Weber's but the orchestral voice was Berlioz's. The recitatives were executed with a steady concern for verbal *versus* musical rhythm, but probably the slow German style was more than he could cope with.[2] There is no need, incidentally, to pay any heed to Wagner's advance and *a priori* dismissal of these recitatives, in an article that he was asked to write for the *Gazette Musicale*, on the ground that Berlioz's fiery, individual writing would kill the airs and choruses which they introduced. Wagner had not heard or seen a note of this music. The method of criticism is typical, and this may explain why Wagner's comments on Berlioz will be given scant notice here.

In 1860 a revival of *Fidelio* by Carvalho (of whom we shall hear more later) roused Berlioz from the low spirits into which he had sunk as a result of the death of his sister, Adèle, ten years younger than he, and other events. At the suggestion of his friend, the tenor Roger, he arranged *Erlkönig* for orchestra as a useful short work for the summer concerts. Inevitably something of the vividness and plasticity of Schubert's piano writing has been lost, but so great a song (or rather cantata) can stand up to a more ponderous treatment, and the dramatic narration almost calls for an orchestra, with its anxious father, terrified child, double-tongued voice underground, and storm-tossed ride for help. The score was published at the time, and it is still surprising that the setting is so neglected. The accompaniment to the Erlking's three songs, for instance, show a telling contrast of (1) woodwind throbs off the beat, held in place by horn-clarinet chords and a tramping bass (pizzicato), countered by a falling violin arpeggio (added) in the even bars; (2) low violin arpeggios against string chords and incisive bass (bowed); (3) vibrating woodwind, flecked with new violin arpeggio figures, syncopated at first with a sustained bass to confirm the ominous note and clarinets to support the voice. In the two chords that so summarily despatch the narrative ('life goes on!'), the trumpets, which have ceased after the boy's last fearful cry, remain silent. Berlioz cut out (in the proofs) the unavoidable upward leap. A'-G'', entailed in the use of an unvalved trumpet in F, which cannot sound G'. To compensate, the previous suspense-chord is given to the strings, and in the cadence the wind, already well above the strings, are joined by 1st and 2nd horn. But in any case the vibrating, modulatory trumpets, screwing up the key by semitones, have been associated with the mounting terror which the awful king strikes in the child, and they can have no place in the sealing of the narrative. It is instructive to compare Liszt's almost contemporary setting in the third of *Four Schubert Songs* (1863). In the king's second song, for instance, the choice of clarinets and harp for the liquid arpeggios, pinpricked by pizzicato strings, is shrewd. The first song, by the way, is 'Die junge Nonne'; an improvement on Ferdinand Schubert's effort (see page 29)?

Minor arrangements include a setting of Martini's 'Plaisir d'amour' (a variant of 'Begone dull care'!) for voice and chamber orchestra; minimal, of Couperin's 'Invitation à louer Dieu' for three voices and piano.

Berlioz's *Rêverie et Caprice* in **A** for violin and orchestra is too slight and solitary to make a fresh genre, and must appear here as an 'also composed'. Berlioz wrote it in 1841 for Alexandre Artôt to play at a Paris concert, and it was repeated at a big Berlioz concert at Leipzig by Ferdinand David, the leader of the orchestra, with the *Lear* and *Francs Juges* overtures and *Symphonie Fantastique*. In this company it must have appeared as a diversion. It is none the less a piece in its own right, well furnished with material to substantiate its obvious juxtaposition of two moods, and to furnish in each a rhythm firm enough to carry off coloratura and other breakaway touches,

Ex. 49.1

Ex. 49.2

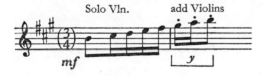

Ex. 49.3

and to claim the interest of the orchestra as well as the soloist (see *x* **Ex. 49.1**). The Allegro invites bravura, of the nonchalant kind, but it always comes back to **Ex. 49.2** especially bar 2, in the role of questioner. The object of the exercise is manifestly that Caprice shall expel Reverie. Caprice achieves this with suitable vigour the first time, and the second time with a final agility. Tchaikovsky's *Sérénade mélancolique* is monotonous by comparison. Berlioz's piece acquired a fantastic programme for its first edition (? 1865) of spreading, illuminating light. It is not authentic. On the other hand, the music apparently began life as the earliest setting of Teresa's first

171

aria in *Benvenuto Cellini*, with many alterations to suit the soloist's tessitura; possibly performed as such, but soon abandoned. An avenue too inspissated to explore.

In 1841, Berlioz began to publish a series of articles on instrumentation in the *Revue et Gazette musicale* (1841, 60–64; 1842, 1–29). He revised and expanded these into his *Grand traité d'instrumentation et d'orchestration* (1844). A German translation followed (n-d.), then an English (1860, then an Italian (1912). Meanwhile in 1904 Weingartner had produced his edition, correcting some points, and in the same year Strauss brought out his expansion, *Instrumentationslehre*, in which the illustrations were brought up to date and increased from 66 to 151, including Wagner in plenitude and some Strauss as well as Liszt, Marschner and Méhul.

Berlioz's book is much more than a manual. It has its instructive side, which does not concern us here, but it is also a revelation both of what the instrumental forces severally meant to him, and what orchestral moments struck him as memorable. On the first line of communication (hence 'instrumentation'), Barzun well compares the barren quality of the *Cours d'Instrumentation* (1836) of cultivated Georges Kastner, bent on disclosing 'poetical aspects' but actually more interested in the mimetic potentiality of an instrumental combination. In contrast, Berlioz on the middle and high notes of a flute: 'They can be used for melodies of various kinds, but without being able to rival the naif gaiety of the oboe or the noble tenderness of the clarinet … an instrument almost devoid of expressiveness … yet it possesses an expressiveness of its own'—with further shrewd elaborations. Throughout *Grande traité d'instrumentation*, Berlioz bears in mind the dramatic possibilities of the given timbre of an instrument, or its suggestion of a poetic mood. Secondly, the kind of exemplary music cited, nominally to exhibit an environment for one instrument, is doubly rewarding. Examples are long enough to be musically significant; and we learn who Berlioz's models were. Of sixty-six examples, seventeen are by Beethoven, seventeen by Gluck, eleven by Berlioz. Gluck, a surprising preference to some listeners today, had on his side a comparatively ample performance at the crucial period of Berlioz's maturing genius, and an almost luxurious degree of score-publication. Beethoven, an easy winner in Forsyth's *Orchestration* (1914), was virtually Berlioz's discovery. His actual citations of Beethoven favour the *Third* to *Seventh* symphonies and *Fidelio*—the omission of the *Ninth* is strange—but they are nonetheless a rich tribute in their context. Four of them cover, in 3–10 lines of full score each, what Forsyth has to confine to a single line each time. The common passages and points of illustration are as follows. **Ex. 6.** Coda of 5.1: violas to back cellos, not violins. **Ex. 16.** *Fidelio* Act 2, grave digging scene: double-bass (and double bassoon) *per se*. **Ex. 25.** 3.4, slow variation: oboe texture. **Ex. 40.** 3.3, trio: security for hand-horns. Berlioz's other examples from Beethoven include: **Ex. 5.** 4.2, cl. theme:

pizzicato against bowed decoration. **Ex. 26.** *Fidelio* Act 2, Florestan's delirious vision (**F** major): the oboe's 'broken sobs' in an absorbing context.

On Berlioz's own craft, he and Forsyth coincide at a strange point: the double-bass harmony for the 'lugubrious silence' in *Le cinq mai*. For his part, Forsyth mentions *inter alia* the eloquent viola solo in Margaret's 'Thule' air (at the critical expense of the 'full-dress obbligato' of such things as Annette's song in *Freischütz* 3) and the sharp pizzicato in the coda of *King Lear*, 'a fibre snapping in Lear's mind' to Strauss. Berlioz's own meagre self-quotation—not a bar from *Cellini* or *The Damnation of Faust*—merits some attention. **Ex. 28.** *Symphonie Fantastique* 3 fin.: the cor anglais, answered by a murmur of drums, for loneliness. **Ex. 34.** *Lélio, Aeolian harp* fin. (from *Mort d'Orphée* fin.): muffled clarinet and string tremolando for 'suppressed melancholy' (or for an exquisite moment of recall?). **Ex. 13.** *Romeo and Juliet* Act 3, *scene d'amour*: violas and vc richly interlocked. **Ex. 10.** *Requiem*, 'Rex tremendae': violoncelli against double-bass. **Ex. 46.** *Ibid.*, 'Hostias': the low-trombones experiment, with flute overtones. **Ex. 20.** *The Tempest* fantasia init.: the essential need of a piano for the 'harmonious quivering' in a chorus of airy spirits.

It is no exaggeration to say that only a perusal of this Treatise can convey precisely what the orchestra came to mean to Berlioz as he stared at a blank page of score, or set about assembling themes, incidents, climaxes, late second thoughts, and how from accumulated choices of timbre he developed a certain symbolism of musical expression.

NOTES

1. The chief revisions in the main Allegro of the overture, 'Le Corsaire', were as follows.

In phase two of the second subject (min. sc., pages 21–24): woodwind entry in **B** flat-**C** minor (22 bars). This replaced what was originally an *episode*, of which the last 54 bars remain in script, the 54th being virtually the violin entry after the new 22 bars. This surviving portion consists of an extended and shapely cantabile in **A** minor, begun by the woodwind and passing to a three-octave line (flute, horn, violoncello). In bars 50–53 the oboe introduces (in **A** minor) the motive which the violins repeat in **C** (page 24). In the revised score, the latter appears as an extension of the motive already treated. Evidently Berlioz found the episode too diversionary at that point of exposition, and in casting round for a fresh theme was attracted to **Ex. 47.**2 and its economic possibilities. So

Ex. 47.1

Ex. 47.2

Ex. 47.3

to **Ex. 47.**1 and its extension, **Ex. 47.2**. But, as the editor of the 1900 edition failed to notice, three bars after **Ex. 47.2** Berlioz goes on, as initially planned, to a fresh and now solitary version of the episode in **C**, diminishing the first phrase to half its length and thus throwing into relief the sequel (**Ex. 47.3**). This leaves **Ex. 47.2** free for enough continuation to be worth breaking up with scales (pages 29–30).

This now short transition replaces what must have been a considerable interlude, of which the few surviving bars show the abandonment of a slower tempo (three beats) but no thematic clue. The almost instant entry of strings and wood for the reprise is there hurled forward by a brass entry a beat *earlier,* not simultaneously, as now. The succinct brass tune of the next section supersedes earlier ideas of expansion, as shown by Malherbe.

The repeat of **Ex. 47.1** (with a fresh bass counterpoint) replaces, as expected, a new episode, of which the extant start and finish point to a move to the present coda (violin **pp** syncopations, page 43 *et seq.*). Clearly **Ex. 47.1** represents continuity of formal statement, where at first there was just episode for episode or a longer coda.

In the coda, at the point where syncopated violins emerge from a blazing diminished seventh, 32 bars before the end (page 58), there was originally a general hold-up, followed by a three-beat *largo,* three bars' survival of which tells us little. A flash-back to the pre-reprise incident of hypothetical content is conceivable at this stage of uncreation; but the major event is the composer's realization that any halt at this juncture, of penultimate liquescent semitonal progression, would be fatal. Eight bars before the end, however, he altered a plain dactylic assertion of **C** major, *tutti,* to the present resurgence of ascending pairs of falling sixths, driving to the confident defiance of the expected by a blazing cadence in **A** flat (leading easily into **C** by way of **E** flat).

This summary of variant scripts and anti-scripts, as cited in the old edition, is enough to show at once Berlioz's concern for expository substance (as in the case of **Ex. 47**) and his ready dashes off the map, repudiated later. That there are no such signs of second thoughts in the *Francs Juges* or *Lear* overtures is simply due to the absence of the necessary scripts.

2. The eleven-plus recitatives and fragments which Berlioz wrote around 1842 to replace (by no means literally) the spoken interludes and interjections (act 2, finale) of *Le Freyschütz* (Schlesinger, 1842) occupy over 36 pages of the 183-page vocal score. This edition contains music

by both Berlioz (marked 'B') and Weber (marked 'W'). In the finale cited they coalesce. Berlioz's more positive additions to Weber's score may be briefly indicated in four of the longer links between the original numbers.

Act 1, scenes 1–2. Caspar's invocation of Zamiel: tremolo chords and wry semitonal modulation. Cunos's warning to Max of a coming test of his marksmanship: a spare half-beat motive, circling round the minor-third degree, to punctuate Cunos's recitative at each end.

Scenes 4–5. Caspar and the magic bullets in the wolf's glen: low tremolo chords and shrill piccolo flourishes on to the even beats (4/4).

Act 2, scenes 8–9. A worried Agatha: an affecting half-beat motive based on the initial **B B B B** and **B B C B** (**E** minor).

Act 3, scenes 15–16. Caspar climbs tree to check eventualities: orchestra follow him up. Max loads his gun: unstable tremolo harmony, propelled steadily by a persistent bass motive, ascending and descending, in a saccadic rhythm.

Unlike the German editors who made it their business, in a similar case, to supply *Béatrice et Bénédict* with the thematic adumbrations and echoes which his own recitatives lacked, Berlioz refrains from anticipating a coming number. He merely furnishes a passing motive or progression *ad hoc* to hold an incident or colloquy together, just as Weber himself does in his more developed ariosos. Berlioz adopted the same method in the music that he eventually supplied for the three spoken recitatives in *Benvenuto Cellini*, except that in the first (Act 1, scenes 3–4) he is more carried away as he annotates Teresa's agitation, using the fussy-Balducci motive of Scene 1 to confirm her words.

3. The actual status of the de Meyer-Berlioz *D'Isly* march is peculiar. In a letter to de Meyer of 3 December, 1845, written from Vienna, where the Marche Marocaine had just been given, Berlioz mentions having sent, and awaiting an acknowledgement of, the score of the *D'Isly*; and the march figures among the unpublished works in a list of Berlioz's compositions appended, at an uncertain date, to the published libretto of *The damnation of Faust* (1846). The only extant score, however, is a copyist's version, raised a semitone, in the Opera library, which shows a number of annotations, in a hand that may well be de Meyer's, but no trace of Berlioz's name or handwriting. Dr. Macdonald, who traced this connexion (Berlioz Society Bulletin 69), remarks that the scoring does not look an obviously Berlioz creation. Indeed, the assignment of the initial melodic line to oboe and clarinet, with flute and strings later, becomes a nonchalant and untypical routine. The only Berliozian touch is the open brass chords in the tutti in bars 128-31, 174-77, and in the peroration, in which a strong third in the final triad is more than audible. (For bar-references, see the original piano piece as published.)

The above list of unpublished works also cites an unperformed *Ouverture des Ciseleurs*, whose obvious analogy with the 'rescue' intentions of the *Roman Carnival* suggests some wishful thinking in aid of the wasted music of *Benvenuto Cellini*. No score has been traced, and it is doubtful if it was ever written.

Further entries of works as unpublished include various works known to have been published in 1848 or 1849, amongst them the *Te Deum*. Even if the list be datable 1847, the chronological stretch points to a stretch of fancy on the part of the here self-promoting composer. Thus the *Ciseleurs* may not have been written. Macdonald sifts the fluid dating implications, including the significance of a possibly Russian provenance for the *Te Deum* from the start, as it was for the second and last complete performance in the composer's lifetime.

175

Benvenuto Cellini and the Unfinished Operas

BEETHOVEN, dead set against any drama giocoso about lecherous nobles, found his first operatic objective in the glorious rescue of an innocent man from prison, in which he has been kept by an evil governor, by his wife, disguised as a man; justice is finally seen to have been done, the guilty punished, and brave conjugal devotion at mortal risk commended to all present. Beethoven was encouraged by *Fidelio* to work at some other libretto but one never materialized to his satisfaction.

As it happened, Berlioz also started operatic work, in his first main year of productivity (1828), with a full scenario by Ferrand dealing with the overthrow of a corrupt power (the Vehmic court of vigilantes in late medieval Germany) by an adventurous hero. Here the plot was more complex, and involved (in modern terms) a concerted and sophisticated invasion of the horrific seat of power by Lénor, the proscribed prince, supported by a populace somehow graciously conditioned to revolt against a ruthless usurping dictator, and by a nervously co-operative fiancée. Berlioz appears to have written about fifteen scenes of *Lénor ou les derniers francs juges*, only to learn that the Opera had turned down the libretto. In desperation—for he had thrown up his position in a vaudeville theatre chorus in order to finish the opera—with the help of Gounet, Berlioz reduced the whole scheme to a one-act Interlude, *La cri de guerre de Brisgau*, but no music has survived for this. Apart from an early concert performance of an aria and trio, and a steady revival of the overtures, Berlioz never heard even this fragment of his projected opera produced. (His chief hope was Karlsruhe, 1830.)

Of all this attack at a promising story of an encounter with fear, cruel oppression and the stoutest friendship, no more medieval to the Paris of 1828 than to audiences of today, the music of five scenes survives in script, with the torn-out pages of two other scenes. (Six scenes marked in the text 'music written' are missing.) The extant music, then, is as follows; all but one in full score (the late Leo Wurmser scored the trio for the British Broadcasting Corporation).[1]

Act 1. (1) Chorus: urgent appeal to the prince, now called Arnold, to free the country, and sudden abject homage to the approaching tyrant, Olmerick; (2) Duet:

Olmerick and a tough collaborator in eloquent illusory confidence in their colleague, Conrad, who has joined only to beat. Act 2. (3) Conventional, insouciant but melodious chorus of shepherds; (4) Equally placid trio: Arnold (disguised as shepherd) and two shepherdesses. Act 3. (5) First fragment: Arnold's invocation to sleep while waiting for action. (6) In the cavern: entry of the tribunal. Ritual hymn to ruthless vengeance. (7) Second fragment: salute to a triumphant Arnold by, presumably, rescuing guerillas.

Of these, Number 5 has been mentioned earlier as an odd source for the 'Oraison' of the fourth symphony. One can just identify the fifteen-odd bars which separate pairs of torn pages yield as isolated points in the 'Oraison', including the solo-part at the start of the sostenuto. In Number 7 a recurring theme is discernible, attached to radiant welcoming words such as 'Fier Germain, reprend tes vallons ... Le bonheur aujourd'hui sourit!' This major-key motive is not, as expected, the big tune in the overture. On the contrary, it can only be identified elsewhere in the prelude to the carnival scene in *Cellini* (bars 10, 15) and later in the perky figure when the chorus cry 'Moccolo, Moccoli' against the duly prepared monk-to-monk confusion. Evidently Berlioz decided that his originally joyous tune must know its place as a witty propelling figure in an ensemble of complication.

It will be observed that all these scenes are quite detached and almost incompatible, matching the cold war of liberation underground in collaborator territory. Today they must be heard, when they are heard—on the radio, say—as bits and pieces in a grim but quite incomplete document in secret resistance to usurped authority, seasoned with a neutralist pastoral calm. Each number has a refrain or is downright strophical: there is a recurring formality of expression. The judges' symmetrical chorus is inadequate. By contrast, the change from the heroic **C** minor of the people's appeal to Arnold to the **D** flat minor of their cowering at Olmerick's approach is the most striking and timeless line in the script.

Before the judges' chorus, they enter to the sound of a 'marche lugubre'. Or earlier in Act 3 Arnold, having got his sleep, has a confused dream that includes the march of Olmerick's bodyguard. A reference in *Symphonie Fantastique* to a 'Marche des gardes', before the March, and to a 'marche des gardes d'Olmerick' in Arnold's dream, have led to a common assumption, started by Boschot but disputed by Tiersot (*Le Ménestrel*, 1906, pages 199-246; *Mus. Quarterly*, July 1933), that the *Symphonie Fantastique* march was taken from *Les francs juges*, with the *idée fixe* crudely attached. I remain unconvinced. There is no evidence in any libretto of a march in the opera as 'music composed'; and it is difficult or impossible to place such a developed march after Olmerick's approach, in Arnold's dream, or before the judges' chorus, a mysterious scene precluding a long preludial march. However, as an event in the theatre of cruelty the *Symphonie Fantastique* march certainly qualifies. Its suitability in *Symphonie Fantastique* has already been debated.

All this frustration of his creative work left Berlioz no less attracted to dramatic, if not strictly theatrical, scenes as musical stimuli. So to *Faust* music; first for the ballet scenario offered, then select *Scenes*. Then, after three competition cantatas, all as dramatic as possible, a free fantasia on *The Tempest*. Not till after writing the first two symphonies, however, did Berlioz begin on the opera which should have established him (in 1838) as the leading composer of France, and indeed of Europe, if the *Requiem* of 1837 had not already done so.

The opera has been the subject of vicissitudes on at least two levels. First, the original production. Apart from the shilly-shallying of managements and pressure groups which ended with acceptance at the Opéra, not the Opéra comique, performances were not only a short run but a première of low potential. With a cabal to reduce the opening night to barnyard noises, and a Cellini who was not only no actor but also incredibly frivolous in his approach, it was not easy for the opera to rise above the ground. After an enthusiastic but by no means packed audience at the third performance, criticism stopped crabbing the libretto and became more positive. 'A new continent', declared Auguste Morel in the *Journal de Paris*, and in *L'artiste* (October, 1838), Chandes-Aigues shrewdly contrasted Meyerbeer's useful eclecticism with Berlioz's creative quality (Barzun). Yet even if he agreed, it was not easy for a manager to favour the creative opera if the eclectic brand was three times the draw. *Cellini* was dropped. The first revival was a brief triumph at Weimar under Liszt in 1852, in a revised edition. In 1853 Berlioz conducted the work (in Italian) at Covent Garden in the presence of the Queen and the Prince Consort. It was hissed more than it was heard, throughout. Not until 1880 did the opera become established in a repertory in German houses up to 1914. Covent Garden made handsome amends in its bold revival, December 1966. Meanwhile there had been pioneer revivals by the Carl Rosa Company since the War. Yet English recognition of the opera as a master-work must be regarded as in lively process rather than an accomplished event.

Secondly, the opera exists, and has been performed, in three distinct versions, of which only the second is now available in vocal score.

(1) The 1838 score is preserved in script. Only the libretto was printed.

(2) The Weimar version was contained in the Litolff edition of the vocal score (French and German) of 1856. Choudens published a French edition around 1863, repeated in 1885, and somewhat amplified in the 1950 edition. A full score published in 1886 remains the only one ever in print, pending the new edition.

(3) Recently a conflation of (2, above) with the recovery of certain lost elements

of (1, above) has been worked out, and this was first performed at Covent Garden in December 1966, appreciably altering the balance of certain turns in the music-drama. This version will, no doubt, figure in the first critical edition of the full score, to appear in the new collected edition. Meanwhile its impact has begun to radiate from the Royal Opera House, for what it is worth. (The House Librarian has kindly allowed me to peruse the new scores in use.)

These differences may as well be summarized at once in order that a listener may know what he may be hearing, in or from the opera-house, and what printed edition he may be studying. For this purpose the accessible 1950 edition is the inevitable common ground of reference, here and in the rest of this chapter. The 1838 scenario (libretto) has accordingly been stated in terms of its own and of the 1950 numbering, then the 1950 score in itself, then the 1966 version in terms of 1950, then 1966 in its actual numbering, conforming for two acts and then augmenting or re-grouping sufficiently to call for a typical re-numbering.

Table 6

Stage Setting	1838		1950 Equivalent of 1838		1950		1950 Equivalent of 1966		1966	
In Balducci's house	Act 1	1–7	Act 1	1–4	Act 1	1–4	Act 1	1+, 2–3, 4+	Act 1	1–4
Piazza Colonna	Act 1	8–13	Act 2	5 6–8	Act 2	5 6–8	Act 2	5 6+, 7, 8++	Act 2	5 6–8
Cellini's Studio	Act 2	1–6	Act 3	12–14	Act 3	9–10 11–14, 15	Act 3	9, 12+ +13++, 14++	Act 3	9–12
The Foundry	Act 2	7–9, 12, 20	Act 3	11, 15, 10b, 16	Act 3	16	Act 4	Entracte (new) 11, 15, 10b, Extra 16++	Act 4	13–18

It may be added that the 1950 score does not contain, firstly, four recitatives which occur in Acts 1, 2 (twice) and 3, which Berlioz had to set for the Opéra, having originally intended them to be spoken (at the Opéra Comique). These are found in the Litolff edition and in the Choudens full score. In the 1966 version they are spoken or omitted. Secondly, an entracte at the start of Act 2 is found only in the full score. Also, the 1950 score is maddeningly short on any stage indications, even the identification of the characters.

In this obvious context of fluid creation, we may return to Berlioz at the start. Odd contacts with Florentine popular songs and a reading of Cellini's *Memoirs* (French trans., 1822) convinced him that selected scenes were the stuff of the opera that he wished to write. Auguste Barbier and Leon de Wailly drafted the verses, with some assistance from de Vigny, but it is safe to say that it was Berlioz's opera. He wanted contrasted scenes which called for set song, speech-song, movement-music, and orchestral development, each characteristic enough to contribute its portion of music-drama; songs, also, which released popular feeling as well as the sentiments and reactions of leading persons. Such comparatively set deliveries would be connected by a minimum of explanatory recitatives, and these never with a perfunctory keyboard attendance, though a break into speech might be convenient.

The career of Cellini was manifestly stimulating for stage settings: the dis-approved suitor of Teresa, the daughter of a rich official at the papal court, heading for trouble but also passionate declarations; yet none the less a proud and re-spected craftsman, capable of destroying his work rather than hand it over to another, as he is penultimately threatened may happen. (He is utterly unlike the mixed-up Walther von Stolzing, courting a rich man's daughter and then prepared to profess 'master-singer' aspirations when he finds it expedient; made credible, in fact, only because he identifies with Richard Wagner, the genius rejected by the Hanslicks and entitled to exclusive room at the top.) His opponents are Balducci, the father, and Fieramosca, the father's choice for Teresa. Both are comic figures; one is pompous and mock-worthy (in the carnival), and the other a sly coward. In contrast Ascanio, a far from studious boy apprentice—no David he—makes a nonchalant ally. The towering figure of the Pope (changed to Cardinal in 1838, 1852, etc., and back to Pope in 1966) stiffly augments the third act. The Shrove Tuesday crowd unceasingly spill around, enjoying the show, then aroused by a murder by a person unknown (Cellini has killed Fieramosca's mate under provoca-tion), and altogether carry a revealing supra-personality. The apprentices celebrate the accomplished artefact, *Perseus*, with simple ardour, incidentally fulfilling the sub-title, 'or the Master-Goldsmiths of Florence' (taken to Rome at papal command). Cellini's final triumph, the demonstrable product of unflagging workmanship and (in the sacrifice of past works to make up raw material in time) of uncompromising choice—under the threat of execution if he fails—is a vindication of the dedicated artist's life, and as such a highly distinctive operatic finish after all the conventional resolutions of usually amorous suspense or again the invocation of a *deus ex machina* to rule out a tragically inexorable fate.

The hazardous arrival at this level of existence after the opening incident of an overheard elopement plan and the ensuing train of popular amusements, misleading disguises, and a fiancée's anxiety over the escape from justice of her beloved, all tends to suggest that Berlioz was not outwardly a reformer of the French stage. Nor would he have been helped by a more specifically art-concerned plot, such as informs the audacious candicacy and progressive liberalizing influences of *Die Meistersinger* and promotes the recurrence of many songs in peculiarly set and preserved style. Berlioz's creative handling lay in the provision of characteristic music that furthers the observer's perception of scene or dramatic action and at the same time adds up sufficiently meanwhile (in the second act especially) to reach the ultimate crisis, for Cellini and all who admire him, with a superlative sense of rhythm in reserve.

Not, it may be said at once, of theme, or even of thematic turn, in reserve. Apart from the Pope's motive, which reverberates from the overture for his confrontation with Cellini, the only thing that comes back is a verse from the apprentices' song in Act 2, for the curtain song. Berlioz had no intention of sweating-out motives, as he had done in some measure in his first two symphonies. On the contrary, he favoured the notion of symmetrically or capriciously developing but still self-contained numbers, in steady juxtaposition apart from recitatives, with closer knit successions of events breaking out as significant focal expressions. On this dramatically stop-go method, there is no pretence at being realistic all the time. Cellini is not less Cellini when, alone, he appeals to 'love' to guard Teresa, or when, left to finish the statue in quick time but, credibly, loth to get going, he dreams of a quiet pastoral existence—not less himself than when he is planning (repetitively) elopement with Teresa or, in answer to his own prayer, heaving his past works in the furnace for a final effort, in which the orchestra carry the main burden. *Verismo* is not a crucial test here. What matters is the musical experience called into being by each genre of vocal situation, and its reaction on later numbers. We may assume that Berlioz was incapable of setting a book in which he did not believe, fundamentally. But as far as he identified with Cellini and his jostling companions and opponents, he was only on the fringe of releasing what was on his mind, consciously or lying in reserve.

Berlioz uses two main methods for securing musical continuation. First, the strophical pattern. On their own scale, straightforward, instant repetitions mark the airs, in Act 2, of Cellini (**5**) and of Ascanio-with-ensemble (**6**). (These and following numbers refer to the 1950 edition of Operatic Numbers in the score of *Benvenuto Cellini*.) The former (an extra for Weimar) stiffly formal, even orchestrally, the latter re-inforced by massive re-texturing in the second verse. In most cases, an unmistakable sense of recurrent strophe is qualified by variant finishes or positive interludes, including, possibly, an abandonment of aria. This blend of free-wheeling and fresh progression persists in each act.

Act 1. Teresa's two airs show two balances of refrain and episode in emotionally opposite contexts. In the duet-trio that follows on well-trodden lines of lyrical, orderly dissent, an outburst of passionate argument, seasoned by Fieramosca's asides, conveniently breaks up the air before the plunge into the rapt third verse, incidentally enhanced by a close canon in soprano or tenor. Further, a background of liquescent violin harmony is picked out by wind syncopation. In the ensuing trio, the coherence of the basic proposition to elope, overheard by Fieramosca, is confirmed by a complete *da capo* later, with extensions in which the connivance of Fieramosca in the plot against himself makes a good histrionic moment as well as a compulsive ensemble. It is all deftly scored. *Act 2*. The Goldsmiths' Guild song (**6**) provides (in varied scoring) the recurrent signature-tune of their 'union', with a rousing climax (**Ex. 50.2**, see page 189). Fieramosca's heroics blend with tender passion and a demonstrative sword-play in erratic metre (**7**). The show people's chorus in the carnival has already been summarized as a developed quasi-symphonic movement, virtually a composite strophe with its ample reprise (**Ex. 46**, page 164). In the second scene the disconsolate apprentices sing a yodelling song of the sea with an 'after-song' to its strophes (approaching the established pattern of a *Bar*). *Act 3*, Ascanio's solo-air (**11**) wittily blends a steady flow of exquisitely nonchalant melancholy (**Ex. 50.3**, page 190) with pictures of Florence (his friend's destination) and lightning impersonations of his acquaintances. Then, as an antidote to Cellini's narrative of exhausting adventure, he and Teresa break into a jubilant duet, dreaming of the victory of the 'Tuscan eagle' over all attack in a vivid passage which in the second verse finds its ecstatic rejoinder (**13**). The Pope's initial pronouncement has its inevitable refrain, with the orchestral off-beat background nicely tempered by a flow of clarinet in the second verse, but this is instantly superseded by dialogue (**14**). Cellini's well-known closing air, 'Sur les monts', is a spacious succession of two open-ended strophes; sealed by a closing phrase and a succinct after-verse.[2] It is the soloist's last vocal opportunity (**Ex. 50.5**) before he has to become a wonder-boy at work, capable only of ejaculatory communication.

As they occur, these various resorts to self-contained utterance, depending on symmetrical stretches of melodic assertion, simple or complex, will be recognized for what they are, as factors of stability in a wide range of dramatic contexts, nervous, combative, hilarious, ecstatic. They represent the most immediately intelligible elements in the opera for the alert listener. By the same token they are also the most susceptible to the wear and tear of performance, especially where repetition is predictable. In this context, Teresa's first air and duet in Act 1, Cellini's air and the 3-verse guild-song in Act 2, the Pope's air in Act 3, betray an insipid quality of texture, enhanced in the later verses in spite of orchestral changes.

The other method of development is more chancy, and depends on the emergence of rhythms and motives in support of a given dialogue or encounter. This is found on the smallest scale in a few link-recitatives (nos. **3** init., **6** med., **8** med., **12** init., **14** fin.) and in four recitatives compiled for performance at the Opera, where spoken word was not acceptable, and included in the Litolff vocal score (1856), but omitted from all Chouden's editions except the full score. (They occur before nos. **4, 7, 8** and **14**.) But it is an essential part of Berlioz's craft that this instrumental process does not slip out of control. A plain 4-bar bass phrase, apt for transportation, introduces a fussy, worried Balducci, incidentally without inhibitions about referring to the hat and gloves, the wearing of which are so important to the character; a provocative feature for the composer's opponents. A suitably minatory, fist-shaking rhythm informs the hue and cry of the modern Bacchantes after the alleged libertine, Fieramosca, and the incisive phrases of the chorus, against whirling scales in the strings, do what is needed to leave Fieramosca where he belongs, in the fountain unless he escapes, as he does. In Act 2, after the guild-song, the angry argument with the inn-keeper over the wine-bill is maintained by a flow of importunate and imprecatory matter (woodwind, tutti), controlled by cadences in unrelated keys, until Ascanio arrives with a money-bag, a full reminder of the strings attached to its enjoyment, and a song to establish the position. The wine debt settled, and a clowning vengeance planned on Balducci for his mean allowance on the statue-work (recitative), an orchestrally festive return to the last verse of the guild-song ends the scene.

Fieramosca having shown to his mate, Pompeo, what a bonny fighter and lover he wishes to be considered, the carnival scene begins to unfold. It falls into five stages. (a) Short songs of Balducci and Teresa, combined and extended in a loquacious ensemble, in which Ascanio and Cellini join, disguised as monks. (b) The chorus of show people and townsfolk (as in *Roman Carnival* overture). (c) Cassandro's pantomime of Midas and the singing award. Harlequin's refined arietta in mime (oboe) sends Midas-Balducci to sleep, while he gives the crown to ass-eared Pasquarello for his preposterous cavatina (tuba nobilmente); a blunt swipe at academic awards, and at the arch-comic Rossini. Balducci chases the actors, to the crowd's satisfaction (blown up by the orchestra). (d) Teresa now faces, each bent on elopment with her, *two* pairs of monks in brown and white (Cellini, Ascanio, Fieramosca, Pompeo)—promoted by bustling woodwind, angry strings and a perky theme, salvaged from *Francs Juges* (see page 178), to match the crossing advance of torchbearers but useful also later. In the struggle Cellini (white) kills Pompeo (brown) and becomes a man under arrest, with inevitably opposite and simultaneous reactions of the rival parties. (e) Crowd feelings now find voice in two musical stages: firstly, 'arrest this monk-murderer'; secondly, Cellini having escaped under cover of the darkness-order, signalled by guns, the confusion is celebrated, with contrary motives, by all parties in literal or virtual unison, reinforced by the later seizure of the still available white monk, Fieramosca. For these two sections Berlioz draws initially on motives first developed in his early Mass for the words in the Creed, 'Et iterum venturus est' and 'Cuius regni non erit finis', in a vision of final judgement. I re-quote the second.

Ex. 5

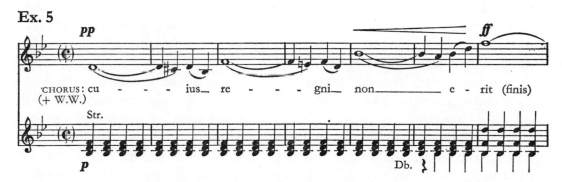

The virtual transcription can only be justified on the assumption that Berlioz thought the early music inadequate for the vision but right for the present confusion of purposes, as indicated by 'Assassiner un capucin' and 'Ah! cher canon', 'Ah! quelle nuit noire.' (Barzun makes the frivolous suggestion that Judgement Day in Rome might be equally confusing.) The only way of accepting this finale is to forget these early associations, and to observe, in the second stage in particular, a blunt sense of suspense in the successive maintenance of one chord in various keys in a forthright rhythm, without any resolution of the chord concerned. In these somewhat equivocal terms **Ex. 5**, oscillatory in pitch until it reaches the home-key (**C** flat, **A**, **B** flat, **E** flat), releases a growing convergence of crowd consciousness in a hectic orchestral atmosphere of which the divided dramatic interest would fall to the producer to clarify. The rest is a matter of modulation and cadence, orchestral punctuation (a crisp trochaic 'Ah! Dieu!') and brilliant climax. Thus, after a diversionary course, acceptable as a statement of the distractions under which the main objective (elopement) is pursued, the music quickly concentrates on a release of a single, almost ecstatic mood. The whole scene is a new vindication of opera in what we may call a slow cinematic style. Compared, as it sometimes has been, with the skilfully organic scheme of *Meistersinger*, Act 2 finale, this easy-going carnival may sound like playing by ear. Yet the sense of succession and proportion does not falter here. Berlioz clearly regarded the use of a motive, destined for plugging, however subtle, as an aesthetic liability.

The outstanding problem of introducing a big finale midway is to go on without a sense of leading from weakness. *Act 3* is, indeed, inclined to be desultory up to Ascanio's air. A minor-key version of the guild-song and a grumbling men's chorus establish a sombre tone of some quality, but I have missed the 'enchanting melancholy' (W. J. Turner) of their feckless ensuing song (**10**). After Ascanio's gambolling song, a delicious interlude for any occasion, he, confident, and Teresa, fearful, while away the suspense at Cellini's non-appearance by listening to monks approaching and mumbling their litanies on a monotone, but the two on stage add a shapely prayer on their own; a typical conflation of rhythms, flecked by some striking modulations in aid of brighter plainsong, but otherwise jejune. At last Cellini's arrival raises the temperature.

In a burst of instrumental expressiveness, in which a semitonal descent in the bass is the connecting link in a progression of vibrant viola harmony (**Ex. 50.4**, page 190), later richly reinforced by trombones and woodwind, Berlioz contrives to convey Cellini's recollections of his perilous escape and then his (to Teresa) appalling exhaustion. As Tiersot pointed out long ago, there is a slight parallel with Tannhäuser's narration of his journey to Rome, not least between the flute delivery of the salvation-to-penitents motive (representing the bells of salvation to the sound of which Tannhäuser awoke in Rome) and the rather similar flute ascent to mark Cellini's recovery of his senses as brought home to him in the glittering roofs and crowing cocks which diverted the groundlings in 1838. It is perhaps more relevant to note that in Wagner a closely packed flute-oboe group announces the new salvation motive, already thundered out by brass in the act's prelude and now good for three short stretches of distinctive rhythm; whereas in Berlioz an impromptu, naïve 8-bar phrase hovers in the flute (with clarinet/oboe support) against shimmering violins and violas, obliterating, indeed, the singing cocks, but signifying chiefly 'I am a flute in my right compass', or, if conjecture is needed, 'to the devil with the Pope and his statue', as Cellini instantly declares to a reluctant Ascanio. In such a devil-may-care mood Cellini and Teresa proceed to their delirious declaration of mutual aid and defiance of authority (extensively prepared by another and contrasted air in the 1966 version).

The descent of Balducci and Fieramosca on Cellini, Ascanio and a supplicatory Teresa makes a short scene of altercation, with Balducci's remonstrances supported by light explosions in the violins and Cellini's threats to kill Fieramosca crowned by a noisy *tutti*, plunging from a pivotal, bustling chord of **F** to a dynamic **A** flat, augmented by upper brass and rolling-drum harmony. So to the Pope's unctuous entry with a calm message of pardon and 'clemency', soon to be interrupted by accusations of murder preferred by one party and rebutted by the other. The Pope here maintains a pontifical tone (clarinet) but not a judicial one. But he exploits Cellini's plight by ordering him to produce the statue forthwith, or lose the job to another. When the incensed Cellini in his turn threatens, under arrest, to smash his model, his patron agrees to grant him pardon, his freedom, the hand of Teresa, and one more chance to finish the statue in the hour agreed, on pain of death. The inquiry into the unfinished statue is at first conducted in a racy Allegro molto, with a catchy phrase in the bass to match Cellini's pleading, which returns in the strings as the company gazes aghast at his uplifted hammer. Otherwise, Cellini's explosions find impromptu settings. The Pope's portentous theme (confusing, rhythmically, in its opposition to the clear 4-bar metre of the rest) is spelt out by Cellini in quiet irony at the 'indulgence' he is receiving. The number packs up in urgent recitative as the Pope sets all in train, Fieramosca included.

Cellini's response, a tranquil and extended escapist air, has been already described as the singer's opportunity. (There is an unfinished score of the number, transposed a fifth down, to suit a baritone who wanted to sing it?) Dramatically, the air is a fantastic hold-up. But at last the foundry is exposed and work has begun, as the orchestra testify. Run out of metal, Cellini prays for guidance, and finds it in the necessity to make do with all he has in his workshop. (But what kind of guidance induces a sculptor to break his mould directly after the molten metal has run into it?) The orchestra set to work again, this time with no bravura setting but with steady concentration on their short imitational theme (**Ex. 50.**6, page 190). In a trice (almost) the *Perseus* is completed. 'Victoire!', with wooden sticks pounding on the drums. Cellini almost worships his handiwork. The Pope grants his pardon and is shown out. Cellini and Teresa exchange quick greetings. After which, can there be anything but a verse of the guild-song? Berlioz decided so, but it is an easy way out. There is a coda of two bars.

This last act can only be described as patchy. The dramatically eventful but fragmentary Number **14** (after the duet) has to wait for Number **16** for its resolution; and the foundry-scene, as a finale, seems perfunctory, compared with either the forging songs of *Siegfried* or the ample but unpredictable reverberations of *Meistersinger*. It is a strong testimony to *Benvenuto Cellini's* solid worth and to German liberalism that it became a repertory work in twenty German towns, up to 1914, presumably in part because of its resemblance to *Meistersinger*. It must none the less be pointed out that Cellini's plan to enjoy life and to win Teresa, occupying two acts and more, and last minute devotion to sculpture, can hardly compare in consistency with the laborious musical apprenticeship of the amorous Walther under

David and Sachs and in contrast to Beckmesser's misguided academicism. It still seems necessary to correct a facile tendency to group the two music-dramas together. Cellini's citizenship is questioned, but never his masterful craft, so long as it is being exercised as agreed.

So much for the long established Weimar *Cellini* currently in print. But something must now be said about the 1838–1966 *Cellini*, the course of which was summarized, in terms of the 1950 vocal score or Weimar version, on page 180 and will continue to be discussed in the same terms. The order of events in the third scene has been altered by the postponement of Numbers **10** and **11**, and by leaving Number **14** as the termination of a greatly augmented third act. In the final scene, now the fourth act, a new juxtaposition of Numbers **11**, **15** and **10** leads to fresh matter and an expanded Number **16**. The main upshot is that the third scene is altogether repointed, and the fourth enriched up to the proportions of an act, instead of being tacked on to the third.

The most striking additions are, first, the duet in Act 3, prodigally preceding the established duet (**13**). (As one of the nine numbers published in 1838 (arr. Morel), it is surprising that it was dropped at Weimar.) Here Teresa and Cellini seek mutually to safeguard their position to the tune of 'Ah! le ciel se declare pour nous', to which they return in conclusion. (**Ex. 50.7**, page 191). The traumatic past can be shed. Thus the jubilant 'Quand des sommets . . . l'aigle', instead of exploding suddenly (with one chord to establish the key) after Ascanio's exit to prepare for a get-out, now comes as a release of growing confidence that all will be well; and only the pedantic listener will grumble about the switch of metaphors. (Rather similarly *in reverse*, the sudden ecstatic duet in *Fidelio*, act 2, no. **15**, was originally (1805 version) shrewdly prepared.)

At the end of this act comes a spirited wrangle between the Pope and Cellini, reinforced by the other parties with messages of comfort and discomfort for Cellini, leaving the pontiff's threat hanging heavily in the air.

In the fourth act, now freshly consolidated, after the postponed song of the sea (**10b**) the workmen have a sustained encounter with a Fieramosca who offers them better terms. The orchestra start up a theme taken up by the men (imitationally) to the cry 'we never close', resembling the abandoned Number **9** chorus (**Ex. 50.9**, page 191). The semitonal movement round one note voices their return to the furnace, and prepares for the crucial casting scene. This final scene has been amplified, after Fieramosca's panicky cry, 'no more metal!', by fresh scorning comment from Balducci and Fieramosca, and by further taunts when Cellini appears to be totally 'sunk'; just enough to delay the pièce de résistance and subsequent celebrations.

Poised thus between the quest for the marriage of his choice, the escape from the law and the fulfilment of his art-commission, Cellini carries the day through four compulsive scenes, attended by concerted opposition, popular sport and anger, judicial prelate and, at all points, supporting parties and his bride-to-be. In trying to pick out brief tokens of the music which most impresses on the spectator the variety of mood, there is no question of listing clue-themes. The Pope's theme and the guild-song, the slightly recurring features, are brought home by sheer repetition. One is a bare one, the other a symmetrical strophe, varied chiefly in type of instrument setting. But something must be put on record, besides **Ex. 46** (see page 164)

50.1 Refrain from Teresa's second air
50.2 Conclusion of guild-song (act 2, no. **6**; act 3, no. **16**)
50.3 Part of the refrain of Ascanio's second song (act 3, no. **11**)
50.4 Opening of Cellini's narrative (act 2, no. **12**)
50.5 Second phrase of Cellini's last song, as in Verses 1 and 2
50.6 Last stage of the casting
50.7 Repeat in additional air inserted before Act 3, number **13**
50.8 Fugue-subject in the addition to Act 3, number **14**
50.9 Theme in additional workers-scene before Act 3, number **16**

Ex. 50.1

Ex. 50.2

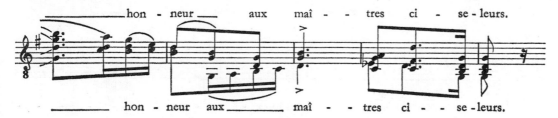

Ex. 50.3

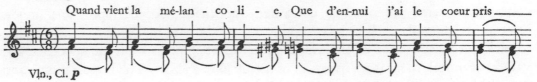

Ex. 50.4

Ex. 50.5

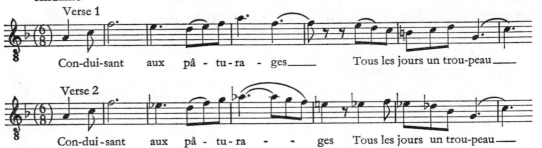

Ex. 50.6

Ex. 50.7

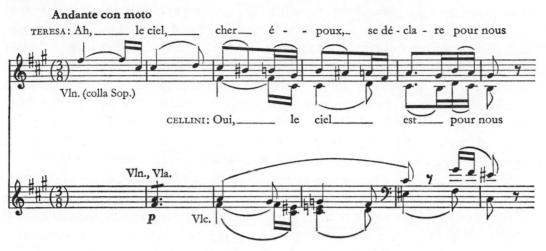

Ex. 50.8

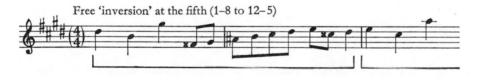

Ex. 50.9

If these quotations seem to play down the more conventional numbers, they also ignore the by no means scarce scenes where juxtaposition and repartee are of the essence. The 1966 production made the most of the piquant incidents that surround the more formal musical events, witnessing the unparalleled buoyancy of Berlioz's invention, eclectic only on the surface.

In 1839 Berlioz based his third symphony on *Romeo and Juliet*, as a pioneer work in stage-struck music that proceeded on its own quasi-symphonic course. But he then turned back to the stage, and provisionally accepted (in advance) an opera book, *La Nonne Sanglante* (henceforward *The Nun*), from Eugène Scribe, a leading librettist. *The Nun* was based on *The Monk*, a novel by Matthew Lewis, an Englishman who had been in useful contact with Goethe and Schiller (and *Faust*). Berlioz wrote the music for some numbers of the first two acts planned, but was then held up by Scribe, who was not going to waste his talent on a composer who had not made good at the opera. In the end Berlioz returned the book to Scribe, who, after having had it refused by Halévy and Meyerbeer (out of courtesy to Berlioz) had it accepted by Gounod, who set it in 1854. (As it chanced, another Monk opera, *Raymond and Agnes*, by Edward Loder, appeared in 1855. It was revived in 1966.)

Berlioz thus began work on a scenario in which the main objective is the elopement of Agnes, daughter of a medieval baron, with Rodolphe de Luddorf, brother of the man to whom she has been betrothed by her father; and the method of escape is disguise. In this case, however, it is Agnes who is to be disguised—as Agnes, the wounded nun wraith who is believed to roam at midnight, walking through doors left open for her. Rodolphe plans that the real Agnes shall appear under this cover, seize him and sweep him away, unchallenged. (In the event the *phantom* Agnes does just this, leaving confusion behind her, but we are not concerned with that.) The monk of the title, Hubert, plays a passive role as Rodolphe's travelling companion. The music of which the score survives, not completely in the last two numbers, amounts to three separate scenes; the last to be followed by a finale which never materializes.

1. (a) Dialogue: Hubert (bass) and an agitated Rodolphe (tenor).
   (b) Air: Hubert calms Rodolphe.

2. (a) Monologue and air: Rodolphe rouses himself from despair to a fiery, fearless devotion.
   (b) Dialogue: Rodolphe and a hopeless Agnes (soprano).

3. (a) Duet. First air and dialogue. Rodolphe, Agnes in ecstatic desperation. Rodolphe's plan appals her.
   (b) Second air. Agnes retails the nun legend.
   (c) First air (v. 3) and dialogue. Rodolphe and Agnes face the consequences. Rodolphe details plan.
   (d) Second air (vv. 3 and 4, unfinished). Rodolphe adds a new verse to the *Nun* legend. Agnes breaks down.

Musically, Hubert's sanctimonious air has a plain serenity, skilfully accompanied; Rodolphe's air is a vigorous tale of stoicism, tempered by a dream of distant happiness (like Cellini's in kind); the 'duet' promises to be a rich interplay of two different moods, the second counter-balancing the first in two stages. Nevertheless, one doubts the potentiality of such a false situation; the rational exploitation of the legend at once disposes of any serious suggestion of a guilt obsession. A glance at Gounod's completed score, with its many and humorous touches and cliché figures, at once confirms these rejections. So unfinished a half-work has little chance even of a studio revival, pending the filling of gaps. But one can only rejoice that Scribe never encouraged Berlioz to continue so artificial a plot. A genuine legend is a valid concern, but a manipulation of it into waking life is a farcical confusion and no music can rescue it from that state.

One can only conclude that Berlioz had to discover these operatic snags the hard way, before he resumed and greatly expanded his operatic repertory on the wings of Shakespeare and Virgil.

During rehearsals of *Cellini* Berlioz sketched some music for an interlude, *Erigone*, originating in the fifth book of a vast and extravagantly symbolic prose-poem by Pierre Ballanche. Erigone is a young and lovely maenad, madly in love with Orpheus as the only being who can bring her back to sanity. Around her are the Bacchantes whose secret fire she shares. Berlioz compiled a scenario and a versification of his plot as far as one scene of five pages, but the only music that he has left to follow this is a continuous but fragmentary sketch of a soprano chorus, consisting of a short but tense and rhythmic section (three voice parts in **D** minor), an interlude in or converging in **E** minor and exhibiting only the first soprano, and a well pointed reprise (three parts) with a coda in **D** major, partly lacking in the lower parts. This is in declaration of the ruthless confidence of the maenads, identifying with Erigone, in their cult and in the worship of Orpheus. All this emerges at the foot of otherwise blank pages of a 25-stave score. Berlioz so far allowed his initial impulse to flop. One is almost reduced to observing, quite irrelevantly, that the two bars after the initial repeat, 'chantons sans rivales, frappons les cymbales' were kept (15 years) for intensification in the course of *The Trojans*, Act I, Scene 1. As it stands, the movement sounds just a minatory-potential note. (There is almost a decided snarl in the background.) One can understand that after telling Gounet in 1834 that he found Ballanche sheer mystical nonsense, Berlioz, contending with his operatic world, warmed to this intimation, however sensationally conveyed, of the fatal and aggressive hold that an obsessive passion for music can produce on one's life; an intimation with which he had so eloquently begun his career in *La Mort d'Orphée*. But now, for reasons unknown, he could not summon creative energy enough to amplify his first thought about the new scenario. Here, anyhow, he was not dependent on orchestral texture, and there is no parallel to this spare appeal to musical perception in a quasi-dramatic situation.

NOTES

1. Wurmser has set the first verse pizzicato, with woodwind sustaining halfway; the second verse *arco* similarly, with the rhythmic figure in the right hand part assigned to oboe or clarinet, with bassoon halfway; the third verse to violin arpeggios, lower string pizzicato and horn filling; with additions, in the choral entry, of violin-woodwind doubling of the choral soprani, general filling-in, and triangle. (I have been able to check these details of a radio performance through the courtesy of Mr. J. H. Davies of the British Broadcasting Corporation music library.)

2. An unexplained autograph in the Bodleian quotes this closing phrase (Cellini's 'Comme aux bras d'une mère/Je dormirais content'), without words, in isolation, in **A**.

12

Béatrice et Bénédict

BERLIOZ's next completed opera was *Les Troyens* (1856–58). *Béatrice et Bénédict* followed in 1860–62. Berlioz had abandoned his undertaking in 1859 to Bénazet, the Baden entrepreneur, to write an opera on the Thirty Years War (book by the popular Édouard Plouvier) but agreed to produce a work 'de demi-caractère' for the inauguration of a new theatre. (That way, he hoped, lay the route to the Paris Opera.) For this purpose he returned to a sketch of situations that he had made from *Much Ado* in 1833. He now composed the music.

While *Troyens* thus stands next in order to *Cellini*, it is so manifestly the fulfilment of Berlioz's life work that poetic justice demands its reservation for the last chapter on specific works. For the composer, no doubt, the writing of the Shakespeare 'opera' that he envisaged was something of a release after the tremendous coverage of *Troyens*. The grounds for this opinion may appear later, but a glance at the plot of *Béatrice et Bénédict* is suggestive. It is concerned mainly with a conspiracy to overcome the hindrances to a recognition of true love between two people whose reluctance lies in themselves; two of the conspirators being openly in love with each other, though only the woman (Hero) is articulately so, and she is supported by Ursula, her lady in waiting. The sardonic theme surely appealed to the dry humour of a composer who had known so much about the chequered course of ardent love. Hence the choice of a slice of *Much Ado*, though without Shakespeare's scheme of motivation. The remainder of the plot, or rather of the scenario, hangs on the gratuitous intrusion of a 'humorous' old ass of a conductor, Somarone, conceivably a blown-up Balthasar (without 'Sigh no more, ladies'). While being a far from unwilling performer, Somarone is about as irrelevant to the main action. Don John's lying and malicious attack on Hero's virtue, resulting in Claudio's rejection of her, with all the counter-strategy on which the suspense of *Much Ado* depends, does not figure. Claudio is vocally a mere participant, and much of the sharp wit of the organized hearsay and direct dialogue which bring the awkward couple together is missing. The snatches of spoken dialogue, which ranges from the first to the last scene of *Much Ado*,[1] suggest some action, but they do not shape the music, which accrues, rather, as a kind of recurrent bonus. Also, the problem that singers are not necessarily good actors or speakers is unusually acute here. The constant musical feature is the masterly, caressing, crackling orchestration. It goes far to match the needle-sharp caprice by which the composer defined his artistic intentions. Yet Berlioz's response to *Shakespeare* is lacking in invention.

In the first act, apart from two pairs of light choruses and a restless Sicilienne for orchestra which also serves as an entracte, there are airs for Hero (soprano) and Benedict (tenor), duets for Beatrice (mezzo-soprano) and Benedict, and for Hero and Ursula (contralto), and a trio for Benedict, Claudio (baritone) and Pedro (bass). Of these Hero's devotional, confident air (3) is a comparatively conventional blend of absorbed larghetto and joyful, triumphant allegro, supported by trumpets. The first duet (4) moves with slick Italian agility from Benedict's fluent rejoinder to Beatrice on disdain to a vivacious allegro. But the extended Trio (6) is the greater tour de force in its construction of a main, brisk allegretto and briefly contrasted tempi, continued in a nicely rescored allegretto (see **Ex. 51.1**, page 198) and further improvizations. This, to match a cascade of sub-satirical dialogue, starting with 'I marry? God forgive me.'

Benedict's air (7), in a light triple metre which returns in his final duet, is a forth-right rondo, exploiting contrasts of key as Benedict turns from himself to think of Beatrice as she is. After its almost Handelian exhilaration the sustained rapture of the second duet (8), effectively breaking into more animated rhythms midway, makes a deep impression; its mannered thirds-and-sixths texture, easily cloying, acquire a penetrating quality widely admired today regardless of its context as the last number (**Ex. 51.2, 3**, page 198). To be sure, this dual reverie is a surprising sequel to the hoodwinking of Beatrice just related. Hero sighs, and explains to Ursula why, and the two salute the night in a united consciousness of bliss, Ursula being a virtual extension of her mistress. Altogether an unusual ending for an act, abjuring the Italian crescendo-climax and sidestepping the main situation. No one can call it a gripping conclusion. Of the choruses, the first, repeated in a lower key after the first dialogue, strikes a manly tunefulness, and the second (6), repeated after considerable fun with piquant coloratura on the oboe, is a piece of smooth polyphony, more noticeable for its refusal to turn out the masterpiece promised by the conductor, and for the exaggeration of its performers, than for its fitness to the funeral epithalamium actually sung.

In the second act there are an air for Beatrice, a duet for her and Benedict, a trio for Hero, Beatrice and Ursula, a garrulous wine-tasting orgy for Somarone and chorus; and two choruses, one prayerful and short, the other an incisive and processional wedding march.

In Beatrice's long-awaited air (**10**) her moods proliferate in an extended series of varying genres: heroic prelude, explanatory recitative, sinuous cantabile, eventful arioso (**Ex. 51.4**, page 199), sustained cantabile resumed, and an exultant allegro agitato of jostling phrases to convey a sense of love newly discovered and explored (**Ex. 51.5**, Ibid. 199); the cantabile having been prepared by its inclusion in the 'starter' portion of the overture. The final duettino (**15**), on the other hand, is an engaging piece of vocal entry, rejoinder and blending entry, prompted by a stream of light verse and superimposed on a resurgence of the opening scherzando of the overture. It is a deft response to the comparatively laboured dialogue of Number **4**. The women's trio (**11**), added with Number **12** to the original scheme, bears a slight formal relation to the men's trio (**5**) in its interplay of vocal textures, but whereas in Number **5** an ensemble acts as a kind of refrain *after* a single entry, in the present movement the ensemble sets the tone and the single voice initiates diversion and literal animation. Thus here the now full ensemble for the returning Tempo Primo is assured of a settled course. Accordingly it is accompanied by the more edgy tone of woodwind-horn timbre, instead of strings, as the main component (**Ex. 51.6**, page 199). In mood the trio refers most obviously back to the faster moving duet (**8**). That duet, characterized by rustling string harmony, overlaid by voices and wood, and by a stuttering clarinet, has set its seal of symbolic naturism on the first act. The trio, following Beatrice's impulsive self-exposure, forms the last stage of 'working' on Beatrice's secret and reluctant envy of Hero's bride-happy state; contemplative but magical. Two choruses, a simple bridal hymn in the distance and a more than elegant nuptial march, with solo-ensemble pitted against the chorus, complete the conversion of Miss Disdain as far as it goes. It remains to the newly united couple to enjoy the prospect of present harmony and future return to discord (**15**). (**Ex. 51.7**.)

Besides being briefed for grotesque direction of his singers, Somarone ('beast of burden'), the Berlioz interpolation, leads off the second act with a noisy drinking song of *Gaudeamus* type, the chorus adding their version in each verse. This mixing-in of a farcical and at the same time academic (i.e. anti-academic) figure with established Sicilian characters of Shakespearian legend lowers the degree of contact with a community's life in a way that the advance of Dogberry and company, clownish but racily meaningful and pertinent, refrains from doing. Beckmesser's serenade is farcical but in character, and dramatically fruitful, to say the least. Somarone has no motive to do anything except to conduct and to be a ludicrous image of pompous contemporaries. It is strange that such a veteran Shakespearean as Berlioz should indulge his fancy to this tantalizing extent.

Such was the loose structure of musical scenes and spoken interludes which Berlioz eventually drew from Shakespeare, as his last main work. It amounts to a series of tableaux made for music. There is little or no music drama. This is number-opera par excellence. The pattern of each act is left to impress itself on the lines indicated, for there is not much doubt about the procession of moods involved, or the contrasts of texture, except in regard to the undertone of melancholy which dogs some confident airs. This is not an overwhelming creation. There is a lack of stress, indicated partly in the absence of vocal movements in the minor (the Sicilienne being the exception). In some numbers the level of interest is less than characteristic. Once more some fleeting images may be recalled, but with far less sense of ignoring total events than in *Cellini*.

For his skilful *Much ado about nothing* (1901), Stanford worked on a book by Julian Sturgis, preserving most of Shakespeare's scenario with certain love-scene emphases, an elaborate church scene and a folky use of the inviting 'Sigh no more

Ex. 51.1

Ex. 51.2

(La lune se lève et éclaire la scène de ses rayons.)

Ex. 51.3

W.W., Hn.
Db., pizz.
(string support, syncopated
in first half of each bar)

Ex. 51.4

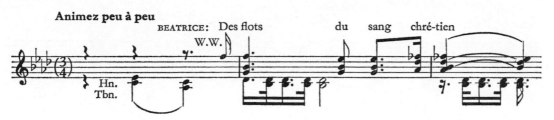

Ex. 51.5

Ex. 51.6

Ex. 51.7

ladies' as a refrain. There is too high a proportion of laboured or strophical songs, to put it bluntly. Yet this work records a more ambitious attempt to translate a whole play into opera; to find lyrics for Shakespeare's prose, including the comic songs. While it lacks Berlioz's magic, it represents a true and coherent image of the comprehensive and broadly faithful setting which he would have declined to write, since it was too dependent on its original, but which he was not prepared to embrace even in his own way.[2]

Béatrice et Bénédict faced theatre experience in 1862. A year later appeared the woefully truncated version of *Les Troyens*, which had to wait nearly three decades before it was realized in a reasonably complete state. But now its true measure has been taken, and in this country, after pioneer attempts at integral performance, its established place in the repertory of the opera-house, in the long run, has been firmly planted since the Covent Garden première of 1957. The musical world can now take this for granted, and it remains to form some estimate of its range and quality as a final and all-embracing stage of the Berlioz experience of music.

NOTES

1. The contacts appreciably discernible are, with the corresponding places between the operatic numbers (in brackets): *Béatrice et Bénédict* Act 1, scene 1 (**1–2**); Act 2, scene 1 (**5–6**); Act 3, scene 3 (**6–6 bis, 6 bis-7**); Act 3, scene 1 (**7–8**); Act 5, scene 4 (**13–14**). In a performance in English these would, indeed, stick out rather obviously in the longer quotations. In Number 11 (trio) the informed listener may catch an echo of *Othello*.

2. In 1888 Karlsruhe produced a new German version of *Béatrice et Bénédict* with Berlioz's music steadily linked by recitatives composed by Felix Mottl and G. zu Putlitz (music and text?); nearly 600 bars in a fully orchestral style. The arrangers supplied what Berlioz recitative conspicuously lacks: the cultivation of motive from scene to scene. Thus, the first recitative forecasts Hero's air (in both tempi), as the last 'remembers' it while Hero signs the contract after Claudio, who is

Facing page 200: An engraving of the composer aged fifty-three by Metzmarcher after a portrait by Nadar

Opposite: A photograph of Berlioz, *c*. 1860

Plate 9 Berlioz, 1862

Plate 10 The cover of *The Trojans*, 1862

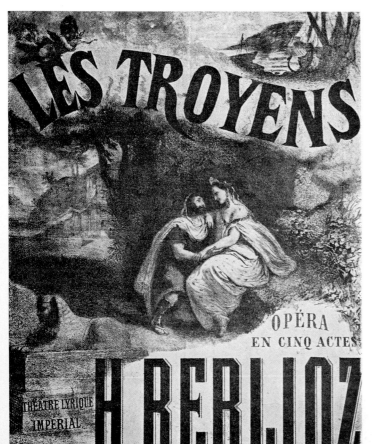

Plate 11 Berlioz conducting the Philharmonic Society in 1850 by Doré

Plate 12 A contemporary caricature of the composer

Plate 13 A portrait of Berlioz in 1862 by Carjot

donated an expansive signature-phrase, since he never had a theme to call his own. Benedict now enjoys a coy 'reluctant suitor' announcement, a captious **B-A-G-D'** phrase, quite different from the busy **F-G-A:. C'** figure with which he stepped forward impatiently after the Epithalamium (6 *bis*), as the start of Mottl's longest effusion. But surprisingly Somarone's disquisition on two-part fugue is left severely unset; not so much as a sly reference to the **G** minor to typify those fugues and ops of which Somarone's mind is professedly compact.

This addition by Zu Putlitz to the score shows a certain boldness of initiative—'At times quite *Meistersinger*-like', remarks Hanslick in his article on the opera (*Die moderne Opera*, vol. 6), nobly forgetting how he was once named in that scenario for the pedant's part—but the utter contradiction between Berlioz's lyrical style and the thematic persistency of quasi-Wagner/Strauss interludes must surely have disturbed other connoisseurs. Berlioz was much happier with his recitatives for *Freischütz* as explained in Chapter 10, *note* 2. However, in 1913 a new version of *Béatrice et Bénédict* for a Leipzig performance appeared in the names of J. Stransky and W. Kleefeld as bolsterers. This also was published, but I have been unable to trace it in any German library. Finally, in 1966 a fresh version was produced in Paris at the Opéra Comique, with recitatives by Tony Aubin (music) and Andre Boll. These additions (there were others, such as a four-pair ballet for the Nocturne) were not, of course, in Aubin's impressionist manner, but, as described by one observer (David Cairns in *The Financial Times,* 1st April), in an assumed late-romantic style, packed with post-Wagnerian flavour and leitmotiv treatment; in other words, 'sweating out the tissue', as Berlioz used to remark disparagingly about the early Wagner that he knew. Perhaps the planners knew their house and public well enough to justify the avoidance of long stretches of spoken recitative at whatever compromise, but this inflation of the work into something like a full-blown opera by so academic a process is misconceived.

Such questions about *Béatrice et Bénédict* were certainly not Berlioz's last thought about opera. He was concerned with the public reception of the Carthage acts of *Les Troyens* (plus nugatory 'prologue'), and with the publication of the *vocal* scores of the Troy and Carthage acts, the full scores having been left unpublished, contrary to an agreement. Not many viewer-listeners had grasped the measure of his creative power. Yet he had fulfilled his dream of bringing Aeneas to his high destiny, and Dido to her pitiful end, on a stage level which could not be calculated in the current terms of record-runs-or-else. He had reached his crowning maturity only in his imagination, and an ample presentation would, inexorably, have to be left to a later generation, but he had found the gleam.

13

Les Troyens

WHERE, on stage, should the Trojans—that mythical people in whose compulsive migrations from Troy to Latium via Carthage Virgil envisaged the march of Roman imperialism to its destiny—rise from the ground in a visible scene that may at once strike the mind as the essential point of emergence? The question had not arisen before in music for the *Aeneid*. In the eighteenth century the libretto furnished by Metastasio in 1724 had set the pattern: *Didone abbandonata*, the story of Dido being won over by Aeneas in the teeth of a jealous Iarbas, only to be abandoned in the cause of a sacred duty which she cannot begin to understand. Berlioz realized from the start how unsatisfactory was this limited perspective. Somehow the spirit that builds nations must be made manifest. For an imaginative designer the Troy that survives the ten years' siege is a close-knit and dedicated community. When the city at peace is betrayed by Greek devilment, having lost by a ruthless act of God the priest who might have warned them, and the enemy within is spreading fire and destruction, a remnant escapes, knowing that they will find where to unite afresh. Thus, in a continuing story which freely skips a decade in order to connect the Trojan and Carthaginian adventures as successive events in Aeneas' career, when the Trojan refugees are cast on the shore of a strange and recently formed kingdom, whose citizens are all the more conscious of *their* imperial destiny, Aeneas' band soon come to represent the Trojan 'cause' in transition. When he and Dido develop a mutual attraction it is first the proud, rejected and already hostile suitor-king, Iarbas, who opposes him with all the might of his armed forces. (In Virgil the rightness of Iarbas' cause makes this attack unnecessary: Jupiter intervenes.) But when Aeneas and Dido have become lovers in the romantic sense (*end* of Act 4), Mercury is sent by Jupiter to rouse Aeneas to his proper destiny, symbolized by making for Italy. It is this sharp and arresting repudiation of the thorough committal of Act 4, at the bidding of a daemon of civilization, that constitutes the crux and tragic twist of the narrative. The despair of the foreign queen emerges as something that matters less than Aeneas' sense of mission. This is the vital issue. It is therefore essential that the Trojan thing should be presented as the basic event.

Two of the five acts are thus positioned at Troy itself, three at Carthage. Berlioz's mental sweep was wide enough to comprehend both cities, each equally important to Aeneas' timeless career and offering its own patriotic interest. He worked out ten scenes, four for Troy and six for Carthage. (As in *L'enfance du Christ*, Berlioz composed his own book for the opera.) He embodied his five-act scheme in the 450-page vocal score which was engraved but not published (i.e. not offered for sale) in 1862 and reprinted (with fresh numbering) in 1889. For the published edition of 1863, the opera was cut into two slices, *La prise de Troie* (unilluminating title) and *Les Troyens à Carthage*, treated as separate evenings and often so regarded, incorrectly, since. Actually only *Les Troyens à Carthage*, with a prelude, was performed in 1863, but *La prise de Troie* was, fortunately, published too, presumably on the chance of a quick sale. In *La prise de Troie* the second scene was made into an act, leaving the remaining scenes as Act 3. In *Les Troyens à Carthage* the first four

Table 7

Scene-identity	*Les Troyens* 1862		*La Prise de Troie* 1863		1899	
	Act	Scene	Act	Scene	Act	Scene
Camp	1	1	1		1	
Citadel		2	2		2	
Aeneas' tent	2	1	3	1	3	1
Altar of Vesta		2		2		2
			Les Troyens à Carthage 1863		1899	
			Act	Scene	Act	Scene
Dido's palace hall	3		1		1	
A virgin forest on the outskirts of Carthage (Entracte)	4	1	2		2	2
Dido's garden by the sea		2	3		2	1
The Trojan fleet in port	5	1	4		3	
A room in the palace		2	5	1	4	1
Terrace overlooking the sea		3		2		2

scenes became an act each, leaving the remaining scenes as Act 5. So far it was only a question of giving act-status to certain scenes, making eight acts in all, and of re-numbering for *Les Troyens*, but since the published vocal score remains in the form *La prise de Troie* + *Les Troyens à Carthage*, while Berlioz's original and coherent scheme is authoritative and will now normally be observed in any production, it is convenient to show at once the essential cross-references of the easily identifiable scenes in the five-act version, as they are found in the tandem edition of 1863, and in the still current version of 1899, an amplification of a shortened version of 1892. These latter scores embody a new piano arrangement by L. Nerici.

It will now be observed that at one point the order has been changed in the 1899 edition (following 1892). In Berlioz's fourth act, now appearing as the second in the second evening, the 'Entr'acte', the ballet-and-miming love scene known in the concert-hall as the *royal hunt*, has been placed *after* the long garden scene. Apparently the publisher, knowing that there had originally been a fuss about the Entr'acte but not concerned at all with its dramatic significance, thought he would try a new place for it. This fantastic tampering with the order of scene would not matter so much if it was merely the printed version still current, but actually this grave error was resurrected in the 1957 première at Covent Garden, and possibly elsewhere. This unfortunate precedent cannot be entirely ignored. It is thus necessary to point out at once that the garden scene, in which every sub-scene leads to the love-duet, is rudely interrupted with the appearance of Mercury to summon Aeneas away to Italy. To go back to the love-making pantomime after this would be a blasphemous disregard of Aeneas' now aroused conscience. He may be impressionable, but he is not lecherous-minded. This deviation having been positioned where it belongs, in every sense, we return to Berlioz's five acts, numbering the component scenes as they occur and leaving the score-studying reader to make the necessary adaptations.[1]

For his world-wide stage Berlioz has assembled no less than ten major soloists: five for the Troy acts, and five more for Carthage in addition to Aeneas and Ascanius. It seems at first a tremendous augmentation of the two or three obvious characters, but it also reflects some rejections. At the first glance Troy must be observed, if not secure, in a condition of active self-awareness. The end of the war is the obvious starting-point; 'armistice night' for today's viewers with long memories, but in the war-torn city. With what preparation shall the fatal horse be introduced, and by whom? There is evidence of a lost scene featuring Sinon the self-styled Greek traitor, alias Greek spy to open the horse, denounced by Cassandra but admitted by Priam (libretto and musical fragment. See the new edition, appendix 3, and Berlioz Society's Bulletin 35). Obviously too much of a diversion. Over, then, to the shocking death, by his own altar, of Laocoon, his warning unheeded. Here the re-entry of Aeneas as the narrator is convenient, and supported by a phrase of fearful, universal mourning. Aeneas, at once assuming the leadership, brings in the sacred horse, as an act of propitiation to the supposed angry goddess. So, an occasion for a gathering popular gesture to the sound of the more-than-city and no less pious anthem to end an act. But with what other soloists, and does no one in the city suspect the return of the enemy?

In lighting on King Priam's daughter, Cassandra, the most truly traumatic character of Greek legend, Berlioz was inspired with the intuition that attends long pondering on a project. Cursed with the insight into the future that no one credits, the princess Cassandra makes a tragic figure of frustrated foreboding. She also has, in Coroebus, a betrothed whom she would fain persuade to escape before it is too late. Her strained encounter with this dedicated Trojan ends the first scene. For the second scene the royal throne introduces a presiding Priam and a mourning Andromache, Hector's widow, but not to sing. (Priam joins in an ensemble in the next scene.) In the second act Ascanius shares vocally a small part with the priest Pantheus. Hector's spirit, on the other hand, makes an impressive and essential entry. The second scene, marking the liquidation of Troy, would make poor music after the Trojan march-in (act 1). Berlioz fills the gap by making Cassandra the prime mover in an act of ritual self-destruction by the women, while the refugees escape to their destination. Her domination of the stage thus continues, and it would not be surprising if she had more to utter, in the spirit, at Carthage, than a muttered warning beside Hector. But her part ends here. (There is no place for her God-forsaken end, dragged, bound, from the temple shrine and done to death by the Greeks, while Coroebus has plunged into their lines and certain death. Here she is just told of Coroebus' death.) The chorus has thus a vital part in these acts as successive images of a joyful, strained, desperate Troy.

For the Carthage acts, the chorus have an equally telling new role, mainly as citizens of a developing kingdom, feting the anniversary celebrations and paying loyal tributes with their prophetic ditty in **G**, confidently gritting their teeth for the war against the Numidians, joining in the salute to the Mediterranean night, adding ritual dignity (of a sort) to the queen's preparation for death, and a final brief and prophetic burst of imprecation against the master-race; but elsewhere as the Trojan troops haunted by the inner call to embark, and as the mystical authors of that call to Italy. For soloists, Dido and Anna in concert, Dido and a more eloquent Ascanius, and increasingly Dido and Aeneas, hold the main stage. They are relieved by three others: the minister Narbal (the composer's creation), in concert with Anna and others; Iopas, the long-haired lyrist whose song precedes, in

Virgil, Aeneas' recital of the story of Troy; and, not from Virgil, the young nostalgic sailor, Hylas. In addition, there are the two disgruntled and entertaining troopers who have never had it so good as in Carthage. The spirits of Hector and the rest, rising from the underworld to urge a vacillating Aeneas to his duties in sepulchral monotone, quietly underline the Trojan (Roman) mission. The orchestra contribute a set of processional dances for Carthage Day, the forest-scene pantomime, and a seductive ballet-suite for Dido's garden reception, besides rounding off many numbers with the sure eloquence of a massive tutti and of every sort of reduced tutti.

Thus the short-lived but passionate encounter of Aeneas with Dido, and his recurrent sense of imperial purpose (for viewers with Augustan eyes), are exhibited in the widest possible context, and with a breadth of vision that can only be termed Shakespearean. No intelligent listener can underrate the range of scene which, in a masterly selection from *Aeneid* 2 and 4, Berlioz has set himself to furnish with music, or to draw music from. 'The Trojans' he calls his subject, meaning, of course, 'in a changing world'.

A listener attuned to Wagnerian music-drama may watch out for clue-themes at least for Cassandra (lover and prophetess), Aeneas, Troy, Dido, destruction and death. Only Troy has its recurring symbol, and it is not a theme but a melody of ten bars, so far more succinct than the goldsmiths' chorus in *Cellini*. Sung for the induction of the supposedly sacred horse, it becomes a convenient token of the march of an imperial power to its destiny in the world. Otherwise, each occasion finds its own music. It is clearly Berlioz's intention that changing fortune and locale shall be honoured by entirely fresh movements as a scene alters. Actually, Dido in the last two acts is the only at all consistent character. Aeneas, the bold but disastrous crusader of the Troy acts, the fire-eater of the 'Numidian' scene, the passionate but divinely arrested lover of Act 4, the reluctant patriot of Act 5, is, for any composer casting around for an identification-mark, emotionally a security-risk, once he has set foot on Carthage, as we shall observe later.

Accordingly, the five acts are organized in separate and self-contained movements, in which cantabile and arioso are linked by a minimum of recitative. Occasionally a 'drier' speech-song is maintained as a special touch of unsophistication. Once more, a strophical manner of development is employed from time to time, in varying degrees, usually with enough episode or improvizatory matter or drop into arioso to break the symmetry and cantabile continuity and lend point to a further verse. The examples may be listed, in order that the obvious examples may be compared with the more concealed organizations. (A hyphen between verse-numbers denotes a noticeable break, ranging from a passing phase of arioso to a prolonged period of expansion or fragmentation, between verses.) In each case the recurrence of a verse constitutes a harbouring of structural energy which balances the effort of the remainder, as the whole movement balances the quasi-extemporary character of other movements. It will be convenient to group with these strophical uses a few instances of a reprise without fresh words and not distinctly separated from its context, and of analogies in instrumental interludes.

Act 1	Cassandra's air: 'Malheureux roi.'	1 (minor)-2 (major)
scene 1	Coroebus' air: 'Reviens à toi.'	1-2
	Duet: 'Quitte nous . . . Te quitter.'	1 (Cassandra)
		2 (Coroebus)
		3 (Cassandra and Coroebus)
		4 (Coroebus and Cassandra)
scene 2	Wrestlers' dance:	1-2-3
	Pantomime: 'Veuve d'Hector.'	1 (**A** minor)-2 (**F** sharp minor)
	Trojan March:	1-2-3-4-5
Act 2	Chorus: 'Complices de sa gloire.'	1 (**A** flat)-2-3 (**A**)
scene 2		
Act 3	National song:	1-2
	enclosing Dido's address ('Cher Tyriens')	1-2
	Dido, Anna: 'Sa/ma voix fait naître.'	1,2
	'Sichée! Ô mon époux!'	1,2
	Aeneas and Chorus: 'Sur cette horde.'	1-2
Act 4	Anna and Narbal:	1a (Narbal), 1b (Anna),
scene 2		2a + 2b
	Aeneas' triumphant entry: National song.	3
	First dance.	1-2
	Iopas.	1-2
	Quintet: Dido. 'Tout conspire!'	1-2
	enclosing 2 verse dialogue of Anna and Iopas ('Voyez, Narbal').	
	Septet: Ensemble and Chorus.	1, 2
	Duet:	1-2-3
Act 5	Hylas:	1, 2, 3
scene 1		
scene 2	Finale: Trojan March.	Last Verse

In contrast to these entirely or comparatively set pieces of expansion, whose integral pattern will readily clarify with further hearing, in a certain number of movements the vocal line, while shaping as it proceeds, is held in a position of involvement by the growth of an orchestral motive. In most cases, this development is restricted, and does not, for instance, continue after the singer has stopped. Rather, it illustrates, by anticipation or by parallel movement, a point of the words. In this respect, Berlioz was *not* the French Beethoven. The following instances may indicate how, most sparingly, he uses the orchestra to enhance dramatic situations.

Act 1
scene 1   Cassandra will not be shaken from her intuition that trouble is coming back to Troy. Her 'exaltation' is sustained by a bass figure that hovers round one degree and then rises a sixth, in a cluster of minor keys (**Ex. 52, page 212**). It continues moodily, while Coroebus tries to comfort her. But after his second round of 'Reviens à toi', the motive returns in the major, as a clear token of hope, and subsequently it initiates each verse of the duet that ends the scene. This is thus a rare instance of the ubiquitous motive.

scene 2   Aeneas directs the moving-in of the horse to the accompaniment of an imperative, saccadic string rhythm. After which, Cassandra releases her forebodings in an eloquent air propelled by a reiterated fall to the even (i.e. off) beats, in the strings, supported by thick trombone chords.

Act 2
scene 1   Hector's spirit advances and retires to the tune of an even phrase played on a muted horn and violins pizzicato. In response, when he at last awakes, Aeneas assures Pantheus, the entirely militant priest, with a rousing ascent, 'Prêts à mourir', enhanced by string pretensions to efficiency that recur, punctuated by trombones, when the whole establishment answer to the call.

scene 2   Cassandra inspires her loyal no-surrender band with a vision of a new Troy arising in Italy. Her instant vocal line, reinforced by woodwind, is pressed forward by a flourish of strings. Later, her chastisement of the doubters is stimulated by a recurring scale figure for strings.

Act 3
In the long and intimate dialogue between Dido and her sister Anna, the opening orchestral bar releases a restless theme, in the minor, which with the ensuing distracted matter makes Dido's assurances of calm incredible. Anna's orchestra takes up the theme in the major. She perceives Dido's

inner discontent, and eventually Dido admits to herself a 'dangerous rapture'. The initial motive (woodwind) is the final word. Another rare instance of a persistent clue-theme.

Dido's sympathy with the Trojan refugees is underlined by a gently recurring multiple oscillation of violins and violas, recalling her experience of a violent storm. In formal contrast, Narbal's feverish call for help against Iarbas is anticipated by surging square phrases for strings, woodwind and soon cornets, which easily carry Narbal's rally of the nation up to Aeneas' disclosure of his identity, with some material to spare for Aeneas' manifesto.

Act 4
scene 2

In the quintet, 'Tout conspire', Dido's calming of her conscience in accepting Aeneas is punctuated by an impulsive, rising woodwind-string figure in the bass, pressing against sharply syncopated string harmony. In the duet, the calm flow of strings, with woodwind support in the repeated verses, contrasts with the pulsating strings and syncopated woodwind in the first episode, and the luxuriant fancies of the second episode.

Act 5
scene 1

Hylas' song is long enough, but the agitated entry of Pantheus and the chiefs is furnished with a full orchestral refrain (with four distinct components). It is duly taken up by the Trojan band, disclosing their fears that the gods are against Troy. But first Pantheus declares, in recitative, 'Prepare to leave', and why. Thus the end of the refrain, a halting phrase repeated in the strings, acquires this unclear association. In the chorus it leads up to the subdued recall of the moment in Troy when Hector appeared, armed. (Not a note of the Hector theme from act 2.) But the motive recurs *per se* as the chiefs go into their tents, and later as Aeneas enters, in great commotion because he has to leave. Thus, this chance thematic component is linked with Aeneas' heaviness of heart, but in too inconsistent a manner to be of any dramatic consequence. In the sentinels' duet, so necessary to heighten Aeneas' entry, the clarinets' voluble theme effectively maintains the militiamen's regret over the girls they must leave behind for a sea-voyage they deplore. When Aeneas at last resolves to alert his forces for sailing out, the strings strike up a martial rhythm in terms of which the Trojan march emerges twice in a wide context. (A formal precedent can be found in the reprise of the second subject of the *Francs Juges* overture.) When Dido appears, the orchestra supply a steady and articulate motive to accompany the out-pouring of her rage and despair, passing from a positive and melodic descent to a general quiver in the same syncopated rhythm. To this Aeneas has no reply but to utter short spasms of protest, to listen for the sailors' cry of 'Italy!', and to embark to the decisive and irrevocable sounds of the March.

scene 2   For Dido's last desperate gesture to send Anna to Aeneas to plead for her, the violoncelli develop a wonderful theme below Dido's broken utterance. Later, a plain trochaic figure of descending thirds takes its place. When, at the end of the scene, she prepares for death (trembling strings), the bass clarinet has a phrase for the inevitable. For her farewell to Carthage the woodwind have a soothing rhythm that eventually leads into a recall of the duet (act 4). The combination of woodwind with viola, without violins, lends astringency.

scene 3   For the ritual sacrifice, the brass initiate an expanding phrase which recurs as Pluto's priests gather for the final movements round the pyre.

Such are the patent opportunities that Berlioz takes to use his orchestra to make a scene. They can be assumed to be the more consistent examples of a process in continual evidence on a more extemporary level. The general method of com-position is in contemporary phrase 'playing by ear', precisioning a tableau by the right motive, not accumulating material in readiness for the climactic moment or the telling recovery later. There seems, indeed, no limit to the number of phrases which take shape under the hand of a conductor who understands the score.

Structuring is then a question of estimating the effect of scenes in succession and as a sum of different genres, where no convention of order prevails as in a symphony. One can observe a remarkable polarization of the classic tendency to consider the logical outcome (of a strophe or thematic development) and of the romantic quest for continuation to the limit.

These strophical or clearly motivated movements for chorus or solo-ensemble all stand for a certain degree of overall musical organization which provokes a desire for a more articulate speech-song elsewhere. Berlioz keeps recitative within a routine of linking sub-movements to introduce a new character or mood, or to break up a too collected air. Yet one cannot fail to notice certain incursions of near-speech in the vocal line, in an often choice orchestral context. Such are Cassandra's recurrent outbursts of foresight and reproach, the people's passing tribute to Andromache, and the dialogue of Hector and Aeneas; Ascanius' tender appeal to Dido (citing Aeneas as his chief *en passant*: only the orchestra recognizes the name-dropping) and Aeneas' farewell to his son before battle; the shades' blunt warning to Aeneas, discharging a shock of reality on his passion-absorbed senses; lastly, Dido's successive stages of 'nationalist' arousal, address to the underworld powers, approach to death, prophecy of an avenging leader and final acknowledgement of the future great power. Opposite to these reliances on speech-rhythm in (orchestral) colour are the scattered interludes for orchestra alone: the wrestlers' dance (act 1), the city workers' parade (act 3), the symphonic movement (with chorus) that makes an overture to Act 4, the 'victory' ballet in Aeneas' honour which turns out to be an invitation to love.

Having established some anticipation of the working interplay of song-verse and orchestral theme, of solo and choral ensemble on a new dramatic level, involving a prodigious range of scene, we may consider the impact of successive movements in their five acts. The events of the Troy acts form in Virgil part of a monumental reminiscence and commentary by Aeneas at the court of Dido. Here, inevitably, they must be seen to happen *in situ*, relying on music to place them in an emotional perspective and what ideology seems expedient.

Act 1, scene 1. *The abandoned camp of the Greeks at Troy*. The camp and citadel scenes of the first act establish the transcendent unity of Troy. War-weariness incredibly forgotten overnight, joy unconfined, with unrestricted movement in the city, releases itself in a vigorous blend of delirious exclamation and spreading theme. The metre is inevitably a rapid six-beats; a little faster than the more settled Carthage on parade in Act 3. (A reverberation from the wild groves of *Erigone* fills a line for the sopranos' 'Que le cri des batailles', here closely echoed by tenors.) A humdrum rhythm marks the subsequent sorting out of the trophies left about and the fading gossip about the closed horse that would hold a battalion.

To a flourish of strings Cassandra emerges, racked with apprehension at the sudden withdrawal of the enemy, enhanced by a vision of Hector on guard. In her first air, with a reprise in the major, she laments Priam and the uncomprehending Coroebus, her dream man. On his entry Coroebus, utterly refusing the flight she desires, seeks to reassure her. After hearing out one verse of his feeble air, she pours out her intimation of disaster. An orchestral theme takes possession, with hectic scales to follow. Coroebus' second verse is met with sinister glances. His

Ex. 52

next air, a bland tribute to the pathetic fallacy of fine skies, fine prospects—hence in
F—amounts to a graceful absorption in undulating violins, to a jejune vocal line;
stretching 'continuation' to tedious proportions, but good enough to prompt a
further brief and pungent exposure of the 'calme perfide' from his disturbed listener.
In tragic resignation, one obscurely gathers, Cassandra again begs her beloved to
leave, knowing he will not. (Richard Capell asked in 1935 how it comes that 'this
idiotic subaltern should have become engaged to the mad princess'.) Coroebus
continues his reproaches. Then (in a burst of operatic convention) a duet ensues,
making three verses of a strophe developing from a major version of **Ex. 52**,
marked by subversive 3-bar units and prodded capriciously by a bass ascent at the
start of Verse 1 and reinforcements in Verse 3. Nevertheless, it betrays in repetition
'une indigence extrême', as Émil Destranges pronounced in his 1897 brochure
(backed by uncompromising suggestions of 'cuts') and many critics since have
confirmed. A further verse confronts the singers. After which, broken utterances,
portending Cassandra's version of 'laughing death' (Schopenhauer-Wagner) in a
marriage state, make for a tolerably convincing curtain, aided by a discordant
cadence not found in Catel's *Harmony*. This cadence inevitably replaced the original
link with the next scene, which is in a different world.

Scene 2. *Before the citadel*. A solemn, edgy chorus, haunted by trombones and drums,
with an inherent oscillation of key, sets the tone of the pompous gathering of all Troy
before an altar; fervent but disturbed. A succinct reprise marks the entry of Aeneas.
A brilliantly scored 8-bar phrase (**Ex. 70**, page 256), with two episodes, forms apt
music for a wrestlers' dance, leading into one of the most striking musical scenes.
To the sound of a kind of dirge in **A** minor, in which the clarinet is the soloist and
the chorus the wayside commentator, Andromache and her son, dressed in
mourning, place flowers on the altar. To fresh, tranquil music (**A** major) she presents
her son to Priam. Cassandra, appearing down-stage with a characteristic hint of
woes to come, starts up a second strophe in a lower key, **F** sharp minor. The coda
of this, during which the two mourners slowly leave, must be cited. (Lower strings

Ex. 53.1

Ex. 53.2

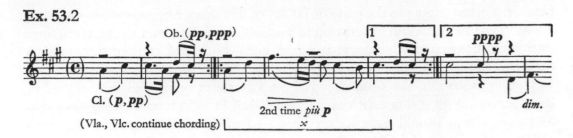

supply chords on each beat.) The next 4 bars repeat *x* without the oboe, leaving the clarinet this semitonal fall for the close, overlapped by a choral sigh (on **C** sharp). 'Un pianissimo d'une rêveuse tristesse.' It would be hard to overstate the impression of this movement, vocally restricted to necessities, yet an original token of Troy mourning for her sons. 'Still can we hear Andromache's lament'. The message comes from Homer through Alcaeus, through Virgil, through Berlioz's sighing singers and woodwind, for whom it may ever concern.

The sharp intrusion on this hushed atmosphere at the re-entry of Aeneas with the shocking news of the horrible destruction of Laocoon beside his own altar, after striking the horse a testing blow, is one of the most shattering moments in opera. As a background to a vivid tenor line, a brisk reiterant progression in a woodwind ensemble, moving out from **F** sharp minor as far as **A** flat encounters a growl of brass for **A** minor, the signal for describing the onset of the seasnakes, and then semitonal tremors (as of a man writhing) rising in the bass. A singularly facile cadence in **A** *major*, the last thing to be expected, presumably drives home the inexorable nature of the priest's death (on one interpretation). There is, or should be, a deafening silence, since at this catastrophic point there is no hint of the confused reaction that one would expect. On the contrary, the people blandly proceed at once to deliver a formal lament, once again in **F** sharp minor, in various stages: a broad antiphony of poignant phrases from different solo-groups yields to the raw unanimity of 'Laocoon! un prêtre!', and then to a fervent line of expression begun by Cassandra and taken up by soloists in unison in an intense tutti of fearfulness at the divine fury, Pallas' especially. Fearfulness, not compassion.

From this impressive predicament of ghastly immobility Aeneas, superseding Priam (see page 235), rescues the people in order to pull the horse with all ceremony into the Palladium itself. (No mention of opening up the walls.) An efficient-industrial string motive of general co-ordination leads to a brisk, florid, jubilant chorus in **B** flat, mingled with a jarring 'Malheur!' from Cassandra. (To be fair, the cornets support Aeneas and Cassandra in turn.) After a general *exeunt* Cassandra, brusquely turning back, plunges into her last spell of distracted grief at the abyss into which this Troy, this proud, patriotic Troy (**D** major diversion from an **E** flat minor start), is moving unprevented. Her melodic phrases are borne along by nervous string reiterations until thoughts of the wasted efforts of Coroebus (and Priam) reach a new level of utter desolation, contained in a measured descending intonation, resting equivocally on the chord of **F**. Once more we must admire the sagacity of Berlioz's replacement, of Aeneas' own recall (to Dido) of the fatal admission into the very citadel of 'that malignant horror', with the perception of the one observer on the spot who divined the issue. Cassandra's air passing to the ensuing chorus without audible change, apart from the establishment of **B** flat and a decrease of speed to *pomposo*, the whole confident march-in takes shape through her dark glasses.

In the dim but to her familiar distance (string tremors), trumpets herald the inception of the Trojan anthem, 'Du Roi des dieux', henceforward the March. It is

Ex. 54.1

Ex. 54.2

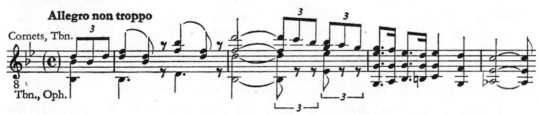

Ex. 54.3

an original tune. One has only to compare the stilted measures and straggling pattern of the **B** flat march in *Olympie* (act 3), with which Berlioz was well acquainted, to realize how little he actually derived from Spontini. Here the opening and penultimate phrases of the 10-bar melody, and a development in the first episode, are cited (**Ex. 54.**1 and 2). For the quasi-ritual enunciation of the hymn Berlioz required a distant band in three divisions—(1) nine full brass; (2) eight saxhorns with cymbals; (3) eight oboes and six or eight harps—besides the orchestra in the theatre. He planned to co-ordinate this outsize band by means of a second conductor, in contact with the principal conductor by a metreonomic device; today, closed television makes this simpler. On these lines the textural pattern works out as follows.

Section	Main performers	Section	Main performers
Prelude	Band 1	Verse 3	Bands 2 and 3 (1)
Verse 1	Band 1	Episode 3	Bands 3 and 2
Episode 1 (a) and (b)	Band 1		
		Verse 4	Bands 2 and 3 (1)
		Coda (a)	Band 3
Verse 2	Bands 1 and 2	(b)	Bands 2 and 3
		(c)	
Episode 2	Bands 3 and 1 (2)	(cf. episode 1*b*)	Band 1
		(d)	Orchestra

The orchestra, especially the strings, effectively punctuate this processional music, off or on stage, with spasmodic entries in support of Cassandra, who is vocal in Verse 1 and the first two episodes and again in the coda, and is manifestly attentive throughout. The chorus enter the scene for Verse 3. The constant rejoinder of verse and episode, band and band, band and orchestra, chorus and soloist, redeems this thrilling procession at nightfall from any hardening routine over the pompous tune. Besides this, on top of Verse 4, extended, comes the sudden stop as the horse-transport is brought to a halt; a clatter of hardware inside is detected, and for one moment Cassandra wonders whether realism will prevail. But the procession is resumed with more glamour than ever. Cassandra gasps out a last desperate 'Stop!' before it passes out of sight, but is overwhelmed. Left to her own thoughts, she is still absorbed in the March (in the shape of **Ex. 54.**3 and the remainder of the first episode), up to her cry of desperation in the face of a ruined city. The orchestra assumes the reins in a distracted ending marked by semitonal slides, as satisfactorily anti-conclusive as the pursuit of an imaginary 'Cassandra motive' would have been trite.

So ends this unparalleled first act. If Coroebus is reckoned as almost a deadweight on the operatic momentum, the whole of the act-long second scene registers an amazing range of moods, which in the vivid context of a city that reveres the gods and yet is unutterably punished by them, forms a coherent pattern of balanced movements, with a sweeping strophical finish, leaving room for a fantastic coda. In performance, the whole act only takes about an hour: number effaces number in smooth succession, leaving little or no time for more than a rough impression of shape and salient detail. It has been the concern of this slow rehearsal to show that a richer acquaintance clarifies and not confuses first impressions. As a number integrates, its impact on the scene becomes sharper.

Act 2, scene 1. *Aeneas' tent*. An ominous, restless prelude, moving contentiously in two symmetrical stages a semitone apart, prepares the ear enigmatically for the silence of Aeneas, deep in the sleep of the righteous, and of Ascanius, as he enters fearfully, finds his father asleep and retires; the orchestra supplying wayward but skilfully devised phrases for the miming. With the appearance of Hector's shade, the musical pressure tightens. An unmistakably dour refrain on the horn, against a percussive horn-string background, with a shrill tutti to waken Aeneas to the depths, starts a tense dialogue. In broken phrases, Aeneas salutes his ancestor fearfully (brass-string tremors). In a slow descent down the octave, Hector warns him to fly from a crumbling and burning city. The refrain, re-pointed, follows his vanishing form.

In an allegro agitato, resolute string phrases, bustling wood and warning brass assist hectic exchanges between Aeneas, Pantheus, Ascanius, Coroebus and dauntless troops, as the city burns but the citadel holds firm. Aeneas leads a desperate move towards it. His 'Prêts à mourir', with militant string support, is taken up by ensemble and chorus. They go. The orchestra might, one would have thought, have enlarged upon this last stand. Instead, they brusquely continue rapid string-woodwind semitonal slides, supported by ponderous brass, until they reach a fresh cadence, grammatically connected to the next number.

Scene 2. *Vesta's temple*. Mount Ida visible in the distance; also, on stage, the reddish glow of the burning city. The altar of Vesta-Cybele is lit. Against lofty pillars of woodwind-and-string-bass chords, the three-part chorus of dedicated Trojan women, in a deep state of dejection, repeat their desperate prayers to Cybele for her Trojans, male and female. Their intonation is marked by an ascent to a flattened fifth, as if in the unused Locrian mode. (**B** to **B** on white notes.) The exotic tone of the repetitive antiphony is striking besides being a moment of calm meditation before strenuous and two-edged conflict. It might be Debussy, if the diminished fifth did not at once resolve inwards on the chord of **A** flat.

217

The last time this occurs, trumpets and cornets announce the entrance of Cassandra. Explaining the relief of the citadel troops by Aeneas, she breaks into a prophecy of the new and excelling Troy that shall arise in Italy. Her imperial tone is supported by banner-waving in the strings. (It anticipates many like demonstrations; those by Saint-Saëns' drummer's girl as well as the triumphant march home of Egyptian troops in *Aida*.) To Cassandra's intimation that with Coroebus' death her life is ended, the chorus offer a warm and disciplined response of admiration for the true prophetess. Then Cassandra, aided by the repeated scalic figure in the strings, turns to upbraid the 'scared doves' who are resigned to capture by the enemy. Eventually the stoic temper of the hawk majority bursts out in a compact but delirious chorus of proud defiance of the enemy, cheating them of the fruits of victory by self-inflicted death. The surge of interlocking phrase is masterly. A

Ex. 55

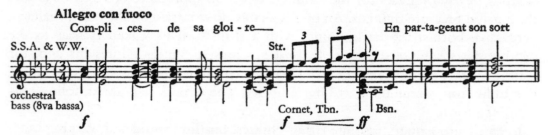

positive battery of harp arpeggio covers all collisions of texture in the forceful scoring. Further and now increasingly minatory denunciation of the waverers for their willingness to become men's servitors, as utterly un-Trojan, receives quite fresh incidental music, but when the objectors have been hounded out, the rest swear their support and return, exalted, to **Ex. 55** (pitched in **A**), with extensions and an extra verse. After this rousing convergence, the music can afford to break up for the bitter encounter of the Greek troops and their resisters. To dying cries of 'Italy!' (to the remnants on Mount Ida), the women liquidate themselves by stabbing, throttling or throwing over the precipice. The orchestra show their teeth and then gradually simmer down. (In the horrific culmination of the superb act 5 of *Khovanshchina*, where the ubiquitous Martha, discarded oracle, descants on the hymn of the Old Believers as she joins them in the flames, Mussorgsky provides a strong challenge to Berlioz.)

The exigencies of one stand of troops in a crumbling city are thus put beside the less conventional cries of Cassandra's band of sisters in fearful resolution. The music for the two scenes cannot be said to be even complementary, much less related symphonically, but it serves to preserve for future acts some immortal hold on the Trojan way of life, which will survive both diversion to Carthage and the historic lapse of a century.

Act 3. *Dido's palace hall.* In its first and only season in the composer's lifetime *The Trojans* began here; that is, with *Les Troyens à Carthage*. To bridge the yawning gap, however, there were, firstly, a prelude, embodying chiefly a new and ponderous setting of the theme (**Ex. 52**, page 212) of the Cassandra-Coroebus duet for full wind (found in all vocal scores of *Les Troyens* and in the 1885 full score); secondly, a lyrical recitation of the disasters which drove the Trojans to Carthage; and thirdly, an orchestral version of the Trojan March. This desperate expedient at the Theâtre Lyrique became happily superfluous in full performances of the opera.

With the transition to Carthage, Berlioz had to measure his musico-dramatic skill against the more advantageous position reached by Virgil as he began *Aeneid 4*, and, on the other hand, the fundamentally inconclusive nature of the end of the book as far as Aeneas was concerned. It is as well to clear our minds on these issues. At the end of *Aeneid 1* Dido has entered into a close relationship with Aeneas. From an inspired and extraordinary compassion for the city-less chief cast on her shores and at her mercy, she has become absorbed by his presence, fed with amorous fire by Cupid in the form of Ascanius, and losing all thought of her murdered husband, Sychaeus. In that mood she hears Aeneas through his frank and sometimes confessional account of what he suffered and did at Troy and on his voyages off course. She has known his morally rebellious outbursts as well as his cultivated sense of duty. Everything is conspiring to forget the raw past in a passionate present. She is, indeed, beside herself, but her driving energy will carry her into total surrender, and soon, through the connivance of Juno and Venus (an accepted symbol of high-power revolt against destiny, or sheer Dido-fantasy?), her love-making will be an open secret. When she learns subsequently of Aeneas' desertion, Dido, incredulous, abusive, humiliated, remains the dominant figure.

Aeneas, for his part, has learnt from his designing goddess-mother of Dido's bitter past, and can recognize not only her own sense of duty but also, by the frieze of the Trojan War in the temple of Juno, the queen's inestimable sympathy for shortlived humanity (*mortalia tangunt*). When he sees her welcoming the Trojan party, she impresses him, and he is particularly vulnerable, for he is unsure of himself. Responding to her unmistakable advances, he settles down to an indefinite period of dalliance in the city. Mercury, sent by Jupiter to recall him to his imperial mission, finds him wearing his self-styled consort's regalia, a veritable Carthaginian. His conscience stirs acutely, and he orders the mustering of the fleet, but, at once irresolute and undignified, he treats an infuriated and contemptuous Dido to litigious self-justification. Mercury has to appear again to make him go where the action is. He needs the new testing experience which he finds in his later wanderings. The Carthaginian stay which meant life and death to Dido was for Aeneas a disturbing, disintegrating episode.

A wider survey of the whole epic reveals the gradual moulding of the heroic temper in accordance with (but not controlled by) the workings of destiny through Jupiter, after a primary struggle between inner rebellion (*furor*) and a sense of duty (*pietas*). (Juno and Venus are subordinate, conflicting influences, but sufficiently cosmic to be no more terrestrial, and so no more within the scope of theatre presentation, than Jupiter himself, whose own messenger retains divine status as a voice in his sole appearance, at Carthage.) Aeneas thus enters Carthage in a far from heroic mood, as his narrative betrays. His mind is more on the Troy that he has lost and cannot rebuild than on his future destination. In the death of his father, Anchises, he mourns the one companion who offered positive hope for the future. He himself is quite unready for the resumption of his imperial venture. Dido's attentions fill every gap in his present concerns. Prodded by Mercury twice and once by Anchises (in a dream), he slips away from Carthage with no more moral recovery than the renunciation of Dido; battered but unshaken by her final entreaties through Anna. Only the vision of heroes (Book 6) can set him on his proper course for Latium.[2]

In short, Berlioz had no brief at all for making Carthaginian Aeneas a superman, the founder-ancestor of Augustus. On the contrary, only Dido's infatuation, and her subsequent dismay in betrayal, violent abuse and final surrender to the full *fury* of a dedicated hatred for her one time lover, and then her ritual death, can conceal the weakness underlying Aeneas' retreat from Carthage.

To whatever extent Berlioz realized this two-prong challenge of Dido's swift and commanding absorption in Aeneas' presence, and of Aeneas' loss of any true sense of destiny, he planned his Carthage acts with a remarkable finesse. The two Troy acts have been comparatively compressed and impersonal; almost 'a choral epic with magnificent solo interludes' (Shawe-Taylor). The fluctuating moods of the city gatherings are largely unmotivated as such. No demonstrators ('Horse: out!') here! That privilege is reserved for the Carthaginians' final outburst at the end. Among individuals, the noble Cassandra (contrary to a recent production, no crouching spirit she) is thrust into a down-to-earth involvement with Coroebus, and later with the divided band of women resisters, with a corresponding tone of passionate exhortation. But otherwise she is a compulsive oracular voice of dark foreboding, and so is Hector's warning voice from the dead. The rest of the Troy scenes are more pageantry than opera. In the Carthage acts the treatment is much more expansive, and after the speech from the throne the drama settles down to the personal level.

The third act introduces Dido in proud majesty and disturbing loneliness, which Anna is quick to probe. The appearance of the Trojan refugees, seeking asylum, recalls her own wanderings and rouses her interest in their famous kingdom. Her minister, Narbal, hurries in with the news of a Numidian invasion, already forecast and, contrary to Virgil's account, assumed to be unprovoked. Aeneas, suddenly revealing himself as not only present but a potential ally, at once becomes an important and glamorous figure at the Carthaginian court. The troops assembled, he leaves, having entrusted his son and deputy, Ascanius, to Dido. The fourth act begins with the pantomime of the 'marriage' in the cavern. The second scene marks Dido's developing advances in a variety of numbers, from a seductive ballet-suite to Dido's renunciation of Sychaeus and an ecstatic duet, interspersed with contrived diversions. Then Mercury's descent to recall Aeneas to his true destination. This leaves to the fifth act to set forth, with similar and now more spontaneous interludes, Aeneas' tormenting doubts; Dido's harangue, maledictions, resolve to die, prophecy of Hannibal; and—thrust upon her!—her dying recognition that the future lies with Rome, while for every loyal Carthaginian the day of retribution will surely come. In thus callously imposing on Dido a vision of a triumphant Rome, Berlioz was, of course, jumping brashly ahead, with a rough compromise in the imperialist mood of his own time. But the general upshot is that Dido, having taken the lead at the start of Act 3, retains it through Act 4, and through much of Act 5. Meanwhile the Trojans, having literally joined the Carthaginians at the end of Act 3, have no voice in Act 4, and appear only in one commander interlude, apart from the recurring march which marks their advance towards their destiny. 'Les Troyens à Carthage' is almost a satirical title! So far Berlioz accepts the subordinate role for Aeneas which *Aeneid 4* involved, and relies on his mastery of Shakespearean variety of scene to avoid the monotony of another *Didone abbandonata*.

So much for the relationship of the Carthaginian acts to *Aeneid 4*, as it comes to the reader and is continued in later books. The Troy acts, as derived in the first place from Aeneas' recital, transfer the emotional colouring from the characteristic personality of the narrator to what the singer-participants (with orchestra) can communicate, aided by their direct address to the spectator. We return to the consideration of the music (act 3).

The simple but now refreshing celebration of Carthage Day, fine after storm— no shadow of war—converges in a solemn national anthem in **G** (**Ex. 71**, page 257). Its square, balancing phrases are measured out by a half-beat bass, with the tune and bass disposed, in the tutti entries, so as to leave room for rhetorical flourishes and plenty of unoccupied space. Surveying the outlook as favourable, Dido formulates an earnest appeal for a renewed effort, with a strong climax (v. 1), and turns to the threat from Iarbas (menacing strings and drum), with a loyal response per national anthem. A second appeal (v. 2) leads to a procession of workers, fitted to a random suite of dances for the engineers, sailors (piped in by piccolo but otherwise a very sober entry) and, with a touching oboe refrain, slow-moving workmen, rounded off by the national anthem to close the public ceremony in the official key **G**, not before time.

Dido now discloses her inner mood, under the probing banter of her sister, Anna, in a series of linked movements. After an apparent contradiction of fluttering prelude and Dido's declared calm of mind, an extended arioso dialogue voices what is troubling Dido, and perplexes the shrewd Anna not at all, as the teasing violin-oboe repartee of her 'such an oath!' reveals. A repeated figure typifies Dido's

Ex. 56

actual state (**Ex. 56**). In a new and lulling rhythm, a symmetrical and exquisite duet of repeated phrases registers Dido's tender, lingering renunciation of her duty to her late husband, Sychaeus, with Anna's endorsement.

The announcement (by the minstrel Iopas) of castaways in trouble arouses Dido's sympathy as she remembers her stormy times on the high seas. A short, flowing arioso, besides adroitly suspending the Trojans' entry, serves to deepen the sense of Dido's humanity, not least through the insistent string figure and its trombone bass. Thus the entry of the fugitives to a minor-key, brass band version of their March (actually to a truncated verse, following two verses and a piece of the third episode played while they are still off-stage) has a certain pathetic dignity. After its ramblings, Ascanius' speech sounds graceful but restrained; a blaze of tutti for the naming of their chief (present, disguised as an A.B.). It is Dido who in reply makes a meal of welcoming him (violin and woodwind figures), thus creating a climate warm enough to be shaken by the next entry.

Ushered in by a refrain of close-knit phrases, each bespeaking vigorous resolution and organization, Narbal, Dido's minister, rushes in to announce the hostile approach of Iarbas and plundering troops. As his mounting alarm, promoted by extensions of the refrain, reaches a climax in a summons to a desperate trial of strength, Aeneas surprises all by revealing himself (as **A** flat, the keynote, becomes **G** sharp, the middle of the chord of **E**; a simple but here arresting transformation.) (Theatrically a more telling stroke than in Virgil, where Aeneas emerges initially from a cloud, looking divine, in response to Dido's wish to see him.) Aided by a phrase in Narbal's orchestral vocabulary and a roll of drums, Aeneas offers all Trojan help, and while Dido gazes starry-eyed at her instant hero, Aeneas frames a united campaign of attack, or rather of extermination, in a long and forcible strophe, in which all, including Dido, join. Meanwhile, arms are issued (out of that standing prop, a laundry basket). As an interlude, Aeneas entrusts Ascanius to Dido's care and exhorts him to be valiant and Godfearing; a gentle exercise in *nobilmente* (trombones) and charm (clarinet). Then the entire headlong strophe returns, with ophicleide, tam-tam and for coda an exploitation of the established flattened-second chord, as a penultimate in cadence, in a fresh extension. No need for sounds off of 'Victoire!', as in Piccinni: the readiness is all. It is a long way from 'Chez Tyriens!' and 'Une étrange tristesse' but it has all taken place in this hall, and conceivably in one crowded hour or two, Trojan re-dating accepted.

Act 4, scene 1. *Symphonic interlude*. (*Mime*) *A virgin forest outside Carthage*. With Iarbas *hors de combat* in every sense, nothing can prevent Dido and Aeneas from falling completely in love. Act 4 is devoted to this, and its construction is one more testimony to Berlioz's powers of invention. First, he stages Dido's sexual surrender to Aeneas, induced by a catastrophic and obviously supernatural thunderstorm which drives them to shelter in a cave, as an incident in a long pantomime: grotto, water nymphs at play and in distress, the hunters, storm and lightning, Ascanius on horseback, entry and exit of Dido, masquerading as Diana, and Aeneas in military gear, devotional cries of 'Italy!', heckled by satyrs bellowing 'ha!'. Such is Berlioz's solution to the problem of staging the forest union arranged by Juno and a delighted Venus, and represented by Virgil as utterly shameless behaviour on the part of Dido, cloaked as marriage. Whatever the producer may devise to bridge credibility in what is easily a ludicrous stage event, the musical intentions of this familiar concert-piece are initially clear. After a semitonally tinged prelude, two themes emerge, one on flutes, the other, in a faster tempo, on the horns, simulating a hunt-call. The first of these is apparently a free re-arrangement, in a more leisurely tempo, of the opening phrase of 'O Magali, ma tant amade (aimable)', a racy pro-vencal folk-tune. It sounds like nothing of the kind, its idiom being modern. Its communication of the 'calm of the forest' (e.g. Arden) remains. The horn-motive runs in 7-bar units, and recurs in the development *in mediis rebus*. This 'development'

223

is actually a medley of bustling wind, brassy colourful rhythms, choral interjections and tuttis, conflicting storm and the secret passionate exchange in almost nonchalant confusion, leaving Magali and the suave hunting-horn to restore equilibrium. A stimulating but baffling interlude, neither symphonic in itself, nor commensurate with the crisis of self-discovery.

Scene 2. *Dido's gardens by the sea.* From that secret meeting the gradual revelation of intentions is devised in this scene, in a series of situations. First, the misgivings of the shrewd Narbal, on whom Cassandra's mantle has fallen, over the queen's hunt-and-feast way of life, and Aeneas' dallying in Carthage when his imperial duty lies outside, are confronted by Anna's confidence in Dido's hold on her hero. After dialogue, this shapes in clear stages: Narbal voices his fears for the future in a sombre strophe (trombones and drums); Anna in reply pooh-poohs his worries with piquant phrases (flute and a pert clarinet); Narbal repeats his apprehensions, joined by Anna midway, with fresh orchestral support. A subtle prelude to the act, too often omitted.

For the entry of Dido, distractedly welcoming Aeneas, the conqueror, the orchestra play a new and ethereal setting of the national anthem, for wood and harp with a florid part for violins, muted. In Act 3 it was a stalwart 'Glory to Dido'. Now it is played for *Aeneas*, as if he were a Carthaginian: in **B**, his recent militant-ally key, but, shades of Hector, it is the wrong tune! On top of this ironical touch (which audiences seem to miss), with Anna smiling beside Dido and Narbal frowning beside Aeneas (one assumes), the victor is entertained with a seductive ballet of three dances. The first (the beat must be kept well down to 120) is at once enticingly melodious and adroit in its placing of the violin melody in established relation to the low accompaniment and then to woodwind bravura in the reprise (**Ex. 57**). So,

Ex. 57

in the coda, with the bass start and the high, wind-attended, string reply. The second dance is brilliant throughout, in its thrust of blending textures and in its expanding design. Its neglect is astounding. The third dance, for 'Nubian' slave-singers declaiming Nubian, is perhaps 'alluringly percussive' with its tarbuka etc., woodwind refrain and quasi-Phrygian mode, but musically a let-down. Anyhow, Dido cries 'Enough!' at this point, and, moving on to a couch, requests Iopas to recite in simple style his country-poem. Assisted by a 'Theban harpist' (and woodwind), Iopas replies with a rural hymn to Ceres, giver of plenty; combining a graceful tune with prodigal high coloratura (v. 2), and climaxing on **C**. It is, of course, in **F**. But Dido is unassuaged, and asks Aeneas to tell her about Andromache. 'Under duress, she married Pyrrhus'.

So begins a rich quintet (**Ex. 58**). Dido, shocked but impressed to learn of Andromache's love match (as Aeneas stresses) with the son of Hector's 'murderer', is preparing to abandon her 'fidelity' to her murdered husband Sychaeus. 'My heart is free'. Ascanius—looking like Cupid, as Anna, Iopas and Narbal observe—contrives to slip Sychaeus' ring off the finger of a distracted Dido. This crucial removal of a binding restraint—in the consciousness of a *conspiracy* of events that seems decidedly modern—falls, after an *arioso* setting, into two highly symmetrical strophes, divided by two antistrophes. In the latter piquant pair, Anna is answered

Ex. 58

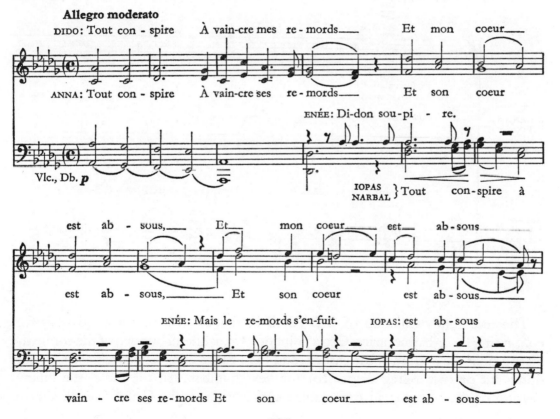

by Iopas with Narbal. In the second main strophe, Dido's confession is confirmed by the rest in the operatic manner. Thus the symbolic play with the ring is absorbed in a much wider revelation of Dido's sense of release, in the simplest vocal terms of an ensemble. It only remains to leave the royal pair where they belong. But first a dismissal of bitter memories in a salute to the calm and balmy seaside night is proposed by Aeneas in wandering harmony, delicately scored (a tremor of solo-strings, muted, *in alt.*). The somewhat pedestrian verbal level is soon forgotten in the exquisite texture of this 'septet' (with chorus). It was encored at the première, which need not happen now, but it is none the less strangely unknown in any concert-room, possibly from a lack of separate publication. The structural impact of its two strophes, for septet (harmonically a quintet) and chorus plus a little solo-coloratura, is slight, and there is no special interest in the melodic line of the three basic phrases. Yet the orchestral context transforms the focus, and the cumulative effect of these blends is exceptional. I quote the second phrase.

Ex. 59

The recurrent oscillation of **C-D flat-C** in the wood makes a good basis for continuing by re-harmonizing **C** to a point of style, while all but two of the company disappear at the bottom of the garden; and then for making **D** flat replace **C** as the dominant or controlling degree for the next number. All the same, the lulling rhythm of the septet is an unfortunate anticipation of the **G** flat duet in almost identical tempo to follow. 'An immense nocturne!' (Destranges) can be taken two ways. In the duet (which it is fatal to exalt by a pompous slowness), Dido and Aeneas at last celebrate a night of rapture under the moon and skies, stirred by comparisons with Troilus and Cressida, Diana and Endymion, as in *The Merchant of Venice*, and, virtually, by sentiments from *Romeo and Juliet*, in the inevitable absence of other matter. Musically, an even-paced serenade of strings (*not* plucked) attends a firm and persuasive duet-verse, discreetly reinforced by wood in the later verses. 'On such a night . . .' invites a rejoinder of voice and voice, the titillation of the woodwind in syncopation with steady strings, and in the second episode random bravura and figuration. The last verse confirms a smiling absorption, framed to continue without a hint of 'laughing death' or inauspicious outcome. But as a casual **G** flat-**A** natural turns unexpectedly into **F** sharp-**A** (**G** flat: out!), Aeneas' dream world is shattered.

With a stunning flourish of **D** major, and two strokes on the gong, Mercury, flashing into vision, mouths his inexorable 'Italy!' thrice and vanishes. The orchestra stagger, and collapse in **E** minor. This corresponds to Mercury's more specifically commissioned appearance in Virgil, made in response to Iarbas's prayer to Jupiter in protest against the intrusion of this 'second Paris', of which rumour had informed him after the secret 'marriage'. There Mercury rebukes him for wasting his time in Africa, playing the 'model husband', ignoring his glorious destiny and, at the lowest aim, preventing Ascanius from being the lord of Italy. Aeneas is almost faint with terror, wishing himself out of Africa but barren of explanations, and meanwhile briefs his commanders to prepare for a secret withdrawal. In springing Mercury on Aeneas, with Dido leaning on his shoulder, Berlioz had to cut out all Mercury's scout-master condemnation, retaining only the key-word.[3] It did not suit his scenario to present so soon Aeneas' absolute sense of guilt and political obligation. Yet Berlioz must have had the original gesture in mind. Anyhow, the message is clear, and when Aeneas next appears he has the evacuation under control, supported by equally alarming premonitions of divine anger in his lieutenants.

To follow this event with the forest pantomime and its furtive movements would, once more, be a repudiation of all dramatic decencies. In the next act Aeneas wavers enough, and credibly, in renouncing his involvement with his beloved queen, but hunting and implied intercourse would be absurd, and, if it is all symbolic, more absurd. As it is, after the forest scene the truth of the relationship between Dido and Aeneas grows from plausibility and opportunity to simple recognition, only to be catastrophically contested. When the habitual opera-goer has recovered from this blow to his sympathies where it hurts, he may recall the self-sacrifice of Cassandra's resisters and the dauntless march-out of the men of free Troy to raise their standard, in a visionary land, from which they have been merely blown off-course. Glamorous Aeneas must be shaken from his seemingly providential commitments in Africa. Only a voice from the centre of reference could do that. It has come, and the habitual opera-goer looks forward to the next act, knowing that it will be tragic, but satisfied that the issues are evenly held.

Act 5, scene 1. *The harbour*. The action of this last act is divided between three points: the port where the Trojan fleet is assembled and where Aeneas wanders distracted between desire and duty, to be tracked down by Dido; the inner room where Dido has her last desperate hour with her friends and in solitude; the terrace overlooking the sea where stands a pyre, prepared by Dido for her own death, overcome by despair and the intuition that 'Rome' will prevail.

Outside the Trojan encampment by the sea, backed by the fleet, are three men: a young sailor on top of a mast (off duty, we hope, as he falls asleep at the end of his song) and two sentinels by the tents obviously on sentry-go but permissively communicative. Representing another world, they give the viewer, in turn, his last chance of relaxing before the essential struggle, while holding up the main action as only opera can. The sailor Hylas (in whom the composer partly saw his son, Louis, then a lieutenant on active service) thinks of the country home that he cannot hope to see again, in one of the finest extensive melodies of the opera (**Ex. 60.**1), delicately accompanied by flute, clarinets, horns and violoncelli, apart from a sudden tutti (a freak wave of strings and trombones etc.) at the end of the second of the

Ex. 60.1

Ex. 60.2

228

three verses. The recurrent collapse of key-centre from **B** flat to **G** minor sharpens the basic nostalgia. It marks a bitter close each time (**Ex. 60.2**).

Pantheus and the chiefs enter in a state of consternation at the portents of divine anger, expressed in a surge of voluble phrases, already given out by the orchestra as they troop in. Pantheus meanwhile explains that for Aeneas' sake evacuation is necessary. But the menacing spirits of the dead are felt to be as near as Hector was in Troy, and once again their voices mutter 'Italy!', spreading despondency and a sense of guilty malingering. The officers having retired, the two men on guard give vent to their low opinion of this Italy plan in an engaging dialogue, encouraged by a wayward clarinet phrase and stabilized by symmetrical periods, which bring home the monotony and privations of the soldier abroad.

As Margaret's grief breaks on an indifferent world, so does Aeneas' distress here. A circular bass phrase, to syncopated harmony, which has been associated with the departure-signal, starts Aeneas off on the first of three linked movements in which he debates his next move, knowing that Dido has been made aware of his departure, and baffled by her cold fury and non-comprehension of his sacred mission. In his distraction, phrase follows phrase in varied texture, though on a broadly common focus of key (**F** minor), which lends point to the resort to a broadly **F** major centre for an interlude of painful anticipation. Then he breaks into a long and passionate reversal of his tracks, resolving that not to see Dido would be despicable. So this outburst ends, as it began, in **A** flat major, and is packed with grand impulsive phrases of Weberian buoyancy, flute included. All this, to be put out of countenance by the only possible means: a warning from all the dead spirits of Troy not to delay; a dramatically convenient substitute for the reappearance of Mercury, to shake him into instant action against a background of tangential harmony and texture, exploiting the etiolated effect of high string harmonies. Aeneas capitulates to the inexorable powers and gives the alert for quitting port.

At this moment his imperial vision springs into life in the shape of the Trojan March in a new version. The strings continue to suggest the familiar tune while stretching its phrases and delivering it in an almost mock-saccadic rhythm, to the stamp of which Aeneas rouses his troops and Ascanius, with the trumpets sounding for him already. He is in a dedicated mood. But having posted his men for Italy, he turns impulsively to bid Dido a rehearsal goodbye and an assurance that an impatient fate calls him to an heroic death, faithless as he is.

And now, to distant thunder, Dido herself rushes in, having followed him to find out if the impossible is true. His plea of divine and pressing orders to leave is ignored beside her humiliation and hence his inhumanity. His protests of previous love are equally dismissed; and those of present love. Audible strains of the March visibly

229

thrill him. Dido responds, 'Go, self-righteous monster!' and leaves. To more cries of 'Italy!' Aeneas joins Ascanius on board, and the March bursts out in full splendour. The music for this sad and crucial exchange and non-exchange (there can be no concerted singing) opens with an extended and rather disjointed dialogue, mainly for Dido, held together by the syncopated theme begun by the woodwind, and a tonality (**B** flat minor) which dissolves after Aeneas' pleading ('O reine') begins. A poignant short interlude on Dido's childless desolation is paralleled by Elizabeth's prayer for Tannhäuser. Then **B** flat major breaks out—rather oddly for Aeneas' final declaration of love and duty as well as for the March to follow.

Scene 2. *A room in the palace.* The pragmatic issue having been settled, the scene changes to a different and more sustained tension, Dido's last desperate effort to delay Aeneas' departure. She urges Anna (and Narbal) to go and plead for her. Her broken phrases are first held in place by a poignant recurring motive in the violoncelli (**Ex. 61**); an insistent trochaic figure of falling thirds (flutes) makes for an equally

Ex. 61

expressive continuation by its duller pathos. But it is all too late: Iopas announces that the fleet has left. Attended by short orchestral outbursts, Dido plunges into punitive injunctions, savage curses and sadistic regrets at lost opportunities, invokes the underworld powers (of magic), and orders the erection of a pyre. But left to herself, she drops into a visible despair (tutti). She settles her mind for death—a more homogeneous movement (bass clarinet)—and eventually breaks into a kind of affectionate lullaby over her city and sister, which leads into a recall of the most remembered duet-music (a flute replacing Aeneas' part). The prevailing wood-horn accompaniment, with concerted violas, suits the subdued commemoration.

Ex. 62

Scene 3. *The terrace by the sea*. The pyre-ritual giving an opportunity for one more solemn march, Berlioz seizes it (**Ex. 62**). The orchestral motive-refrain is memorable. Against this sombre and oppressive background, never explained, of ceremonial music in honour of the infernal deities, certain human manifestations appear. Anna and Narbal, continuing Dido's imprecations, pray fiercely for Latin-Umbrian [*sic*] opposition to Aeneas' imperialism, and his horrible destruction. Dido feels the end approaching (a slow semitonal descent); prophesies the rise from her ashes of an avenger, Hannibal; stabs herself, to the horror of all; but in her dying moments visualizes the unique supremacy of Rome, signalized by a token screen image of officers and artists. So to the prepared entry of *the* March-tune, as in the Trojan citadel—with a suggestion of the third episode (wind and harp)—but now counter-pointed by the curses of all Carthage, since the fleet are out of hearing. A very terse reprise brings the scene and opera to a finish.

It is not easy to find a musical shape for a lingering death and despair. A cumula-tive self-pity (Purcell) was not right for the scorned and spirited queen. Still less was conventional mourning apt for her furious subjects. Vindictiveness was not a subject for an air either. Berlioz settles for disillusion and dissolution, operating in a mysterious (and indeed mystifying) environment of sacrificial ritual, which in its turn is psychologically upstaged by a pantomime of glorious Rome, while vocally supporting the fanatical nationalists on the terrace, not without a final pompous touch of more-royalist-than-thou. Thus the drama ends joyously but far from glamorously. Almost existentially! For while the thrusting empire-building principle has triumphed, and history confirmed the *pax Romana*, there is a sharp hint that the builders leave behind, in a once hopeful community, men embittered against the subverters of *their* royal regime as far as thought can reach. If Berlioz could not have predicted how soon French imperialism would meet its retribution, modern history has plenty to say about imperialists and satellites. It is this penetrat-ing sense of widening horizons that finally seals the assurance to a responsible viewer of a valid Virgilian music-drama, of a work of genius in its own original way. Meanwhile the orchestra round off for the last time 'Troy in **B** flat', so far removed from the 'Troy in **G**' with which the chosen people had expressed, almost deliriously, their happiness at the end, as they assumed, of the Greek war. On further acquaintance, this flight from **G** to a recovered **B** flat is a token of the growth of the *esprit de cité* from relaxation to dedication.

That Berlioz faced the problem of rising beyond the tragic suicide of a foreign queen, there is ample evidence in the survival of a different ending, amounting to forty-odd pages of full score, dated April 1858. Here, after Iris has appeared to end Dido's agony, scattering poppies over her (an interesting gloss on Virgil),[4] the ritual assembly swear undying enmity to Aeneas' race, until their destruction shocks the world. The text of this oath is identical with that of the Carthaginians' last effort in *The Trojans*, but here the music is a vigorous, coherent and brilliant **D** major chorus. A transitional piece (no stage indications) leads to **B** flat, in which, ushering in Clio, the March appears orchestrally, in plenitude: four verses, identical apart from string and harp vibrations in the last, and portions of the three episodes of the citadel version, the last of which figures in the penultimate stage of *The Trojans*. This hieratic scheme is punctuated by three pronouncements (on a monotone) by Clio, muse of history: (1) Scipioni Africano gloria. (2) Imperatori Augusto et divo Virgilio gloria. (3) Fuit Troia: stat Roma. The last is echoed by distant singers, and gives the signal for the final fanfare. It is a masterly penultimate scene, all told.

This complete draft (all but some missing initial, linking pages) suggests three points of illumination. First, the general attempt to hoist the narrative on to the plane of Roman epic, in harmony with the *Aeneid* as it was read by Virgil's contemporaries. Second, the hint of victory in Africa, surely a booster of French conquests. Third, the plan to elaborate the vengeance theme (with a passing recall of Pizarro) and then balance it by a reprise of the undaunted March (which presupposes the citadel exposition; as a revived strophical, it would be burdensome at this stage). The first remained in principle, unsung but spectacular; the second was rightly abandoned; the third was 'scrambled' into one verse of the March plus subsidiary choral imprecations, which continue later. So to objectors of 'perfunctory' here Berlioz might have replied that (*a*) he had tried up to four verses and it was too pompous and protracted (b) still less was there room for a vindictive sub-movement on top of Dido's death and confusion of all. If time hung heavy (which, of course, it did not), three or four verses might have been made tolerable by introducing a chorus of Trojan-Romans under Clio's banner, as in any mechanical ending of a classic opera, but it would all have been an overbearing breach of artistic privilege. So on to the approved text.

For a full performance in one evening an early start is essential. For the acceptance of that, Wagner at least must be thanked for establishing precedents. Even so, the entire score will, with intervals, take over five and a half hours. Berlioz's estimate of four and a half was optimistic. Dismissing the notion of giving the Troy and Carthage acts on consecutive evenings, as was done at the Karlsruhe première, we may ask what can most be spared. Emile Destranges, whose short monograph on the opera (Paris, 1897) was one of the first pieces of sustained critical description of the five acts, proposed ten cuts.[5] Many of these are, plausibly, recurrent strophes or periods, whose removal subtracts confirmation while leaving the basic musical

232

context, but they are listed cheerfully, and the surprising inclusion of large chunks, or even the entirety, of the Laocoon episode, is a warning against any censorship of taste. On the other hand, Destranges does not want to throw out numbers because they are irrelevant to the main action, such as Hylas' air and the sentinels' dialogue. However, the following cuts were suggested by the composer in his script in the Conservatoire library, and listed in the 1889 edition of the original vocal score of 1862 (printed but unpublished). None of these excerpts is in the printed full-score of the *Carthage* acts (1885).

1. Act 3. Workers' procession.
2. Entr'acte. La chasse royale.
3. Act 4. Anna-Narbal scene.
4. Act. 4. Iopas' song.
5. Act 5. Sentinels' duet.
6. Act 5. Dido-Aeneas encounter.

Of these the most astonishing is the last, due to dissatisfaction with a Dido who was left without reserve for her final scenes, and so far not a permanent suggestion. The omission of the hunt was the result of an unimaginative and time-wasting anti-production. Most people will agree with Destranges that difficult as the stage proposition is, it cannot just be played as an Entracte. There must be a scene. But the saving of time could be a tremendous asset, and the music is scarcely relevant to the act that it precedes.

So much for the opera as a stage-and-pit happening. I conclude with some attention to the development of character and motive in relation to Virgil and, on the musical side, to eighteenth-century opera on the Carthage scene.

Cassandra is almost entirely Berlioz's creation. As a court influence who perceives Priam's blind leadership, and as a lover, forced by her exceptional intuitions to press Coroebus to flee from the city that she cannot leave, and impatient of his refusal, she cuts an interesting figure, *vis-à-vis* her devoted but dull-witted hero. About all this the music is eloquent. On her continued pleading, however, the composer's surrender to a near-conventional 'love-duet' lowers the pitch. As the leader of the resisters in the second act, Cassandra makes a deep impression that qualifies her as one of the warning ghostly appearances to Aeneas, beside Hector. She and her picked group of fanatics provide songs and intonations for the resolute-oppressed of all time.

Dido, for the informed, mounts her throne to celebrate the foundation of Carthage as a name resounding from many archives. Now a mythical Phoenician goddess, now a struggling queen, forced to marry the Numidian king, Iarbas, to preserve her people and saving herself by suicide from that humiliation. At the next stage, Virgil's Dido cherishes the memory of her murdered husband, Sychaeus, and finds the pressing overtures of Iarbas intolerable, but the advent of Trojan Aeneas to her shores soon unsettles her resolve to remain a widow. The subsequent rivalry of Iarbas and Aeneas makes a ready-made tense situation, usually of gruesome triviality, in the eighteenth century operas based on Metastasio's *Didone abbandonata* (1724). In Piccinni's *Didon* the repudiated and defeated Iarbas is more of a personality, and his prayer to Jupiter (act 1) is forcible enough to make his cause valid and Dido's change of heart significant, with a corresponding lapse in Aeneas later from hero to betrayer, followed by Dido's spiritual downfall. Interesting anticipations of Berlioz's scenario include the appearance of the spirit of Anchises to urge heaven's will to Aeneas, of the priests of Pluto to add ritual sanction to Dido's suicide, and of the final burst of national rage against Aeneas.

In *The Trojans* Dido is first shown as a revered queen, mistress of the developing empire she has founded, but in firm and reassuring communication with her people on whom she depends for her stability. But then, as a widowed woman, she confesses a restlessness to her sister, and to herself a 'dangerous passion'. (The disclosure of this unexplained discontent calls for music to substantiate it.) The arrival of the shipwrecked strangers (such as she had been) rouses her sympathy which Ascanius (soprano), leaping over the centuries as he identifies his connexions, augments in his young prince style. Narbal's entry with war news brings her back to the country's needs, but when Aeneas himself jumps up unexpectedly, present and of commanding stature, and promises alliance and enemy extermination in one breath, we know that any distinctions between the master race and the lesser breeds are being forgotten, and the jumping of the hurdles a question of time. After the ensuing hunt-and-storm interludes, indeed, it is most surprising how long it takes Dido to realize a 'conspiracy' of events to make her put Sychaeus out of her mind. Perhaps it is rather that Aeneas' attention has to be wooed at the expense of his mission to rebuild Troy in Italy. There is in the national anthem (new and etiolated version), the ballet, and in Iopas' hymn to the corn spirit, more than a flavour of the oriental ease which good Romans liked to contrast with Italian simplicity. A veiled suggestion, from Anna to Narbal, of a Cupid persona in the boy Ascanius, as he takes Dido's wedding ring from her finger, reflects Dido's trend of mind. (N. B. Aeneas' bland reportage in **Ex. 58**, page 225). So, after a significant general salute to the night's lulling murmurs, there follows the duet, fructified by the timeless thoughts of a certain Lorenzo and Jessica, but annihilated by the devastating interruption of the divine voice, for Aeneas, not Dido, whose moment of truth is a boundless ecstasy shared with him.

234

Virgil borrowed from Homer the man Aimas, a subsidiary personage who confronts Achilles in *Iliad* 20 (in an arguably late interpolation), and is pictured as superseding Dardanian Priam as chief. But Virgil's first concern is to replace Menelaus in the vindictive search for Helen, and to represent the ideal Roman type, in whose son the poet's readers would identify Augustus, for whose benefit he was offering his epic. In *The Trojans* Aeneas, a strong, silent leader, takes charge after the shock of Laocoon's death, directs the transport of the horse and retires to his quarters. When the enemy are destroying the city Aeneas, asleep, is receiving his first 'Italy' message from Hector. He rallies his troops, nevertheless, to defend the citadel to the death, and that is the last one hears of him until his son names him to Dido. A stranded chieftain bound for Italy, his plunge into Carthaginian politics is, to say the least, impulsive. Slow but solid Narbal, a realist in his governmental sphere, does not relish the situation as the match-making Anna does. On the short view Anna's diagnosis is right, and Narbal has to join in the quintet, the Cupid image staring him in the face. Thus obliquely, after these twists and turns, including the forest union—to all appearances an episode as transitory as the mock marriage described by Virgil—Aeneas, left alone with Dido, joins her for a full declaration of passion on equal terms. It is enough to call down on Aeneas an instant messenger from heaven. The voice that cries 'Italy' is an inexorable command to leave Carthage, queen and all.

From this point Aeneas, the 'true' Roman, can have no doubts where his way lies, yet he wished Dido to understand his dilemma. While, as the first decisive step, he has given orders to leave to a responsive Pantheus, who reads divine anger in the weather, he feels compelled to see Dido again. He has found her deaf to his invocation of high imperial duty. He dreads another encounter, and prays it will be soon, but he would rather die than not see her again. Only the voices of the Trojan dead can screw his resolve to the sticking-point. Virgil blandly allows Dido and Aeneas to argue it out. She meets Aeneas with reproaches for his secretive abandonment of her, and then with an appeal not to leave her ruined, childless and politically friendless. He replies in kind. There was never any intention of concealment, nor was there any marriage contract. His oracle has dictated Italy for his future kingdom, as she had made for Carthage. Berlioz shrewdly absorbs this fruitless dialectic in Aeneas' long and musically many-pronged soliloquy, an advance on the smug indecision of the Aeneas of eighteenth-century Italian opera. The reluctance of Aeneas to give Dido up is nicely anticipated by Berlioz in the equal reluctance of two soldiers to give up their girls for the 'caresses' of storm and ocean.

Aeneas rouses the fleet, and for a moment, with crusader cries of 'Italy!', the March (smartened up) in full swing, the fleet on course, and Aeneas aiming his passionate adieux at the palace, it seems as if the drama will terminate in an outburst of empire-building sentiment, glorifying whatever Augustan pride Paris might find in the sixties. But this is not the end but the beginning.

Dido now appears in person, pursuing Aeneas. Scorned by the man who had promised everything and now was abandoning her in the name of implacable destiny, she does not spare her denunciation of his inhumanity. She ignores his protests of affection thwarted by the call of duty, and, mocking his trembling response to the fanfare calling all Trojans, leaves cursing. The revelation of her tragic predicament is a tribute to the composer's mastery of accompanied recitative. The next scene shows her last despairing effort to delay Aeneas' departure. When she learns that the fleet is already out to sea, she passes from malediction to preparation for death (a lingering moment of sweet memory), dire prophecy, the fatal stab and a vista of the Rome to be, not given to her fellow countrymen. To the last Dido is true to herself. Her continuing story shapes the latter half of *The Trojans* and gives the final glamour a dark streak. It is much harder to believe in adventurer Aeneas.

Ascanius is little more than an important messenger or assistant. But Anna here is more than a confidant of the queen. Less of a politician than Virgil's Anna, she nevertheless encourages Dido to consider marrying again before the castaways have arrived, and once Aeneas has made his unmistakable impression, she sees a prosperous future for queen and country. When he defaults she blames herself. (Virgil's callous lines, indicating that Anna never dreamt that Aeneas' defection would upset her more than Sychaeus' death, are excluded.) Anna remains a true friend and sister. As a fanatic servant of the state, Berlioz's Narbal is an attractive and consistent figure.

Finally, there are the Trojans: always under pressure, enduring, united and, one must assume, visionary to the end, reflecting the pride of the early Empire (and any other) in wider boundaries but also the struggle for survival about which the twentieth century has little to learn. Polarizing this master race, the equally proud and united Carthaginians, who, when betrayed, leave their maledictions for the future Troy as the last statement in words, and with them a penetrating insight into the hard core of bitterness in modern revisionist states, classes and races, without conceivable end.

Clearly Berlioz did not think all this out, though he must have handled the whole Virgilian thread. But the character making and breaking goes on through the drama, illuminated by music, and it is this total theatre on a world stage that will carry *The Trojans* from one operatic generation to another, as a living document of men, women and nations, such as only music can bring home.

NOTES

1. The full score of *Les Troyens* à *Carthage* was printed, but not published, in 1885. It has ten major cuts, and in any case there is only one copy in Britain, in the British Museum. The full score of *La Prise de Troie* (1899), uncut, is exclusive to the British Museum and the National Library of Scotland, in Britain. There is no score of *Les Troyens* in the old collected edition. The new edition exhibits the full five-act version in its two volumes of score.

2. Of recent studies, Brooks Otis's *Virgil: a study in civilized poetry* (Oxford, 1964) deserves special acknowledgement here for his perceptive analysis of Virgil's intentions and execution, unrevised as the *Aeneid* remained at the author's death.

3. Berlioz rejected 'I-*ta*-lia' in favour of the more expletive 'Ita-*li*-e'.

4. The scattering from the ceiling of a great multitude of poppies, one for each casualty, remains a penultimate feature of every Armistice Day commemoration in the Royal Albert Hall, London.

5. (1) Coroebus' air, Verse 2; (2) Cass. Cor. duet, Verses 1–3 and recit; (3) Lament for Laocoon. Part or whole; (4) Aeneas' tent. Chorus (except last 8 bars); (5) Dido's address to her people, Verse 2; (6) Dido and Anna, 'Sichée! ô mon époux, pardonne', 1st time; (7) Aeneas, 'C'est le dieu Mars' to Recitative; (8) Anna-Narbal, Verse 2; (9) Iopas' song, Verses 2b, 3.

Contemporary caricatures of the composer

14

Berlioz's Methods

A COMPOSER of stature enters the musical life of the generations after him as the creator of major and minor works, some of which at once leap over the barriers of period and style, while others waver, or, while clear in intention, may be irrationally relegated to an insignificant position in concert society, temporarily or more irrevocably. At the outset it was observed that as a knowing Beethovenite, Berlioz was out to enlarge the scope of music in every genre adopted, but that his approach was, unlike Beethoven's, consistently on a literary foundation, including opera. So far his musical output hangs together as an erratic career of creative effort, whether transmitting a 'programme' into structured assertions or developing 'sonata' patterns from given material; except that he would undoubtedly have written more opera had he had proper facilities and patronage. By incidentally liberating that genre from the Italian aesthetic of minimum effort, and writing almost entirely for orchestra, with or without singers or acting, Berlioz secured a certain level of public address in the concert-room, opera-house or contingent devotional centre, while not achieving the pronounced conquests of Beethoven in symphony and chamber sonata, of Wagner in music-drama. Yet every composer, whether producing in accordance with or ahead of his time, must be regarded as aiming not only at the completion of specific projects or works but also at a growing communication of his creative personality. With this total inheritance of musicianship in mind, I propose to exhibit some of the general features of Berlioz's art, in so far as these are not already apparent.

The most patent fundamental of Berlioz's music is melody, from a characteristic phrase-pattern to a developed strophe. If one begins to assemble the raw material of the thirty-odd works concerned, one becomes aware, first, of numberless pulsating phrases. They usually show a common four-bar basis, but exceptions are not hard to find: 'La captive', *Sanctus*, the dominant, emerging themes of 'Scène d'amour' and Father Lawrence's final appeal (5 bars); 'Zaïde', *Iudex crederis*, *Lacrimosa*, the Allegro openings of *Les francs juges* overture and *Harold* (3 bars); *Salvum fac* (6 bars). The common element is the distinctive character of these rhythmic starts. They do not yield to grouping according to melodic or harmonic interest. Whether

by compulsive movement by steps, or by harmonically conjunct or disjunct intervals, in restricted or overflowing compass, invention suits the mood of the moment.
Similarly, whether four bars become a multiplying eight or a more flexible or
contentious pattern, or again a quasi-declamatory period, and whether subjects or
groups balance measurably, is a matter of temperament; but second-subject groups
tend to be fragmentary, wayward and sometimes a very perfunctory concession to
convention. From this point analysis of line is bound to widen. Three routes branch
from here: first, the developed strophe; secondly, a succession of scenes and sub-
scenes; thirdly, symphonic movements of varying construction.[1]

1. Schubert started off song-composition by setting a scene, *Hagar's lament*, the
makings of an extensive solo-cantata; a heavy narrative in which singer *and*
pianist would have somehow to work their passage or admit a declining vocabulary.
But 30 songs later the *Faust*-driven composer produced a new type of concentrated
despair in the resoundingly strophical 'Margaret at the spinning-wheel'; and
nearly 150 songs after that (covering a bare year) he revealed in 'Erlking' an even
more riveting whole dramatic scene, which proved to be only the beginning of a
historical event in genre-creation.

Fed on the 'guitar romances' of Dalayrac *et al*, and chronologically slower to
develop, Berlioz found it inevitable to begin with strophical 'Mélodies', primarily
for the singer. The differences between 'La dépit de la bergère' and the piano versions
of 'La captive' or the wider strophe of 'Villanelle' (1840) lie more in quality of
sustained utterance than in method of appeal. It is a matter of a more sensitive vocal
line and a more subtle range of harmonic overtones. Meanwhile Reber and

Ex. 31.1

Ex. 31.2

Boisselot (**Ex. 32.1**, page 112) had respectively stayed with the romances in 1837;
Reber, with varied piano figures for later verses. Nor was Berlioz incapable of

furnishing stirring national songs, as in *Vox populi* or 'Chant guerrier'. He orchestrated five verses of *La Marseillaise* with energetic precision, and as late as 1859 he arranged Martini's 'Plaisir d'amour' ditty for chamber orchestra.

In the rest of *Nuits* (nos. 2–6), as in other songs, the stimulus of later verses led to a richer design; and in 'La belle voyageuse' as revised (1834) Berlioz had begun to implement by orchestration the jejune routine 'accompaniment' of his best songs, to include *Nuits* eventually (1856). He even confronted 'Erlkönig' with the full orchestra, and scored points that Liszt, working at the same song, could not challenge except by different orchestral paraphrases. Thus voice-and-piano, while valuable to the home musician of every period since, became the rehearsal stage of the new genre, song with orchestra for the concert-room, mainly for one voice, occasionally for chorus. In *Sara* the multiplicity of images evoked by the selected verses of Hugo's *Orientale* is matched by a stream of variants and episodes for the recurring motive, yet the passing and plenary reprises of the initial phrases are not only functional but persuasive, such are the melodic invention and the subtle interplay of three-tier chorus and chamber orchestra. Berlioz never found another

Ex. 15.3

opportunity for such a distillation of euphony, but it crystallized a method of appeal which remained a permanent asset.

2. The dramatic and psychological demands of the operas and cantatas inevitably stretched Berlioz's resources. The cantabile strophe, neatly or casually packed, was never abandoned, from the formal declarations of Teresa and Cellini and the Pope to the sub-acid absorptions of the homesick Hylas, and from the utterly contrasting songs of Mephistopheles and Margaret for *Eight Scenes* (later for *The Damnation of Faust*) to the serene shepherds song in *L'enfance du Christ* and the poignant opening of 'Te ergo quaesumus' (*Te Deum*). But in order to cover fresh incidents without losing contact with an initial mood an open-ended but still repeatable melodic period becomes expedient. A persuasive recovery of melodic shape can at once supersede a declamatory interlude and be challenged in its turn. Such cantabile-plus schemes have been so constantly noted throughout our survey that citation would be otiose, but Norbert Dufourcq, amongst others, named the fusion of air and

recitative as the first of Berlioz's bequests to French music (*La musique française*, part 7, ch. 7) and Wilfrid Mellers (*Man and Music*, vol. 2) moved in the same direction.

Alternately, formally contrasted interludes may hang together in a loosely coherent ABA(CA) succession. Berlioz rarely, however, found any use for the recitative-air-finale pattern of Viennese opera and Weber. In a more temperamental situation, a series of interlinked sub-movements, each more or less cantabile, more or less orchestrally motivated or stimulated by the rhythms of speech and action, are the chosen solution. Choral expression, as implying either the firm rhythm of a harmonic progression or the metrically more wayward impact of polyphony and imitational phrase, is a standing variant from solo-melodic assertion. Precisely structured dance-movements and marches recur, usually with a resounding refrain. Finally, the accumulation of such variously biased numbers becomes an act or part, usually converging in a chorus or multiple ensemble. We shall consider separately the bearing of harmonic and orchestral texture on musical shaping, but meanwhile 'Mélodie' in the most comprehensive sense stands paramount.

3. In purely orchestral composition, instrumental timbre replaces vocal line with what analogies a growing instrumental control can offer, and a characteristic stretch of rhythm can make do for the support of an articulate sentence or a poetic verse, but a too self-contained feature is inimical to any extension unless it contains mobile phrases. All Berlioz's eight overtures have a slow introduction or interlude, which affords space for a cantabile. *King Lear's* opening is particularly detached, and reverberates in and across the reprise of the Allegro; and operatic overtures (*Benvenuto Cellini*, *Le carnaval romain*, *Béatrice and Bénédict* and probably *Les Francs Juges*) quote arias in advance. But in the main movement the sonata shape grows out of contrasting groups of crisp phrase-development, the trend of which to form swinging 4- or 8-bar units of momentum has already been noticed. What distinguishes Berlioz from Beethoven or Schubert is a certain waywardness about his expositions, with consequently slight development. *Les Francs Juges's* insatiable second subject remains an exception, inviting speculation on what it signifies.

For coda Berlioz follows Beethoven in his blend of relevant after-thought and exuberant rhetoric, Beethoven remaining more in command of transforming

Ex. 44.1

Ex. 44.2

souvenirs. The song with orchestra has become an ordered succession of melodic and textured phrases for orchestra, linked and crowned with fortuitous or organic material. One may not so readily remember the contexts of entries and re-entries as happens with Beethoven, but most of the salient phrases are easy to recall, once identified with their work. Not for nothing did Berlioz start his musical career by absorbing the operatic repertoire of Paris, thus engaging in a cult of the easily memorable. It corresponded to the assimilation of selected folk-songs by composers of this century.

Since most of the symphonic movements are made up on the sonata plan of the overtures, or from plain enlargements of a principal opening and interlude, the processes already sketched can be observed in the four symphonies without further specification. The composer's bland attribution of the start of the *Symphonie Fantastique* to a youthful setting of Florian's 'Je vais donc quitter pour jamais' is not to be taken as literally as Tiersot did (see page 131), but the appearance of a pronounced open-ended melodic line, soon repeated with fresh harmonic punctuation and after-phrase, is significant. The ensuing *idée fixe* of the Allegro, biographically identifiable as an interlude in Herminia's second aria ('J'exhale en vain ma plainte') in the 1828 cantata, here introduces itself as an unfaltering melodic line of 8-7, 8-9, and 7 bars, a firm pattern for a quasi-strophical reprise and later for implementing an instant interlude in the Waltz and finally a neat parody on the high clarinet for the 'danse grotesque'. But it also justifies itself as a unit of development in the Allegro, as well as a 'cyclic' symbol par excellence, flexible enough to be pertinently recurrent, not a break on a movement as many 'motto-themes' become. The theme can take all that is put upon it (except in the March). For the rest, the main section of the Waltz is obviously a repetitive and expansive violin tune, sufficiently composite to yield easily to the *idée* in an extraneous Schubertian key (**F** amid **A** major), and sufficiently tough to acquire without loss of face a liberal assortment of orchestral flourish (woodwind and harp) in the reprise, and a considerable and thematically gratuitous coda (animato). In the arch-pattern of the Pastoral Scene

243

rhetorical elements blend with the flute-violin melody which functions as first and second subject in commanding gestures, yet *forte* for only one bar. The oboes of the

Ex. 36

dialogue fore and aft are, so to speak, only the cover story of the inner message. The remaining two movements are mainly the products of colour-contrast, yet a brash major-key melody breaks into the horror-march; the *Dies irae* Tone retains its mock identity in the wild, sepulchral dance; and the subject of the fugal finale acquires the role of a folk-dance tune fragment—like the Dargason used by Holst in *Second Suite in* **F** (for military band) and *St. Paul's Suite* (for strings)—while precipitating interesting semitonal deviations penultimately. It must be agreed that here mélodie is given unusual lease for a symphony. And if *Lélio* is regarded as an extension of this motto-propelled 'Episode', every musical number there but the final fantasia is strophical or an air. It need hardly be said that where a fond farewell to Miranda, in Italian, is perpetually involved, cantabile reigns, and even Caliban has his Dargason.

In the *Harold* symphony thematic development is much more pronounced. The square but tuneful phrase announced so innocently by the viola in the Adagio declares its independence in the middle movements, as a sort of awkward over-riding 'counterpoint' to the prevailing material, but it is scarcely a motto-theme. In the march the main section is virtually an extending violin strophe, with wood punctuation. Its token return leads into a nice after-song of receding content, one of Berlioz's inspired pages. The hymnal interlude is demonstrably a pilgrim's refrain, and the piping, too, of the mountaineer next encountered by the Byronic wanderer suggests popular music. The rest is symphonic music on lines detailed earlier, but melody in the large and in the instant is a constant resort.

Romeo and Juliet, a symphony enclosed in a dramatic sketch, is sprinkled with actual or virtual song-verses: the 'Premiers transports' of the prologue; the oboe tune from *Sardanapale* in the first main movement, committed to brass for Berliozian 'counterpoint' later; the young Capulets' carolling after the fête, and the various emanations from the surviving phrase of the orchestral sequel, on which Rolland's 'tendresse Virgilienne' (beside Wagner's 'fureurs chanelles') may be acceptable to many listeners without ignoring the highly symmetrical strophes of 'So starben wir' (*Tristan und Isolde,* act 2, scene 2, *cf.* act 3, scene 3); and, for the final burst of

Ex. 41

oratorio, Father Lawrence's air and oath-song. Nevertheless, in this most amphibious of symphonies thematic development predominates. In *Symphonie funèbre et triomphale* the 'march' maintains a sonata-design, but the 'oraison' is a recitative and aria for trombone, and the 'Apothéose' is patently more strophical than not.

So much for the marked pursuit of melodic line in and beyond settings for a text. But what of harmonic progression as a characterizing agent? It is not easy or, indeed, strictly possible to formulate a balanced view of Berlioz's procedures. He may, in selected examples, appear so conventional as to be deemed colourless; in other instances, to be so restless as to be monotonous. If one cannot be just, one must be prepared to be arbitrary. On the conventional side, then, there is ample evidence of an acceptance of tonic harmony (the triad of ascending degrees in different octaves, 1-3-5-1-3-5... in any selection, the 5 being optional) as a start, not a forward retention, and dominant or fifth-degree harmony (ascending 5-7-2 with commonly accessory 4 or 6 flat) as the most direct approach to the tonic and the elementary alternative for a close. In the following harmonizations, **Ex. 42** keeps to the tonic, apart from

Ex. 42

the dominant to pick out bar 2 (-*bo*-le). **Ex. 19.1** similarly diverges in bars 3-4 up to the last beat. **Ex. 19.2** is hooked to a tonic bass for the diabolical spell under remote control. **Ex. 19.3**, with a wider sweep in view, circles round the tonic in bars 1-2 and then makes for the dominant for its first cadence.

Ex. 19.1

Chorus of
Sylphs
and
Gnomes

ALTOS: Bien-tôt, oui, bien-tôt,__ sous un voi - le D'or et d'a-zur
(+ Alto Oboe)

TENORS: Heu - - reux Faust! bien - tôt, sous un __ voi - - - le
(+ Bsn.)

Ex. 19.2

(The spirits hover round Faust, asleep, then gradually disappear.)

Sylph Dance

Allegro mouvement de Valse

6 Vln. soli

Ex. 19.3

Soldiers' Chorus

Allegro

Vil - les en - tou - ré - es De murs __ et rem-parts __ Fil -
-let - - - tes su - cré - es Aux ma-lins re - gards __

These being accepted as the normal harmonic framework for a starting melodic line, and often for a concluding phrase, we may fasten some attention on the following unusual cadences. The first two, so unlike in accentuation, are grammatically identical. The first clinches a disturbed *Mardi Gras* (*Benvenuti Cellini*, act 2, *fin.*). The second punctuates a deserted Margaret's last gasp of despair (*The*

Ex. 63.1

Allegro assai

Tutti

ff   *ff* — — *ff*

degree of   1   1   3 major   1
root or real
bass of chord

Ex. 63.2

(The equals sign denotes an implied change of degree on the same note, with a corresponding change of key.)

Ex. 63.3

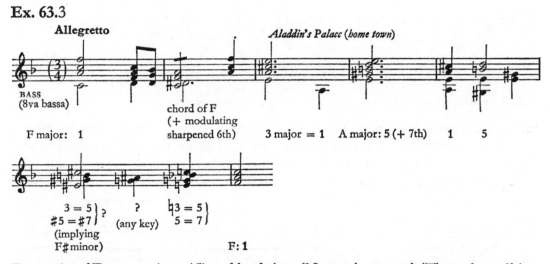

Damnation of Faust, act 4, sc. 15) and leads into 'Nature immense'. (There the striking sharpened fifth (**C** sharp) prepares somewhat for the leap into **C** sharp minor, unrelated to **F**, for Faust's new reaction.) The third example exhibits the same outlandish key in an instant modulation and then slides back by way of a rhetorical surprise to shape the refrain of 'Zaïde'. For a prolonged, somewhat dreamy finish, of the kind favoured by the composer after a dynamic moment, the following harmonically simple but haunting progression (*The Trojans*, act 3, *fin.*), made interesting by the semitonal bass, demonstrates that Berlioz was no fumbler (**Ex. 64**). (Each bar has been halved to show the 3-bar units.) A similar example, more contrapuntally discursive, can be found at the end of *The Trojans*, Act 1. It ends with a brisk semitonal drive upward, over a dominant bass, to the tonic minor, to seal Cassandra's grief.

Turning to incidental semitonal twists away from the diatonic or 'straight' scale, we may refer to the second phrase of the septet in Act 4 of *The Trojans* (**Ex. 59**, page 226) for its early but ready slip into the tonic minor and back. More subtle is the essentially harmonic implications of the unilinear accompaniment to Faust's

Ex. 64

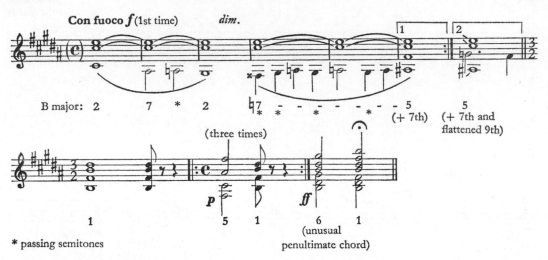

* passing semitones

interested tour of Margaret's room (**Ex. 65**). The tonality is intentionally obscure, but it may be guessed by alert ears to make sense. (Unessential turns are marked with an asterisk.) A comparable piece of writing is the prelude to Romeo alienated (*Romeo and Juliet*, Part 2, init.).

Ex. 65

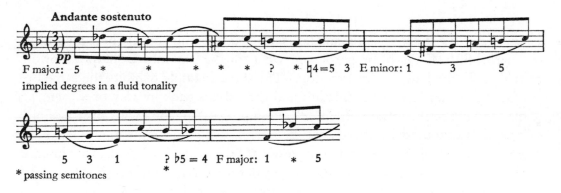

* passing semitones

Next, amongst progressions that are arresting in their immediate context, I may give a harmonic abstract (**Ex. 66**) of the approach to the previously cited cadence in the opening of *Requiem* (**Ex. 28.1**, page 95). Without bars 4-7 the progression would pass unnoticed, but with the disintegrating chords in bars 4-5, repeated, the restoration of **G** minor via the chord of **A** flat gains the needed urgency. The disturbance of routine underlines the progress of the text. (Verdi has a radical change of key and phrase at this point in the Mass.) Too precious to repeat, this

Ex. 66

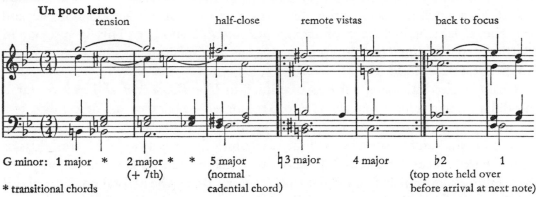

Un poco lento

tension   half-close   remote vistas   back to focus

G minor: 1 major *   2 major *   *   5 major   ♮3 major   4 major   ♭2   1

                 (+ 7th)   (normal   (top note held over

* transitional chords   cadential chord)   before arrival at next note)

observance of 'lux' is balanced in the reprise by two extended periods of plainer but insistent harmony in diminishing tone, **Ex. 28.2** (page 96) being the second. This kind of invention continually reinforces the easier maintained tension of close imitational counterpoint.

A further and emotionally reverse example of this two-prong mastery arises at the end of the Offertory of the same work. The piece unfolds as an instrumental fugal number in **D** minor against a halting but steady release of the text in a 'drone' of voices round the *dominant*, **A**, which the freely moving contrapuntal harmony deliberately ignores without unseating it. Eventually a flash of total *dominant* agreement leaves 'Quam olim Abraham et semini eius' at vanishing point, in tense expectancy of 'promisisti'. Suddenly **D** *major* breaks gradually downwards in the descending degrees of two octaves (5-3-1-5-3-1) in close, cumulative drone entries of each voice, pinpointed by strings and integrated melodically by the woodwind. It remains to form cadences in the revealed key, and to let the tonic major resound at last in the chord of **D**. A sturdy process of 130 bars of phrase-development, geared into mounting suspense by the drones, has thus received its quittance in an unpredictable transformation of the drone, contrapuntal, melodic and harmonic. Resonance itself. This concentration of expression, which none can miss, prepares the sympathetic listener for the humility of *Hostias*. The cynical participant, looking back at the dead in anger, and rejecting the serene conclusion, will find relief in the savage humour of Britten's *War Requiem*. Yet Berlioz was no psalm-droner. He retained his sense of dedication in a welter of adversity and disillusion.

In his well documented but somewhat defensive essay on Berlioz's pioneer qualities as a harmonist (*La revue musicale*, Berlioz number, 1956), M. Jacques Chailley stresses the composer's special use of 'Inverted pedal' (i.e. bass drone placed on top) as his main reform; implying that this pedal has sometimes to be 'understood'. I find this a fanciful generalization, but the Offertory chorus is a good example, and the choral lament in Part 5 of *Romeo and Juliet* is another. This is just one of Berlioz's many devices for constructing a progression of character by the application of method.

Chailley also tabulates various examples in *The Damnation of Faust* of rapid modulation to a remote key. First, **F** to **B** minor in two bars by bass descending to a mixed-up **F** (**F-B** natural-**G** sharp-**D** *asc.*) and so to **F** sharp, point d'appui for **B**. Faust, in Margaret's room at twilight, welcomes the sensation of the fresh kiss of dawn (part 3, scene 9, bars 21–23). Secondly, **B** major to **F**, via **D** sharp (**E** flat), then bass falling semitonally from **E** flat to **C** (minor), **B** flat (the pivotal note in a chord of **C** that invokes **F**): Margaret, entering later, distracted with passionate feelings about Faust, sees life as a mockery, and sinks into a childhood reverie, 'The King of Thule' (part 3, scene 13). Such ready slips into alien territory show once and for all that Berlioz was ready to adopt the then modern trends towards a fluid tonality when he thought fit. But what of the following lapse in the middle of the Waltz of *Symphonie Fantastique*? (**Ex. 67**) Well, it is *not* as the composer had it, but as Liszt

Ex. 67

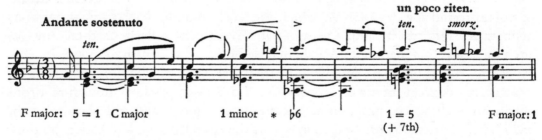

decorated it in his curious 'prelude' on that interlude (in **B**), as preface to his arrangement of the marche horrifique. It is a question of degree of unbalance. Admittedly 'Villanelle' (**Ex. 32.2**, page 112) comes very near the Liszt level with its glance at the flattened *second*.

There is no space to demonstrate Berlioz's habitual and sometimes trite command of modulation by repeating a phrase in descending or ascending steps, ending on the new dominant desired. Nor is it worth even tabulating the range of key in the developments and codas of his sonata-movements, since these are usually slight, but the flattened sixth of the key of the moment is a likely bet. The Allegro of *Les Francs Juges* overture shows the most forcibly structuralized key system: **F** minor (1) and its related major, **A** flat (2) —**C** minor (3) and its related major, **E** flat (2)—**F** minor (1) and its opposite, **F** (4) —**D** flat (5), **F** (2); (1, 2, and 3, being the primary thematic trends; 5, a reverberation from earlier events, and 4, rhetorical variants of 2.) By contrast, in the Allegro of *Symphonie fantastique* the irregular return of the *idée* in the dominant key for what amounts to a reprise sounds wrong to my ears, though I find no confirmation in the analyses of P. Magnette (1908), Wotton, Hopkins, Shore, except that the last considers the 'development' (including this entry) 'incoherent'.

'Opportunism' is a fair summary of Berlioz's harmonic mystique. By contrast,

Ex. 68.1

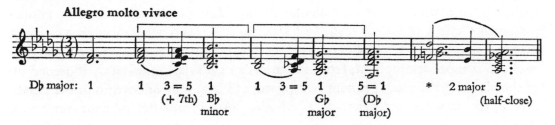

Ex. 68.2

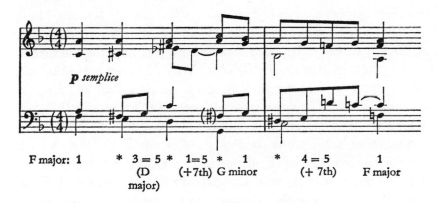

let us recall the basic harmony of two piano pieces of 1839. **Ex. 68.1** is the start, **Ex. 68.2** the reprise, of a straightforward phrase in each case. Its methodically incisive progressions, not the decorative phrasing of Chopin or Mendelssohn, mark it as Schumann. To cite a Berlioz parallel, integrate the following as demonstrations of harmonic approach: **Ex. 63–66.**

Attempts to pin down Berlioz's intentions by his choice of key, with implied ulterior motive, are sure of failure. **D** (major) is quite ambivalent in itself. At one moment it is a relaxed key: Harlequin's arietta in the carnival (from a song in **D** flat), attending a mock declaration of passion; Ascanio's badinage (air 2); Mephisto's

251

evil magic; 'La captive' (later version); two *Nuits*. But it can also have the triumphant or even minatory associations inherited from Handel and Mozart in **D**. So, Teresa defies age in her second air, and she and Cellini proclaim their mastery on the eve of the final crisis; Hero, looking forward to Claudio's return, seasons her reveries with as obvious a picture of the home-coming conqueror as the glowing expectations given by a well known count's servant to a dandified recruit (in **C**). In the sinister range, those diabolical girls in *Érigone* move to **D** *major* for a last moment of corybantic elation, and the Carthaginians in the original finale of *Troyens*, pledged to liquidation of the Trojan myth, leap into **D** for an orgy of hatemanship. In contrast, **G** is a joyous key, from *Harold* and the Goldsmiths' chorus (*Benvenuto Cellini*) to *Béatrice et Bénédict*, (*init*. and *fin*.), and *The Trojans*, the opening and the second ballet-movement; but the preceding ballet-movement is languor itself. **E** is more triumphant, from Herminia's final aria, significantly loosened up at the close by the establishment of a broader (3-bar) unit of rhythm in the prayer theme, to the wrestlers' dance of *The Trojans*, Act 1, and the jubilant war-cry of Act 3.

F is for absolutely anything, from an Easter hymn, a 'flea song' (Mephisto's), a reverie ('Thule') and song of despair (*The Damnation of Faust*), to 'Ma belle ville', 'Dites, la jeune belle', an elopement plan (*Benvenuto Cellini*, act 1), 'Queen Mab', Iopas' naturism. The key of **A** is for the nonchalantly happy: the *Carnival* overture, *Sara*, 'Villanelle'. **A** flat is variously absorbed, on Beethoven lines: the duet (trio) in *Benvenuto Cellini*, Act 1, the trio in *Béatrice et Bénédict*, Act 2, 'Le coucher du soleil', the Bethlehem stable scene. **B** unites the resolution of the new Rail at Lille, the *Romeo and Juliet* finish and that of *The Trojans*, Act 1, scene 1 (Cassandra's 'If'), but also the worldly assurance of Mephisto's 'serenade'. But for the delicate palace welcome to that Carthaginian hero, pious Aeneas (act 4, scene 2) the switch to **B** seems designed more for the contrast of the drop back to **G** in the ensuing ballet. **B** flat appears lyrically for the spreading amorous crowd of troops and students in *The Damnation of Faust*, Part 2, *fin*., but the 'Roman myth' sanctifies its finest hour. Minor keys are chancy and comparatively rare: **C** sharp minor for Faust's 'Nature immense' and the flight from Egypt; **A** minor for the Hungarian march, the cabalistic dance of Herod's crooked advisers and the lament for Andromache; **G** minor for the marche horrifique (*Symphonic fantastique* 4th movement), the nominal anarchists of *Harold* (4th movement), a worried Herod, a sadly frustrated Joseph, a bitterly nostalgic Hylas, in a discernible connexion with Mozart's utterly saddened or subdued women (Ilia, Pamina). But no case for a key-propensity in a given mood can be substantiated as it can for Beethoven.

This dogged tabulation of harmonic features may seem extravagant, but in my estimate harmonic progression is one of the most instant features of composer-identity in the classical-romantic period of 1700–1900.

All this melodic patterning and harmonic punctuation, however, is not normally presented in the 'black and white' of a piano, or chorus, or ultimately, in many cases, voice and piano. It is suffused with the blended colouring of orchestral masses of every dimension. For some listeners the Berlioz touch is most patently manifest here. His advance in this field was historical. 'Might have been Strauss' was the spontaneous comment on the scoring of even the early *Cléopâtre* cantata, in the review of the English première at the Queen's Hall in 1903 (*Pall Mall Gazette*, 13 November). Berlioz's way of writing for orchestra was positively new. He thought in orchestral terms from the start; that is, in blobs of sound *per se*, rather than in an imposition of colouring on a progression already formulated. Beethoven had added dynamic grading and a new degree of harmonic change to musical expression. Berlioz introduced this orchestral sonority, a typical attribute of the first Viennese school, as a new dimension.

His specific achievement defies encapsulation, but a sense of direction is desirable. What or who meant most to him craft-wise? In the *Traité* (see page 172) his display of his own work is not only modest but meagre, except that most examples are extensive. Since copies of the book are widely accessible, I shall not quote from it. Of the seventeen examples, I may mention four. (1) The separation of the violon-celli from the double-basses for the semitonal clash of 'Flammis acribus' (*Requiem*, 'Rex tremendae' *med.*), but also (2) for the first Adagio of the 'Scène d'amour' (*Romeo and Juliet*). (3) The entry of the piano for *The tempest* fantasia (*Lélio*, sixth movement). (4) In contrast, the bold penetration into the lowest notes of the tenor trombone for the end of 'Hostias' (*Requiem Mass*), to the power of eight—for security against drop-outs. To which one might add Strauss's oboe citations (*King Lear*, Andante *ppp* and Allegro, *dolce* theme) to place with Berlioz's precise examples of oboe roles from Beethoven. From the *Traité* alone, if evidence were needed, one could take for granted Berlioz's fresh investigation and long-range forecast of the capacity of each instrument (13 lines of music to illustrate awkward phrase-patterns on the clarinet), and his now shrewd, now astonishing, discernment of the 'mood' of different instruments, of different registers on each, and even of different keys. (There is an obvious mis-statement about mixture stops on the organ which has naturally threatened the confidence of every practising organist.)

To an unparalleled knowledge of operatic scoring, remembered if not available for study, and also of advanced orchestral music, Berlioz devoted his practical experience and gifted imagination. He recognized the new security of production, for even tone and proper intonation, of the Boehm flute, and foresaw the like progress of the single and double reeds. He was aware, too, of the need of the trumpets and horns for some brand of extension-system in aid of a proper, unrestricted vocabulary, while apparently unable to depend on the presence of the valved instruments which Halévy had mixed with the valveless ones in opera as early as 1835. Berlioz stretched his invention to auralize the magic of numbers, gathered round one instrumental line, especially the strings; or moving in unprecedented harmony in certain genres, such as double-basses or timpani and the now regularly appearing harps and rarely the piano. If Beethoven and Weber had given many instruments a new life, Berlioz continued the revival in fresh contexts.

Moreover, the Berlioz orchestra, ranging from a chamber orchestra of today to a full orchestra with extra bands, was extraordinarily flexible. Beethoven had added a wind group, without trombones, to the standing tuttis of strings and full orchestra. Berlioz not only stabilized both a woodwind (horn) and a brass group, but subdivisions of these. Further, whereas the classical procedures for blend had been based on a typical change from one texture to another, with Berlioz the incidental colouring is much more organic; that is, essential to the melodic shape. The upshot was that while Beethoven's developments and interludes might be unpredictable, his symphonies showed a certain progress from strings to tutti, or just tutti, for first subject, woodwind (strings) and tutti for second subject, in the first and last Allegro, string cantabile and woodwind antiphony for slow movement, agile antiphony for third movement, and stormy scenes or boisterous humour or apocalyptic trends for finale. In Berlioz the route is unfamiliar. The music sounds less like a symphony than an orchestral documentary. (Just so, Bach's fugues in the first set of the '48' were at first criticized because they were all too 'different' to sound like fugues.) The answer to this dilemma, if it still persists, is enough familiarity to assimilate the changing moods and unbalanced sections as a matter of style rather than judgement.

Meanwhile the following cross-section may illustrate the importance of texture. **Ex. 69** gives the waltz-tune of *Symphonie Fantastique* in varying accompaniments at the start, repeat and reprise. In the last, the listener may feel a gap in the lay-out of the third beat. There is: it is filled by a decorative gesture in the now detached first violins, here omitted. In **Ex. 70** the commencement of the wrestlers' dance in *The Trojans*, Act 1, scene 3, is shown at the start and finish; the first with a little spasmodic reinforcement, the second with a continuous and substantial backing, yet with a nice, roomy sensation, ebullient but not pompously pressurized. **Ex. 71**, the repeat phrase of the national anthem in *The Trojans*, Act 3, exhibits a luxurious spaciousness with just enough decoration in the even bars. With these examples the studious reader can place such anticipations as **Ex. 10.3, 11, 16** (sostenuto

Ex. 69

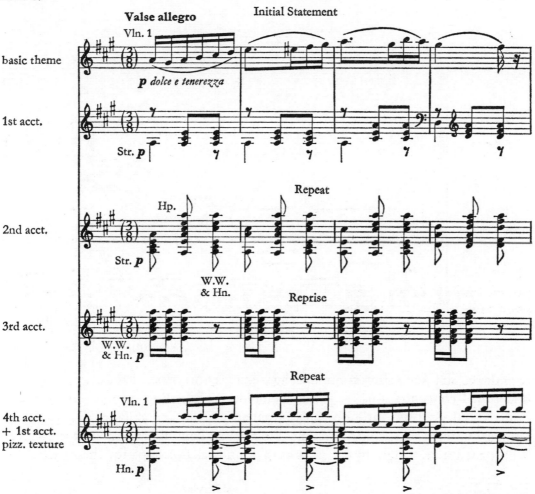

against busy antiphony), **21.3, 21.4, 23.1b**, 25.2, **28, 42, 43, 45, 48**, 50.2.4.6.7, **51, 53–57, 59, 61, 62.**

Finally, all these declarations of melody, harmonic nuances and orchestral virtuosity, are presented as translations of a literary text or scene imagined or acted, from a full operatic libretto down to a programme-note or mere title. In this romantic style the music comes to the listener or viewer as an affirmation in reference to a situation which may be poetical or fanciful or dramatic, but, in varying degrees, is pointed enough to convey a psychological burden that swings from the thought of a century ago to today's concern. One cannot deny the prevalence of this extrinsic appeal on the surface to share once more and creatively the longing, desolation,

Ex. 70.1

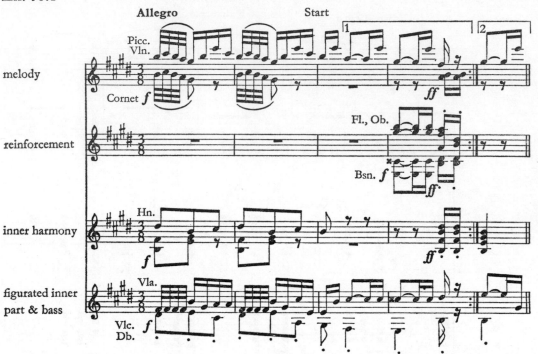

confidence, evil scheming, communal aggressive effort, basic deterioration, relaxes, devotional concentrations on praise, penitence or pleading, of men and women, crowds and peoples, through music's enhancements and conservations. Yet as familiarity deepens, such programmes sink below consciousness, and the receiver is absorbed increasingly in the pursuit of sound-relationships for their own sake,

Ex. 70.2

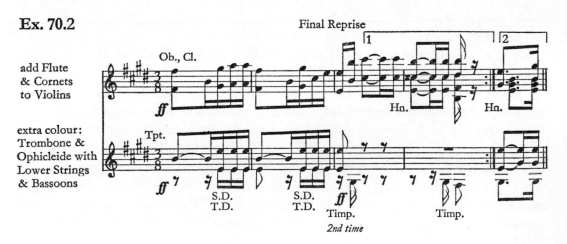

Ex. 71

datable, as music always is, but no less refreshing. Berlioz did not make the mistake of rushing into music when an outside stimulus possessed him. He waited to grasp its effect in what a contemporary English poet called tranquillity. He kept his romanticism dry! He recognized lightning in the influence of Beethoven and Shakespeare as creators of mood and of a new shaping dynamic, and particles of life force in many lesser men, but once having observed these, he never or rarely forgot that he was a musician, concerned to testify once more that sound-relationships, and their formulation and communication, are ends in themselves. This remains, in conventional terms, the abiding truth that makes coherent sense of Berlioz's endless and dazzling adventures in music.

NOTES

1. In a critical essay on Berlioz's treatment of bar-rhythm (*Soundings* 2 (1971–72), 18), Eric Gräbner exposes (1) Berlioz's doctrine of extended phrase-proportions *per se*, as overruled in actual impact by 'harmonic' metre, except where this is static (*Cellini* init.); (2) his provocative citation of Gluck but not Haydn or Mozart for tense rhythm *per se*; (3) the articulate, quasi-dramatic freedom of Faust's final outburst ('Oh! qu'il est doux') in *The Damnation*, scene 1.

Works from which music examples are taken

Berlioz:

Others:

APPENDIX 1

Works

THE chief object of this list is to display the composer's output in the order of composition in its various genres. Unfinished works are shown in brackets. The overlapping of a number of entries, owing to there being two classes of setting for a given item, raises a question of priority. In the case of orchestral settings of songs for voice and piano, I have, following the line taken in chapter 7, treated the later and orchestral setting to be the more authentic version, and accordingly reckoned that as the basic reference, mentioning the other setting later.

The authoritative bibliography of published editions by Mr Cecil Hopkinson (1951) has been a constant guide to a positive and well documented date-limit for the production of a work or of its revision. At times I have conjectured a date of composition from the composer's correspondence, or accepted the rulings of the chronologies at the end of the books by J.-G. Prodhomme (3rd edition, 1927) and Julius Kapp (1917). But the date of the final version of *Sara la baigneuse* is one of very few uncertainties that might be significant; to which I might add *La captive*, whose published final version is so distant from the original composition that one wonders whether it happened as casually as such an aftermath implies.

ORCHESTRAL

1. SYMPHONIES

1830 *Fantastique*
1834 *Harold en Italie*
1839 *Romeo and Juliet* (with soloists and chorus)
1840 *Funèbre et triomphale* (with chorus)

2. OVERTURES AND FANTASIAS

1827–8 *Waverley; Les francs juges*
1830 *Fantasie sur 'La tempête'* (later in *Lélio*)
1831 *Le roi Lear*
1831–2 *Rob Roy*

1831–44–55 *Le corsaire (Le tour de Nice)*
1843–4 *Le carnaval romain*

3. MARCHES AND MISCELLANEOUS

1839 *Rêverie et caprice* (violin solo)
1841 Arrangement of Weber's *Invitation to the Dance*
1845 Arrangement of L. de Meyer's *Marche marocaine*
1845–6 Arrangement of L. de Meyer's *Grande Marche triomphale d'Isly* (?)
1846 Arrangement of Rakoczky's *Marche Hongroise* (later in *La damnation de Faust*)
1848 *March funèbre pour la dernière Scène d'Hamlet* (later *Tristia* 3)
1864 *Marche Troyenne*

VOICES AND ORCHESTRA

1. Stage Works

1827–30 (*Les francs juges*)
1834–8, 1852, 1856 *Benvenuto Cellini*
c. 1840 (*Érigone*)
1841 Recitatives for Weber's *Le Freyschütz*
1841–7 (*La nonne sanglante*)
1856–63 *Les Troyens*
1860–2 *Béatrice et Bénédict*
1859 Revision of Gluck's *Orphée*
1861 Revision of Gluck's *Alceste*

2. Cantatas, Suites, etc.

(a) Major works
I. FRENCH
1846 *La damnation de Faust*
1850–4 *L'enfance du Christ*
II. LATIN
1837 *Requiem* (*Messe des Morts*)
1849–54 *Te Deum laudamus*

(b) Competition Cantatas (Rome Prize)
1827 *La mort d'Orphée*
1828 *Herminie*
1829 *La mort de Cléopâtre*
1830 *La dernière nuit de Sardanapale* (only a fragment survives)

(c) Miscellaneous Cantatas, Suites, etc.
1825–6 *Scène heroïque* (*La revolution grecque*)
1828–9 *Huit Scènes de Faust*
1831–2 *Le retour à la vie* (*Lélio*)
1834 *Le 5 mai* (*Chant sur la mort de Napoléon*)
1855 *Le 10 décembre* (*L'impériale*)

(d) Shorter Works
I. FRENCH
1831 *Méditation religieuse* (later *Tristia* 1)
1834, ?1850 *Sara la baigneuse*
II. LATIN
1824–7 *Messe Solenelle* (only 'Et Resurrexit' survives)
III. ITALIAN
1828–32 *Quartetto e coro dei Maggi*

3. Songs

(a) Chorus
1830 Arrangement of *La Marseillaise* (soloists and double chorus)
1844 *Chant sacré* (*Irlande*)*; *Hymne à la France* (later *Vox populi* 1)
1846 *Le chant des chemins de fer**
1850 *La mort d'Ophélie* (Women's chorus)*; *La menace des Francs* (later *Vox populi* 2) (Double chorus)

(b) Solo-ensemble
1844 *Hélène* (*Irlande*)*

(c) Solo-voice
1834 *La belle voyageuse* (*Irlande*)*; *Le jeune pâtre breton**
1845 *Chasseur danois**
1848 *La captive**
1850 *Zaïde**
1856 *Nuits d'été** (*Absence*, 1843)
1859 Arrangement of Martini's '*Plaisir d'amour*' (publication date; c. 1849?)
1860 Arrangement of Schubert's *Erlkönig* (trans. E. Bouscatel)

* See further entry under 'Voices and Piano'

VOICES AND PIANO/ORGAN
(piano where not otherwise stated)

1. Chorus

1829 Ballet des ombres
1829–30 *Chant guerrier* (*Irlande* 3); *Chanson à boire* (*Irlande* 5); *Chant sacré* (*Irlande* 6)
1835, 1850, 1858 *Chant des bretons* (*Fleurs des landes* 5)
1848 *La mort d'Ophélie* (orch. 1850); *L'apothéose* (from *Symphonie funèbre et triumphale*, fin.)
1850 *Chant des chemins de fer* (*Feuillets d'album* 3)
1855 *Prière du matin* (*Feuillets* 4)

260

1859 *Hymne pour la consécration du nouveau tabernacle*

1860, 1868 *Le temple universel* (piano or organ)

? Arrangement of Couperin's *Invitation à louer;* (*Le livre choral,* see below under 'Voices')

2. SOLO-VOICES

(a) Two or three voices

?1822 *Pleure, pauvre Colette*

?1823 *Le montagnard exilé; Amitié, reprends ton empire; Canon libre*

1829–30 *Hélène* (*Irlande* 2)

1850 *Le trebuchet* (*Fleurs* 3)

(b) One voice

1819–22 *La dépit de la bergère*

1822 *Le Maure jaloux*

1823 *Toi qui l'aimas*

1827, 1831 *Le pêcheur* (*Lélio*)

?1827–31 *Chant du bonheur* (orch. 1 version: *Lélio*)

1829–30 *Neuf melodies irlandaises*

1850 *Irlande:* 1. Le coucher du soleil; 4. La belle voyageuse (orch. 1 version, 1834); 7. L'origine de la harpe; 8. Adieu, Bessy; 9. Elegie. (For 2, 3, 5, 6 see sections 1 and 2a)

1832 *La captive,* in **E**

1833–4 *Le jeune pâtre breton* (orch. version, 1834)

1834 *La captive* (with violoncello part)

? *La captive,* in **D** (orch. version, 1848)

1834 *Je crois en vous*

1834–41 *Nuits d'été:* six mélodies (orch. 1856): 1. Villanelle; 2. Le spectre de la rose; 3. Sur les lagunes; 4. Absence (1834); 5. Au cimetière; 6. L'ile inconnue

1834, 1850 *Les champs* (second version, Feuillets 2)

1838 Premiers transports (orch. 1 version in *Roméo et Juliette*)

1844 *La belle Isabeau* (Feuillets 5); *Le chasseur danois* (Feuillets 6) (orch. 1 version, 1845)

1845 *Zaïde* (Feuillets 1) (orch. 1 version, 1850)

1847 *Page d'album; La mort d'Ophélie* (see section 1)

1850 *Le matin* (Fleurs de landes 1); *Petit oiseau* (Ib. 2)

VOICES

? *Veni creator; Tantum ergo* (for Le livre choral ou Répertoire populaire) (publ. 1888)

?1843 Arrangement of Bortniansky's *Pater noster* and *Adoremus* (perf. 1851)

HARMONIUM

1845 *Sérénade agreste à la madonne; Hymne pour l'élévation; Toccata*

ACADEMIC EXERCISES

1828–9 Fugue à 2 choeurs à 2 contrasujets; Fugue a 3 sujets

LOST OR DESTROYED

1816 Two quintets; *Romance pour Estelle*

1822 *Le cheval Arabe*

1823 *Beverley*

1824–7 *Messe solennelle* (exc. *Et resurrexit*)

1825 *Le passage de la mer rouge* ('Oratorio')

1830 *Sardanapale* (except for the draft of the conclusion)

1833 *Le pirate*

?1848 *Ouverture des Ciseleurs*

TREATISES

1844 La grande traité d'instrumentation et d'orchestration moderne

1855 Le chef d'orchestre, théorie de son art

Bibliography of Sources

(published in London or Paris unless otherwise stated)

1. GENERAL STUDIES

BOOKS

1882   Jullien, A., *Hector Berlioz: la vie et le combat: les oeuvres*

1883   Noufflard, G., *Berlioz et le mouvement de l'art contemporain* (Florence; 2nd ed., 1885, Paris, Florence)

1884   Ernst, A., *L'oeuvre dramatique de Hector Berlioz*

1890   Hippeau, E., *Berlioz et son temps* (Berlioz, l'homme et l'artiste, 2)

1901   Hahn, A. and others, *Hector Berlioz: sein Leben und seine Werke* (Leipzig)

1904   Louis, R., *Hector Berlioz* (Leipzig)

1904   Tiersot, J., *Hector Berlioz et la société de son temps*

1904   Prod'homme, J.-G., *Hector Berlioz: sa vie et ses oeuvres*

1906   Symposium of 26, *Le livre d'or du centenaire d'Hector Berlioz*

1930   Koechlin, C., *Traité de l'harmonie: 2*

1934   Turner, W. J. R., *Berlioz: the man and his work*

1935   Wotton, T. S., *Hector Berlioz* (pioneer chapters on Berlioz's methods)

1938   Elliot, J. H., *Hector Berlioz* (revised 1969)

1939   Pourtales, G. de, *Berlioz et l'Europe romantique*

1947   Daniska, J. (trans. W. A. C. Doyle Davidson), *Hector Berlioz* (Stockholm) (a succinct guide)

1950   Barzun, J. M., *Berlioz and the romantic century* (Boston; London 1951. Abridged and revised edn., *Berlioz and his century*, 1956)

1952   Kühner, H., *Hector Berlioz: Charakter und Schöpfertum* (Olten und Freiburg im Breisgau)

1969   MacDonald, H., *Berlioz Orchestral Music* (BBC Music Guides)

1971   Ballif, C., *Berlioz*

1972   Newman, E., *Berlioz, romantic and classic* (selected writings, ed. Peter Heyworth)

CHAPTERS IN BOOKS (NAMED BELOW)

1872   La Mara (Marie Lipsius), *Musikalische Studienköpfe 2* (Leipzig)

1882   Fouque, O., *Les révolutionaires de la musique* (on the influence of Lesueur)

1887, 1890   Kretzschmar, H., *Führer durch den Concertsaal: 1a, 1b, 1c, 3b* (Leipzig)

1898   Hadow, W. H., *Studies in Modern Music: 2*

1905   Newman, E., *Musical Studies* (2nd edn., 1908)

1949   Shore, B., *Sixteen symphonies* (perceptive summary of modern criticism of Berlioz)

ARTICLES IN DAILIES AND PERIODICALS CITED (FOR ABBREVIATIONS SEE PAGE 273)

1903   Symposium, *Die Musik* 3, 5 (December)

1903   Symposium, *Monde musical* 15, 22 (30 November)

1903   Various, *MT* (July–December)

1903   Various, *Neue Zeitschrift für Musik* (December)

1904–6   Tiersot, J., *Le Ménestrel*: 3 January 1904–December 1906 (96 articles) (a pioneer survey, including unpublished works). Also 22 July–16 September 1911 (B as Conservatoire librarian and at the Institute)

1920   Emmanuel, M., *Le Correspondant* 278 (new series 242), 237

1929   Calvocoressi, M. D., *The Christian Science Monitor* (2 March)

1969   Symposium, *MT* 110, 1513 (March)

1969   Mann, W., *The Times* (1 March)

1969   Bradbury, E., *Yorkshire Post* (11, 18, 19 March)

1969   Dickinson, A. E. F., *Musical Opinion* (April)

1969   Symposium, *Adam Intern. Rev.* 34, 33133

2. PARTICULAR WORKS

Béatrice et Bénédict

CHAPTERS

1875   Hanslick, E., *Die moderne Oper* 6 (Berlin) (trans. Robin H. Legge in *Studies in m* (1901), ed. R. Grey)

1891   Imbert, H., *Symphonie*

ARTICLES

1890   Lostalot, A. de, *Gaz. des Beaux Arts* 3e per. 32, 4, 82

1890   Reyer, E., *Journal des Débats* (8 June)

1969   Walsh, S., *Listener* 82 (31 July)

1970   Dickinson, A. E. F., *MR* 31, 2 (May) (Cambridge)

Benvenuto Cellini

BOOKS

1889   Brenet, M., *Deux pages de la vie de Berlioz: le 1er opéra de Berlioz*

1927   Würz, A. H., *Franz Lachner als dramatischer Komponist* (Munich) (on Lachner's *Cellini*)

CHAPTERS

1912   Weingartner, F., *Akkorde* (Leipzig)

ARTICLES

1882   Anon, *MT* 23, 468 (February) (A well-illustrated tour of the music)

1882   Shedlock, J. S., *MMR* 12, 134, 135 (February, March) (Wagner-biased)

1910   Lalo, P., *Temps* (11 October; 8, 22 November; 8 April 1913)

1940   Bornoff, J., *Nineteenth century* 127, 757 (March)

1957   Hammond, A., *Opera* 8, 4 (April)

1961   Paap, W., *Mens en melodie* 16, p. 165 (January) (Utrecht)

1966   Macdonald, H. J., *MT* 107 (December) (on the new Covent Garden version)

1966   Searle, H., *Opera* 17, 12 (December)

1970   Dickinson, A. E. F., *MR* 31, 2 (May). On all the stage works (Cambridge)

CANTATAS, ETC.

Le cinq Mai

ARTICLES

1903   Louis, R., *Die Musik* 3, 5 (December)

Herminie

ARTICLES

1964   Dickinson, A. E. F., *MR* 25, 3 (August) (Cambridge)

L'impériale

1903   Louis, R., *Die Musik* 3, 5 (December)

Lélio

CHAPTERS

1833   D'Ortigue, J., *Le balcon d'Opéra* (reprinting *Rev. de Paris* 45, December 1832)
1964   Fiske, R., *Shakespeare in music* (ed. P. Hartnoll). (On *The Tempest* fantasia)

ARTICLES

1832   T., J., *Quotidienne* (10 December)
1832   Anon, *Le Corsaire* (12 December, January 1833)
1881   Anon, *MT* 22, 466 (December)
1881   Hippeau, E., *Renaissance musicale* (13 November)
1903   Sternfeld, R., *Die Musik* 3, 5 (December)

La mort d'Orphée

ARTICLES

1964   Dickinson, A. E. F., *MR* 25, 3 (August)

La mort de Cléopâtre

ARTICLES

1903   Anon, *Pall Mall Gaz.* (13 November)
1903   Anon, *Musical standard* 20, 516 (21 November)
1964   Dickinson, A. E. F., *MR* 25, 3 (August) (Cambridge)

La mort de Sardanapale

ARTICLES

1943   Wotton, T. S., *MR* 4, 4 (November) (incorporating Tiersot's discovery) (Cambridge)
1964   Dickinson, A. E. F., *MR* 25, 3 (August)

Scène héroïque (La révolution grecque)

ARTICLES

1828   S. (Fétis), *Rev. musicale* 3, 422
1903   Louis, R., *Die Musik* 3, 5 (December)

La damnation de Faust

BOOKS

1896 Prod'homme J.-G., *Le cycle B. La DF*
1910 Boschot, A., *La Faust de B*
1924 Tiersot, J., *La DF de B*
1946 Malapiero, R., *B: La DF* 6 dic. 1946 (Milan)

CHAPTERS

1880 Jullien, A., *Goethe et la musique . . . les oeuvres qu'il a inspirées*

ARTICLES

1846 D'Ortigue, J., *Quotidienne* (December)
1854–5 Kreutzer, L., *Rev. et Gaz. musicale de Paris* 21, 389, 2, 10, 27, 41, 91, 97
1880 English première, Manchester, 5 February (Hallé)
1880 Anon, *MT* 21, 448 (June) and 454 (December)
1880 Anon, *MMR* 10, 116–17 (August–September)
1904 D'Udine, J., *Le courrier musical* (January)
1904 Sternfeld, R., *Westermanns Illustrierte Deutsche Monatshefte* 95, 485 (January) (Brunswick)
1921 Boucher, M., *Rev. musicale* 2, 7 (May)
1933 McNaught, W., *MT* 74 (July) (*DF* as opera)
1946 Turner, W. J., *Hallé* 2 (October)
1959 Dickinson, A. E. F., *MMR* 89, 995 (September–October) (The revisions (of *Eight Scenes*) for *DF*)

L'enfance du Christ

BOOKS

1898 Prod'homme, J.-G., *Le cycle B.* 2, EC

CHAPTERS

1861 D'Ortigue, J., *La musique à l'église*
1948 Dukas, P., *Les écrits de PD sur m* (reprinting articles in the Revue Hebdomaire, 1892)

ARTICLES

1854 D'Ortigue, J., *Journal des Débats*
1881 Anon, *MT* 22, 456, 458 (February, April)
1909 Boschot, A., *Le Correspondent* 237, 1172
1966 Cairns, D., *MT* 107 (February)

Lélio, see CANTATAS

Marche funèbre (Hamlet), see OVERTURES ETC.

MASSES

Messe (1825): *Et resurrexit*

ARTICLES

1825 Anon, *Journal des Débats* (14 July)
1825 Anon, *Quotidienne* 196 (15 July)
1828 S. (Fetis), *Rev. musicale* 3, 422

1829   Fetis, F.-J., *Rev. musicale* 6, 348
1903   Louis, R., *Die Musik* 3, 5 (December)
1969   Parry, W. H., *Birmingham Post*, 20 March

Messe des Morts, see *Requiem Mass*

Operas and Interludes

Béatrice et Bénédict, q.v.

Benvenuto Cellini, q.v.

Érigone

ARTICLES
1970   Dickinson, A. E. F., *MR* 31.2 (May)

Les francs juges

ARTICLES
1896   Brenet, M., *Guide mus.* 42, 4 (26 January) (German trans. in *Neue Zeitschrift für Musik* 63, 22)

'*Les francs juges*' and the '*Marche au supplice*'

ARTICLES
1880   Weber, J., *Temps* 20, 6934 (14 April)
1906   Tiersot, J. and Boschot, A., *Le Ménestrel* 199, 207, 215, 240, 246
1906   Brenet, M., *Mercure musical* 2, 4 (15 February)
1933   Tiersot, J., *MQ* 19, 3 (July)
1933   Calvocoressi, M. D., *MT* 74 (December)
1934   Wotton, T. S., *MT* 75 (January)

La nonne sanglante

ARTICLES
1896   Brenet, M., *Guide musicale* 42, 5 (2 February) (or *Neue Zeitschr.* 63, 23)
1926   Prod'homme, J.-G., *MQ* 12, 3 (July)
1952   Curtiss, M., *MQ* 38, 1 (January)
1966   Dickinson, A. E. F., *MT* 107, 1481 (July)

Les Troyens q.v.

Overtures, etc.

Les francs juges

CHAPTERS
1899   Hanslick, *Am Ende des Jahrhunderts*

ARTICLES
1828   S. (Fétis), *Rev. musicale* 3, 422

1829   Casembroot J. L. de, *Rev. internationale de m* 21 (views of Mendelssohn, Schumann, Moscheles)
1829   Fétis, F.-J., *Rev. musicale* 6, 348
1836   Schumann, R., *Neue Zeitschr. für Musik* (reprinted in *Gesammelte Schr.* (1854), 1, and in *Music and musicians* (trans. F. R. Ritter, 2 (1880))

Rob Roy
ARTICLES
1950   Herbage, J., *Con brio* 1, 3
1963   Snowman, N., *Berl. Soc. Bull.* 44 (October)

Roi Lear

CHAPTERS
1936   Tovey, D., *Essays in musical analysis* 4
1964   Fiske, R., *Shakespeare in music* (ed. P. Hartnoll)

ARTICLES
1964   Snowman, N., *Berl. Soc. Bull.* 48 (October)

Waverley

ARTICLES
1829   Fétis, F.-J., *Rev. musicale* 6, 348
1839   Schumann, R., *Music and musicians* 1 (trans. F. R. Ritter)

Marche funèbre (*Hamlet*)

CHAPTERS
1964   Fiske, R., *Shakespeare in music* (ed. P. Hartnoll)

Rêverie et Caprice (*viol. and orch.*)

ARTICLES
1927   Wotton, T. S., *MT* 69 (August)

Requiem Mass

BOOKS
1939   Schlitzer, F., *La Messa di Requiem di EB* (Florence)

ARTICLES
1837   D'Ortigue, J., *Quotidienne* (6 December)
1837   Morel, A., *Journal de Paris* (6 December)
1837   Bottée de Toulmon, A., *Rev. et Gaz. musicale de Paris* 4 (10 December)
1852   Kreutzer, L., *Rev. et Gaz. musicale de Paris* 19, 356, 369, 387, 395
1879   Massougnes, G. de, *Rev. et Gaz. musicale de Paris* 40, 25, 33, 41, 57
1883   Shedlock, J., *Academy* 23 (2 June)
1894   Dukas, P., *Rev. hebdomaire* 17 March (also in *Les écrits de PD sur m*, 1948)
1900   Tiersot, J., *Guide musicale* 46, 2 (14 January)
1925   Turner, W. J., *The New Statesman* 26 (21 November) (also in *Musical meanderings*, 1928)

Rêverie et Caprice, see OVERTURES, ETC.

BIBLIOGRAPHY OF SOURCES

Songs—general

CHAPTERS

1935 Wotton, T. S., *Hector Berlioz*, 123–32

1954 Noske, F., *La mélodie française de B à Duparc* (Paris and Amsterdam)

ARTICLES

1903 Puttmann, M., *Neue Zeitschr. für Musik* 70, 50 (9 December)

1932 Walker, E., *MMR* 62, 737 (June)

1969 Dickinson, A. E. F., *MQ* 55, 3 (July)

Particular

La belle Isabeau

ARTICLES

1970 Hopkinson, C., *Brio* (December)

1971 Charlton, D., *Music and Letters* 52, 2 (April)

Le chant des chemins de fer

BOOKS

1926 Ratz, E., *Une visite de B à Lille* (Lille)

ARTICLES

1953 Frémiot, M., *Vie du Rail; notre Métier* 413 (September)

La Marseillaise

ARTICLES

1915 Newman, E. and Wotton, T. S., *MT* 56 (August, September)

1970 Hopkinson, C., *M and Letters* 51, 4 (October)

Melodies irlandaises (*Irlande*)

ARTICLES

1834 Stoepel, F., *Gaz. mus.* 1, 169

1964 Snowman, N., *Berl. Soc. Bull.* 48 (October)

La mort d'Ophélie

CHAPTERS

1964 Fiske, R., *Shakespeare in music* (ed. P. Hartnoll)

Nuits d'été

ARTICLES

1936 Cooper, M., *Radio Times* (21 March)

1957 Cardus, N., *Manchester Guardian* (31 August)

1957 Cardus, N., *B. Soc. Bull.* 23 (December)

1964 Bernheim, R., *B. Soc. Bull.* 47 (July) (on recorded interpretations)

Le trébuchet

ARTICLES

1966 MacDonald, H. J., *B. Soc. Bull.* 54 (April) (on the textual conflation)

269

Symphonies

Harold en Italie

CHAPTERS

1936   Tovey, D., *Essays in musical analysis* 4
1966   Cairns, D., *The symphony* (ed. R. Simpson)

ARTICLES

1834   Anon, *Journal des Débats* (21 November)
1834   Janin, J., *Ib.* (December)
1848   Holmes, E., *Atlas* (12 February), reprinted in *MT* 4, 89 (October, 1851)
1855   Liszt, F., *Neue Zeitschr. für Musik* 43, 3–5, 8–9 (shortened version of a study in French)
1890   Montaux, A., *Le Ménestrel*, 17, 24 August (on an earlier version of the second movement)
1956   Court, A. W. G., *MR* 17, 3 (August) (Cambridge)

Roméo et Juliette. Symphonie dramatique

CHAPTERS

1869   Lavoix, H. fils, *Les traducteurs de Shakespeare en m*
1948   Dukas, P., *Les écrits de PD sur la m*
1964   Fiske, R., *Shakespeare in m* (ed. P. Hartnoll)
1966   Cairns, D., *The symphony* (ed. R. Simpson)

ARTICLES

1839   Merrau, C., *Rev. et Gaz. musicale de Paris* 6, 63 (28 November)
1839   Heller, S., *Ibid.* 69, 70 (19, 22 December)
1881   Anon, *MT* 22, 458 (April)
1909   Servières, G., *Guide mus.* 55, 9–11 (reply to Heller)
1939   Dumesnil, R., *Mercure de France* 295 (November)

Symphonie fantastique

BOOKS

1880   Noufflard, G., *La SF de HB* (Florence)
1908   Magnette, P., *SF* (*Les grandes étapes dans l'oeuvre de B*: 1) (Liège) (thorough analysis)

CHAPTERS

1833   D'Ortigue, J. M., *Le balcon de l'opéra* ('romantic')
1929   Wotton, T. S., *B*: four works
1949   Shore, B., *Sixteen symphonies* (illuminating view of an articulate orchestral player of long experience)
1954   Roux, M. de, *Domaine musical* (ed. P. Boulez)
1966   Cairns, D., *The symphony* (ed. R. Simpson)

ARTICLES

1835   D'Ortigue, J. M., *Gaz. mus.* (10 May)
1835   Schumann, R., *Neue Zeitschr. für Musik.*, 3, 1, 9–13, and in *Music and musicians* 1 (trans. F. R. Ritter), 1877
1903   Bouyer, R., *Le Ménestrel* 69, 40

Symphonie funèbre et triomphale

ARTICLES

1840 Blanchard, H., *Rev. et Gaz. musical de Paris* 7, 47, 48 (2, 9 August)

1882 Anon, *MT* 23, 473, (July)

1882 Sloman, R., *Musical Standard* 23, 4, 932 (10 June)

1936 Searle, H., *MMR* 66, 776 (May)

1936 Wotton, T. S., *Musical Opinion* 59, 706 (July)

1965 Gräbner, E., *Berl. Soc. Bull.* 50 (April)

Te Deum laudamus

CHAPTERS

1861 D'Ortigue, J. M., *La musique à l'église*

ARTICLES

1855 Bourges, M., *Rev. et Gaz. mus. de Paris* 22, 18 (6 May)

1855 Anon, *Neue Zeitschr. für Musik* 42, 23 (2 June)

1884 Shedlock, J. S., *MT* 25, 501 (December)

1885 Première at the Crystal Palace

1885 Anon, *Athenaeum* 3000 (25 April)

1885 Pohl, R., *Musical Review*, 1 May

1906 Edwards, F. G., *MT* 47 (October)

1909 Boschot, A., *Le Correspondant* 237, 1172

1943 Turner, W. J., *The Listener* 30, 756 (8 July)

1957 Raynor, H., *MMR* 87, 984 (November–December)

1959 Raynor, H., *Musical Opinion* 82 (July) (On *Requiem* and *Te Deum*)

1962 Macnutt, R. P. S., *Berl. Soc. Bull.* 38–39 (April–July)

Grande Traité d'instrumentation

CHAPTERS

1903 Kling, H., *Le livre d'or du centenaire d'HB, symposium* (Grenoble) (on Berlioz as conductor)

1939 Bartenstein, H., *HB's Instrumentationskunst* (Strassburg)

ARTICLES

1906 Istel, E., *Zeitschr. der Internat. Musikgesellsch.* 8, 2 (November)

1909 Closson, E., *Guide musical* 55. 39–41 (26 September, 3, 10 October) (On Strauss's edition)

1958 Bernheim, R. C., *Berl. Soc. Bull.* 27 (December)

1963 Warrack, G., *MT* 104. 1450 (December)

1969 Lockspeiser, E., *M and Letters* 50, 1 (January) (on B.-Strauss edition)

1969 Lockspeiser, E., *Apollo* 90. 328–30 (October)

?   Bartenstein, H., *Archiv für Musikforschung*

Les Troyens

BOOKS

1897 Destranges, E., *Les TR de B* (refers to page numbers in 1889 edition of complete vocal score)

1900 Smolian, A., *Die TR von HB* (Opernführer 4) (Leipzig)

1900 Bruneau, A., *Musiques d'hier et de demain*
1916 Halm, A., *Von Grenzen und Ländern der Musik* (Munich)
1920 Robert, P. L., *Les TR* (Rouen)
1943 Newman, E., *Opera nights*
1955 Guichard, L., *La musique et les lettres au temps du romantisme* (B and Virgil)

ARTICLES

1863 Première (Carthage acts)
1863 Anon, *The Athenaeum* 1885 (12 December) (a trenchant but thorough review)
1890 Première, Karlsruhe (5, 6 December)
1890 Magnard, A., *Figaro* 36, 3 (6, 8, 10 December)
1890 Anon, *The musical world* 68 (13, 20 December)
1891 Jullien, A., *Revue d'art dramatique* 21 (15 January)
1924 Servières, G., *Rev. musicale* 5, 10 (August)
1929 Capell, R., *MT* 70 (January)
1935 Turner, W. J., *The New Statesman and Nation* 9, 44 (30 March)
1935 Capell, R., *MMR* 65, 766 (May) (realistic dramatic review)
1935 Howes, F. and Fiske, R., *MT* 76 (May, September)
1942 Lalo, P., *Temps* (12, 19 March) (reprinted in *De Rameau a Ravel*, 1947)
1951 Capell, R., *MT* 92 (January)
1951 Crankshaw, G., *Musical Opinion* 74, 880 (January)
1951 H, *Opera* 2 (February)
1951 Meyerstein, E. H. W., *MR* 12, 1 (February)
1953 Barker, F. Granville, *Opera News* 22 (14 October)
1957 Première: Royal Opera House, Covent Garden
1957 Klein, J. W., *MMR* 87, 981 (May–June)
1957 Elliot, J. H., *MT* 98 (June)
1957 Anon, *Ill. London News* 230 (8 June)
1957 Collet, R., *Score* 20 (June)
1957 Dean, W.; R., HD, *Opera* 8, 6, 7 (June, July)
1957 Bourgeois, J., *Opera* 8, 9 (September)
1957 Dickinson, A. E. F. and Sharp, G. N., *MR* 18 (August) (Cambridge)
1957 Anon, *MMR* 87, 983 (September–October)
1958 Dickinson, A. E. F., *Durham Univ. Journal* 20, 24 (Durham)
1958–59 Dickinson, A. E. F., *Tempo* 48, 51
1959 Dickinson, A. E. F., *Greece and Rome* 2, 6, 2 (October) (on music for *The Aeneid*)
1960 Klein, J. W., *Musical Opinion* 83 (May)
1960 Wallis, C., *MT* 101 (June)
1960 R, HD, *Opera* 11, 6 (June)
1961 Husson, T., *Musica* 93 (December) (Chaix)
1961 Macnutt, R. P. S., *Berl. Soc. Bull.* 35 (June) (On a lost Sinon scene)
1963 Fraenkel, G. S. and MacDonald, H. J., *M and Letters* 44, 3 (July) and 45, 1 (January 1964)
1966 Dickinson, A. E. F., *Berl. Soc. Bull.* 53 (January) (on differing versions of scene-order)
1969 Symposium, *Scottish Opera Magazine,* spring (Glasgow)
1969 Wilson, C. *Weekend Scotsman* (3 May)

969   Cairns, D., *New Statesman* (16 May)
1969   Cairns, D., R. *Mus. Ass. Proc.* 95 (1968–69) *B and Virgil*
1969   Klein, J. W., *Opera* 20, 9 (September)
1969   MacDonald, H., *MT* 110, 1519 (September) (on Th. Lyrique perf.)
1969   Kemp, I., *Listener* 82, 2113 (25 September)
1969   Reid, C., *Spectator* 7370 (27 September)
1970   Dickinson, A. E. F., *MR* 31 2 (May)

ABBREVIATIONS

Bull.   *Bulletin*
MMR   *The Monthly Musical Record*
MQ   *The Musical Quarterly* (*New York*)
MR   *The Music Review* (*Cambridge*)
MT   *The Musical Times*

Index

1. MUSICAL WORKS OF BERLIOZ

2. FEATURES OF BERLIOZ'S COMPOSITION METHOD. STRUCTURE AND TEXTURE

3. OTHER MUSIC THAN BERLIOZ'S